No Middle Ground

No Middle Ground

Women and Radical Protest

EDITED BY

Kathleen M. Blee

New York University Press

NEW YORK AND LONDON

NEW YORK UNIVERSITY PRESS
New York and London

© 1998 by New York University

Chapter 4. Sonya Paul and Robert Perkinson, "Winona LaDuke" reprinted from *The Progressive* 59:10 (1995), 36–39 by permission from *The Progressive,* 409 East Main Street, Madison, WI 53703.

Chapter 6. Beth Roy, "Goody Two-Shoes and the Hell-Raisers: Women's Activism, Women's Reputations in Little Rock." Copyright © Beth Roy, 1997.

Chapter 7. Karren Baird-Olson, "Reflections of an AIM Activist: Has It All Been Worth It?" reprinted with permission from *American Indian Culture and Research Journal* 18:4 (1994), 233–52. Copyright © Regents of the University of California, 1994.

Chapter 10. Cynthia Costello and Amy Dru Stanley, "Report from Seneca" reprinted with permission from *FRONTIERS: A Journal of Women's Studies* 8:2 (1985), 32–39. Copyright © 1985 FRONTIERS Editorial Collective.

Chapter 12. Margaret Rose, "From the Fields to the Picket Line: Huelga Women and the Boycott, 1965–1975" reprinted with permission from *Labor History* 31:3 (1990), 271–93.

Chapter 15. "Fighting for Environmental Justice: An Interview with Lois Gibbs" reprinted with permission from *Multinational Monitor* 17:4 (1996), 15–19.

Library of Congress Cataloging-in-Publication Data
No middle ground : women and radical protest / edited by Kathleen M. Blee.
p.   cm.
Includes bibliographical references and index.
ISBN 0-8147-1279-7 (clothbound : acid-free paper).—ISBN
0-8147-1280-0 (paperbound : acid-free paper)
  1. Women radicals—United States.   2. Women political activists—United States.   3. Women social reformers—United States.
  4. Radicalism—United States.   5. Protest movements—United States.
I. Blee, Kathleen M.
HQ1236.5.U6N6   1997
305.42'0973—dc21   97-21111
                              CIP

New York University Press books are printed on acid-free paper,
and their binding materials are chosen for strength and durability.

Manufactured in the United States of America

10 9 8 7 6 5 4 3 2 1

For Pam, Eli, and Sophie

Contents

No Middle Ground

Chapter One

Introduction
Women on the Left/Women on the Right

Kathleen M. Blee

In his reconstruction of the history of the Communist Party in Alabama, the historian Robin D. G. Kelley (1990, 21–22) relates the story of a group of poor and working-class women who became active communists in Birmingham in the mid-1930s. On the surface, the women were unremarkable: mostly black, some white; young and old; schoolteachers, domestic workers, bookkeepers; wives and mothers. But their actions were striking. They organized sharecroppers, challenged the distribution of food and supplies to the unemployed, and struggled to change health care in their communities. Moreover, by joining an interracial and gender-integrated party that was tied to Northern communists, these women defied Alabama's most fundamental rules of gender propriety, racial segregation, regional supremacism, and anticommunism.

On the other end of the political spectrum are the white women described in Glenda Gilmore's (1996) history of turn-of-the-century politics in North Carolina. Identifying themselves as the wives and daughters of white men, they enlisted in North Carolina's White Government League, urging their husbands, fathers, and the larger white male citizenry to preserve white supremacy against African American political inroads. Although they minimized their usurpation of men's traditional domination of political life, these white women brought a distinctly gendered presence to the defense of the racial prerogatives they claimed.

Examples such as these generate a host of questions about women who adopt political stances that are outside the conventional norms of political life. How should we define activism that does not fall within mainstream politics? What role do women play in militant and radical politics? What prompts women to organize in behalf of unpopular causes? To what extent does women's involvement in such politics undermine long-standing norms about women's place in political life? How does confrontation with established authorities affect women's activism? And how are women themselves changed by personal experiences of militancy and activism?

Until recently, scholarship has provided little guidance in answering these questions. Studies of radical politics and militant activism have focused largely on men. Women have been assumed to be apolitical, more interested in domestic concerns and personal relationships than in public issues and political controversies. Except for studies of feminist and other women's rights movements, research on social movements has focused largely on male-dominated activism (such as labor unions) or on the male leadership of mixed-gender movements (such as the anti–Vietnam War movement). In political groupings outside the mainstream, it is men who are depicted as the most militant actors and leaders. Despite evidence that women have been involved in a wide range of very radical political activities, from revolutionary parties to racial hate groups, such women have been the subject of relatively little scholarly attention. This neglect stems from several sources.

First, the invisibility of women is due to the overly restricted way in which we *define* radicalism. In popular understanding, and often in scholarship, to be radical, nearly by definition, is to be male. The challenging, provoking, demanding stance of radical activism evokes images of men who make public claims on the state. When women act, their activism is regarded differently. They are assumed to be puppets of politically active husbands, fathers, brothers, or sons or to be expressing unfocused, irrational anger or resentment. The subversive activities of Southern Confederate women during the Civil War, for example, violated expectations of the behavior of southern women and thus were regarded as "disorderly" or "defiant" (see, e.g., Bynum 1992); men's subversion was more likely to be seen as purposeful and radical.

Moreover, the majority of studies of women in nonmainstream politics focus on women's involvement in progressive or reformist politics, leading to an identification of women's radicalism exclusively with left-wing and feminist politics. Until recently, women who join collective struggles on behalf of right-wing causes have been seen as pawns of male leaders. Little attention has been paid to women as active agents of right-wing, racist, or reactionary politics, although recent research suggests that women have been involved and even leaders in virtually every major right-wing and antifeminist movement in U.S. history (Blee 1997; 1991; de Hart 1991; Luker 1984; Mansbridge 1986; Marshall 1986; Petchesky 1981).

To understand the full range of women's radical action, it is necessary to define radical action in an inclusive way. The dictionary definition of a "radical" is one who seeks reforms that go to the root of a problem. Radicalism can exist on the right as well as on the left. Radicals are those who seek social, political, or economic changes meant to produce great equality within society, or those who seek changes meant to re-structure society in a less egalitarian fashion. An inclusive definition of radicalism recognizes that radical actions are not necessarily violent, although violence has been used strategically by radical activists as well as by those who oppose them. Moreover, it is too restrictive to consider as radical only those whose actions are public and highly visible. Women in radical groups often work in less visible, but no less militant, ways, striving to solidify groups from within by strengthening personal rela-tionships among activists.

To define radicalism in a gender-inclusive way, it is better to scrutinize goals than tactics. Radicals are those who envision fundamentally new social arrangements or who fervently guard existing social arrangements against forces of change. Radicals focus on the core mechanisms and relationships of a society. Left-wing, Marxist radicals, for example, struggle to alter the economic system to ensure an equitable distribution of resources. Radical feminists work to change the sex/gender system and to abolish women's oppression. Black nationalists concentrate on ending racism and racial inequality. Environmental radicals target corpo-rate control of natural resources. And radical white supremacists aim to deepen existing inequalities based on race.

An understanding of radicalism also requires attention to the particu-lar social and historical context in which activism takes place. An action may be radical in one context but not in another. For example, struggles to protect one's community against toxic chemical exposure might in-volve a deep critique of corporate or government policies and an analysis of the racial disparities in toxic waste disposal siting, or it might simply mobilize privileged communities to displace toxic disposal onto more powerless communities (Szasz 1994).

Second, the traditional invisibility of women radicals is the result of limitations of *where* we look. The focus on radical action within formal institutions such as labor unions, political parties, and social movement organizations has neglected an important spectrum of women's militant protest. Some of women's activism involves informal networks of friendship, kinship, or neighborhood rather than elections, positions, and hierarchies of organizations. In the terms used by Louise Tilly and Patricia Gurin (1990, 7), such protest is "protopolitical," operating outside formal political structures and based on the solidarities of everyday life in contrast to "political" militancy, which operates through formal politics or social movements and is grounded in allegiance to voluntary associations.

The study of women's radical protest requires a broadened sense of the spatial contexts in which activism outside the mainstream political process takes place. Certainly, militant women have contributed substantially to traditional forms of protest, such as labor union organizing, although even here women may draw upon personal relationships and family bonds to form collective solidarity (Cobble 1991; Costello 1991; Frank 1994). Women (like men) also are found in militant activities that are situated outside formal organizations: in the social networks of friendship or shared experience, the spatial commonalities of everyday life in homes, stores, neighborhoods, and schools, or the ties of sexual identities and attachments (Duggan and Hunter 1995; Kelley 1994; Ruddick 1989; Taylor 1996). It is into these arenas and relationships that we need to probe if we are to understand women's role in radical politics.

Third, invisibility is a product of *how* we go about looking. Jacquelyn Dowd Hall argues that until recently "[i]nstances of female militancy were seen and not seen. Because they contradicted conventional wisdom, they were easily dismissed." When gender is placed "at the center of analysis," she notes, "unexpected dimensions come into view" (1986, 355, 356). By focusing on the "disorderly women" who were part of early-twentieth-century labor militancy in the Appalachian South, Hall is able to discern how dimensions of private life—such as sexuality, friendship, romance, and consumption aspirations—shaped the nature of militant action in Appalachia as well as these women's understanding of themselves and their place in history.

A gendered analysis—Hall's notion of putting gender at the center— can provide a better viewpoint not only on women's radical activism but also on men's radical actions. It turns attention to arenas, such as domestic life, that traditionally have not been viewed as politically important but that may prove decisive in radical organizing and objectives. It also focuses analysis on the gendered nature of radical activism and on the ways in which militant activity and even political commitment itself are products of gender-specific social circumstances, opportunities, barriers, and associations.

No Middle Ground brings together a wide variety of studies that produce new insights into women's role in radical and nonmainstream political movements in modern U.S. society. Some essays are first-person accounts that reflect upon the personal dimensions of political commitment; others are scholarly examinations, based on interviews and document analysis. Many focus on a particular incident or time period in which women were involved in militant activism, such as a hospital strike, farm worker boycott, or protest for nuclear disarmament. Others analyze one aspect of militant politics across a broader time period, such as the American Indian Movement or organized antifeminist mobilization. Some focus on cities that are commonly associated with radical politics—Boston, San Francisco—but most examine areas of the country in which the political landscape is less charted—places like Kentucky, Arkansas, and rural New York. Together, these essays detail women's activism across a broad and contradictory political spectrum: right-wing and left-wing movements, feminist and antifeminist groups, movements that support racial equality and those that favor white supremacism. They suggest both the similarities and the differences in women's activism across the ideological spectrum.

Within very different types of radical politics, the contributors examine the role of emotion as an aspect of both leadership and the organizational dynamics of radical groups. They explore the relationship between individuals and the groups to which they are committed and the consequences of participation in radical politics on the activists themselves. They also provide insight into the ways that gender roles and expectations shape women's activism and how activism in turn affects social arrangements of gender.

No Middle Ground examines women's radicalism in the United States during the second half of the twentieth century, from the mid-1950s to the mid-1990s, in contexts as diverse as the gay/lesbian movement, anti-integrationist groups, Marxist parties, and the movement for environmental justice. In these essays we learn about women who identify themselves as revolutionaries, those who define themselves primarily as concerned mothers or wives, and those for whom the label of "radical" or "troublemaker" is an unwelcome consequence of their actions. Some of these women would, and do, identify themselves as political activists or as radicals. Many would not, although their actions or beliefs suggest an understanding of society that is outside the political mainstream.

Several themes unite the essays in this volume. One theme is how gender shapes political identities and political consciousness. Collective activism, whether on behalf of white supremacism or the civil rights of African Americans, requires an alignment of one's own interests and personal agendas with those of the larger political group. Within activist organizations, individuals develop an *identity* that links them to a larger effort for social change (see Johnston, Laraña, and Gusfield 1994, 15; Melucci 1989). The essays in *No Middle Ground* explore this process of identity transformation for women activists on the right and the left. Political activism caused many women to develop new understandings of themselves both in politics and in personal life. For some, these identity transformations were supported by family members and friends. For others, they prompted profound alterations in domestic and personal life. In some cases, women found their new identity as political activist to be a comfortable, even liberating, one. In other cases, it was unwanted, stifling, or oppressive.

Other essays in this volume consider the ways that gender structures *consciousness,* that is, how individuals come to understand the structural basis of society and social problems. Women and men often are situated differently in social, economic, and political life, creating gender-distinct assumptions of entitlements and possibilities. Temma Kaplan proposes the useful concept of "female consciousness" to suggest that "recognition of what a particular class, culture, and historical period expect from women, creates a sense of rights and obligations that provides motive force for actions" (1982, 545). Women's lives thus may structure certain forms of political consciousness, suggesting why, as West and Blumberg (1990) note, women's protest activities, both on the left and on the right, tend to be linked to issues of economic survival, national/racial/ethnic conflict, humanism/nurturance, or women's rights.

This pattern is evident in the essays collected here. Much of women's activism stems from concerns over economic inequities, racial disparities, the future of nuclear weaponry, and feminism/antifeminism. The essays in *No Middle Ground* suggest that women often participate in political activism in gendered ways and that their participation can either fit within, or subvert, the gender expectations of the larger society. Women engaged in activism to defend their working conditions might broaden social expectations of women's concerns; those fighting for racial homogeneity of their children's schools might leave traditional gender norms untouched. For each, the conditions that encourage (or curb) militancy reflect in part the boundaries of gender norms in social and domestic life even as they might challenge those boundaries.

A second common theme that runs through the book suggests that it is necessary to understand radicalism in the context of both organizational and personal histories. Sara Evans (1979) describes how women activists in the civil rights movement and the antiwar "new left" learned organizing skills and political identities that spurred the development of the second wave of feminist activism in the 1970s. In a similar vein, Nancy Whittier (1995) argues that the women's movement of the 1970s had a substantial impact on a number of subsequent social movements, including progressive coalitions, the lesbian/gay and AIDS movement, the spirituality movement, and recovery/self-help movements. Others have charted the impact of women's movement activism on social activism around issues of health, policy, wife battering, and rape (Ferree and Martin 1995) and documented how organizations can bolster political commitment between periods of intense activism (Rupp and Taylor 1990).

The histories of activist women presented in these essays underscore the importance of the intersection of personal biography and political movement. For many women, an evolving political consciousness and identity developed through involvement in a single issue brought them into a wider world of political activism. In some cases, this development was the outgrowth of organized efforts to build multi-issue movements; in others, it was a product of deepening political commitment. For those at a point in their lives in which expanded involvement in politics was most possible—those with the freedom to travel or to form new relationships—activist experiences could be transformative, shaping life-long commitments and beliefs. For those with greater impediments to political activism—those who were young or had demanding or disapproving families—a singular experience of activism might not result in fundamental personal or political change.

A third unifying thread is the belief that radical or militant activism develops within an organizational and relational context that involves emotional issues of intimacy, sexuality, betrayal, dissension, grief, exhilaration, and conflict. Many scholars have called for increased attention to the informal dimensions of organized activism as the "platform from which movement organization occurs" (Johnston, Laraña, and Gusfield 1994, 24; also, McAdam 1988; Morris 1984). In political activism, people find not only political satisfaction (or dissatisfaction) but also patterns of collective action that are gratifying or appalling, fulfilling or debilitating. Radical activism can be a platform for forging deep, intimate relationships or for encountering damaging interpersonal conflict.

A number of the essays and personal narratives in No Middle Ground address the informal dimension of radical activism directly, and often painfully. Some women describe being committed to organizations that they came to equate with dysfunctional families. Others reflect with sorrow on the enormous personal costs that they have incurred as political activists. Still others describe activist commitment in positive, even glowing terms. In these essays are women whose actions were made possible by dense, supportive networks of relationships, women who felt isolated and alone in their activist commitments, and women who found life out of the political mainstream to be at once difficult and attractive.

Finally, the essays in No Middle Ground point out how radicalism is shaped within a larger social and political context that can be supportive, hostile, or neutral. Surprisingly, very different contexts can produce similar results. Repression directed against activists by established authorities can strengthen the internal solidarity and commitment of the group by posing more starkly the contrast between "us" and "them" (della Porta 1992). Supportive (or even neutral) contexts may have a similar effect by making radical beliefs seem mainstream and acceptable (Blee 1996). Conversely, hostile climates can create fear, confusion, and distrust within groups, while, lacking ties to external critics, radical groups may become insular and intolerant of internal dissent. The context within which radicalism exists involves not only authority figures but also the audiences that activists seek to reach and convert. Women's radical activism can be bolstered by support from the community or undermined by an unsympathetic public.

For many of the activist women portrayed in this volume, their political life took place in a context best described as threatening. These were women whose ideological and organizational commitments impelled them to take action, despite fear of violence, imprisonment, or loss of job. Others faced less hostile environments, but they too often worried about the toll that radical activism might take on them, their families, and their communities.

The essays in this volume thus advance our understanding of the gendered underpinnings of activism that occurs outside the "middle ground" of conventional electoral and pressure group politics. They suggest the importance of often overlooked aspects of radical politics such as emotionality and domestic life, and they underline the significance of issues of identity, consciousness, personal biography, and external context to our understanding of women's involvement with radical politics and militant social movements.

The volume is divided into four sections according to theme. The essays in Part I focus on the complexities of naming political activism. Those who are considered radicals or feminists by their adversaries or by the society at large do not always claim this identity themselves. The decision to name oneself in political terms is a significant step toward claiming a public political identity, but the process can involve difficult decisions of personal allegiance as well as public commitment to a political ideology.

Pam Goldman explores the meaning of radicalism in a 1975 FBI and grand jury investigation in Lexington, Kentucky. In the course of their probe, federal authorities defined members of the local progressive, gay/lesbian and counterculture community as radical. Goldman's study suggests the power of political naming in her description of how a web of suspicion spread from employees of a natural food restaurant to organizers of a rape crisis center and to members of socialist-feminist and gay liberation groups. Goldman explores how people were labeled as radical, why they embraced or rejected this characterization, and how being considered "radical" affected their political actions and identities.

Shirley Jackson's study of African American women examines the issue of naming in a different context. Many politically active African American women are hesitant to embrace a feminist identity, although they share the tactics and goals of white women in feminist organizations. Jackson traces the historical reluctance of African American women to adopt feminist identities both to the white-centeredness of the feminist movement and to the emphasis on conventionality in the African American community that labels the feminist movement negatively as lesbian-dominated. In recent years, Jackson argues, the development of "black feminist" and "womanist" political ideologies have changed the political terrain for some African American women activists, permitting a new reconciliation of racial and feminist identities.

In an interview with the prominent Native American activist Winona

LaDuke, Sonya Paul and Robert Perkinson trace LaDuke's involvement with the Indigenous Women's Network. LaDuke's activism is an example of women's militant activism that transcends traditional political labels. LaDuke's political efforts have been directed at integrating traditionally separate spheres of Native American politics and feminist politics and developing alliances across racial lines.

The second group of essays in this volume look at the relationship between personal life and political commitment, an issue that lies at the heart of understanding women's activism outside the bounds of conventional politics. The essays in Part II examine how personal ties affect political activism and how activism reshapes the nature of interpersonal relationships.

Belinda Robnett emphasizes the importance of emotional motivations in developing strong social movements by charting the roles of women at several junctions of the civil rights movement: the 1946 Women's Political Council of Montgomery, Alabama, and the subsequent 1955 Montgomery bus boycott; the 1961 Council on Racial Equality (CORE) Freedom Rides; and the 1964 Mississippi Freedom Democratic Party. Robnett argues that traditional definitions of leadership overemphasize the rational and planned nature of social movements, thus downplaying the leadership contributions of women such as those in the civil rights movement, whose charismatic leadership style was based on emotional as well as rational acts. Women leaders were able to mobilize others when the formal, male leadership was unwilling or unable to risk alienating the power structure.

In her study of a very different type of activism at a similar point in time, Beth Roy draws upon extensive interviews to contrast the stories of two high school girls involved in the struggle over racial desegregation of Central High School in Little Rock, Arkansas, as they are portrayed and remembered by their classmates. Sammie Dean Parker, a white student, is remembered as a troublemaker, in contrast to other white students who saw themselves as innocents who acquiesced in desegregation. Minnijean Brown, one of the nine African American students who desegregated Central High School, also is remembered as an instigator of trouble. Roy explores how the memories of their classmates linked the personal lives and the political actions of the two girls, pinning their respective politics to issues of body size and presumed sexuality.

Karren Baird-Olson presents a frank account of her experiences at the 1976 American Indian Movement (AIM) Bicentennial protest at the U.S.

Bureau of Indian Affairs, a follow-up to the 1972 AIM Trail of Broken Treaties caravan. At the protest, Baird-Olson and other women were separated from their children and taken to jail, before eventually being released. Baird-Olson discusses the value of AIM for creating positive racial identities and a unified political agenda among First Peoples and the role of strong women and mothers in AIM. Baird-Olson also provides an honest assessment of the backlash faced by some AIM activists, including violence, economic problems, and unsatisfying intimate relationships.

Expanding on the relationship between personal life and political commitment, the third group of essays examines the nature of the ties that bind people to activist politics, which are complex and often contradictory. As the essays in Part III demonstrate, activist commitment can be formed through dedication and belief but also through group pressure and even confusion.

Susan Marshall's study focuses on the women in antifeminist organizations whose participation has been essential to contemporary New Right political advances. Phyllis Schlafly's "Eagle Forum" and Beverly LaHaye's "Concerned Women for America" have been particularly effective in mobilizing large numbers of women into conservative politics and helping to create a backlash of public opinion against feminism. Marshall's work illuminates how involvement in groups that are opposed to gender equality can spill over into participation in campaigns with very different political agendas, such as those opposing school integration, welfare programs, and racial equality.

Kathleen Blee also examines the organizational context in which women operate on the right, but her focus is on the differences between organizational propaganda published by contemporary racist groups in the United States and the ideological and political beliefs held by adherents of these groups. Through case studies of women active in neo-Nazi, skinhead, Christian Identity, and Ku Klux Klans group, Blee argues that women racist radicals do not always share the beliefs of male racist activists, especially on issues of gender, family life, and child rearing. Commitment to a racist group thus may represent only a shallow personal commitment to the agendas and beliefs of that group.

Cynthia Costello and Amy Dru Stanley give a first-hand report on feminist disarmament politics at the Seneca, New York, Army Depot in 1983, where 2,000 women assembled to protest NATO deployment of first-strike nuclear weapons in Europe. For these protestors, the Women's Encampment for a Future with Peace and Justice was a site that challenged militarism and violence through the construction of an alternative lived feminist community of peace. However, the encampment provoked conflict with many of those in the surrounding community who were confused and alarmed by the encampment's all-female, communal practices and its acceptance of women of varying lifestyles and sexual orientations. Costello and Stanley explore how these negative community reactions prompted the encampment to modify its tactics.

Jane Margolis discusses her ten years as a member of a Marxist/Leninist/Trotskyist party. Margolis focuses on the reasons that she initially joined the party, the ties she developed within the party, and the painful reasons that led to her decision to leave. Margolis complicates our understanding of organizational ties in her examination of betrayal by those inside and outside the party and by her analysis of how organizational dynamics stifled dissent within the organization.

Taking a different approach to examining the relationship between public activism and domestic life, the essays in the fourth and final part of the book analyze how political commitments change, or fail to change, domestic relationships in a variety of protest movements on both the left and the right.

Margaret Rose focuses on married women with children in the Washington, D.C., campaign against grape and lettuce growers and wineries by the United Farm Workers of America (UFW). In the UFW campaign, tasks often were divided along traditional gender lines, with men playing a public leadership role and women managing household tasks and the needs of and the relationships among family and household members. However, Rose suggests that women's participation in public boycott activities and on picket lines also undermined traditional gender relationships by bolstering self-esteem among women and promoting cooperative relationships in marriage.

Julia Wrigley examines the role of white working-class women in Boston Restore Our Alienated Rights (ROAR), a 1974 antibusing group that fought against racial desegregation of schools. Wrigley's study illustrates a movement based on a communitywide political division of labor by gender. She finds that working-class women were dominant in the antibusing movement because it supported the status quo, did not challenge male authority, revolved around issues of education, remained confined to working-class neighborhoods, and did not require strategies like strikes or direct violence. Unlike women in the civil rights or the anti-war movement, activism against school busing, Wrigley concludes, did not significantly transform the lives and politics of its women activists.

Sally Maggard's essay is study of a strike waged by white working-class women to gain union representation at a hospital in Appalachian Kentucky. Maggard focuses on the ways that region, class, and gender interacted to shape this instance of radical action by working-class women. She examines the lives of the women who participated in union activism and discusses how this struggle forever changed how they saw themselves and their region. In contrast to women in the UFW boycott, the women who participated in the Appalachian hospital strike, Maggard argues, experienced relatively little change in their nonwork relationships because strike activities were integrated into existing frameworks of domestic life and responsibilities.

The volume concludes with an interview with Lois Gibbs, founder of the Citizens Clearinghouse for Hazardous Waste, an organization established to help develop environmental consciousness among ordinary people. In this interview, Gibb discusses how concern for her family's and community's well-being led her to organize against a local chemical waste dump and, from there, to sustained involvement with the antitoxic and environmental justice campaigns.

Together, the essays in this book illuminate women's role in radical politics in various milieus and movements. It is a role that has been overlooked far too long.

BIBLIOGRAPHY

Blee, Kathleen M. 1991. *Women of the Klan: Racism and Gender in the 1920s.* Berkeley: University of California Press.

———. 1996. "Becoming a Racist: Women in Contemporary Ku Klux Klan and Neo-Nazi Groups." *Gender & Society* 10 (December): 680–702.

———. 1997. "Mothers in Race-Hate Movements." In Alexis Jetter, Anneliese Orleck, and Diana Taylor (eds.), *The Politics of Motherhood: Activist Voices from Left to Right.* Hanover, N.H.: University Press of New England.

Bynum, Victoria E. 1992. *Unruly Women: The Politics of Social and Sexual Control in the Old South.* Chapel Hill: University of North Carolina Press.

Cobble, Dorothy Sue. 1991. *Dishing It Out: Waitresses and Their Unions in the Twentieth Century.* Urbana: University of Illinois Press.

Costello, Cynthia. 1991. *We're Worth It!: Women and Collective Action in the Insurance Workplace.* Urbana: University of Illinois Press.

de Hart, Jane Sherron. 1991. "Gender on the Right: Meanings behind the Existential Scream." *Gender and History* 3: 246–60.

della Porta, Donatella. 1992. "Introduction: On Individual Motivations in Underground Political Organizations." In Donatella della Porta (ed.), *Social Movements and Violence: Participation in Underground Organizations.* Greenwich, Conn.: JAI Press, pp. 3–28.

Duggan, Lisa, and Nan D. Hunter. 1995. *Sex Wars: Sexual Dissent and Political Culture.* New York: Routledge.

Evans, Sara. 1979. *Personal Politics: The Roots of Women's Liberation in the Civil Rights Movement and the New Left.* New York: Random House.

Ferree, Myra Marx, and Patricia Yancey Martin. 1995. *Feminist Organizations: Harvest of the New Women's Movement.* Philadelphia: Temple University Press.

Frank, Dana. 1994. *Purchasing Power: Consumer Organizing, Gender, and the Seattle Labor Movement, 1919–1929.* New York: Cambridge University Press.

Gilmore, Glenda Elizabeth. 1996. *Gender and Jim Crow: Women and the Politics of White Supremacy in North Carolina, 1896–1920.* Chapel Hill: University of North Carolina Press.

Hall, Jacquelyn Dowd. 1986. "Disorderly Women: Gender and Labor Militancy in the Appalachian South." *Journal of American History* 73 (September): 354–82.

Johnston, Hank, Enrique Laraña, and Joseph R. Gusfield. 1994. "Identities, Grievances, and New Social Movements." In Enrique Laraña, Hank Johnston, and Joseph R. Gusfield (eds.), *New Social Movements: From Ideology to Identity.* Philadelphia: Temple University Press, pp. 3–35.

Kaplan, Temma. 1982. "Female Consciousness and Collective Action: The Case of Barcelona, 1910–1918." *Signs* 7 (3): 545–66.

Kelley, Robin D. G. 1990. *Hammer and Hoe: Alabama Communists During the Great Depression.* Chapel Hill: University of North Carolina Press.

———. 1994. *Race Rebels: Culture, Politics, and the Black Working Class.* New York: Free Press.

Luker, Kristin. 1984. *Abortion and the Politics of Motherhood.* Berkeley: University of California Press.

Mansbridge, Jane J. 1986. *Why We Lost the ERA.* Chicago: University of Chicago Press.

Marshall, Susan. 1986. "In Defense of Separate Spheres: Class and Status Politics in the Antisuffrage Movement." *Social Forces* 65: 327–51.

McAdam, Doug. 1988. *Freedom Summer.* New York: Oxford University Press.

Melucci, Alberto. 1989. *Nomads of the Present: Social Movements and Individual Needs in Contemporary Society.* Philadelphia: Temple University Press.

Morris, Aldon. 1984. *The Origins of the Civil Rights Movement.* New York: Free Press.

Mueller, Carol McClurg. 1992. "Building Social Movement Theory." In Aldon D. Morris and Carol McClurg Mueller (eds.), *Frontiers in Social Movement Theory.* New Haven: Yale University Press, pp. 3–25.

Petchesky, Rosalind Pollack. 1981. "Antiabortion, Antifeminism, and the Rise of the New Right." *Feminist Studies* 7: 206–46.

Ruddick, Sara. 1989. *Maternal Thinking: Toward a Politics of Peace.* New York: Ballantine Books.

Rupp, Leila J., and Verta Taylor. 1990. *Survival in the Doldrums: The American Women's Rights Movement, 1945 to the 1960s.* Columbus: Ohio State University Press.

Szasz, Andrew. 1994. *Ecopopulism: Toxic Waste and the Movement for Environmental Justice.* Minneapolis: University of Minnesota Press.

Taylor, Verta. 1996. *Rock-a-by Baby: Feminism, Self-help, and Postpartum Depression.* New York: Routledge.

Tilly, Louise, and Patricia Gurin. 1990. "Women, Politics, and Change." In Tilly and Gurin (eds.), *Women, Politics, and Change.* New York: Russell Sage, pp. 3–32.

West, Guida, and Rhoda Blumberg. 1990. "Reconstructing Social Protest from a Feminist Perspective." In West and Blumberg (eds.), *Women and Social Protest.* New York: Oxford University Press, pp. 3–35.

Whittier, Nancy. 1995. *Feminist Generations: The Persistence of the Radical Women's Movement.* Philadelphia: Temple University Press.

Part I

What's in a Name?

Chapter Two

"I Am Kathy Power"

Expressions of Radicalism in a Counterculture Community

Pam E. Goldman

This is a story of radicalism, not in Berkeley or New York City or Boston but in Lexington, Kentucky. It is a story about one incident in the government's never-ending campaign against leftists. It is a story of scores of young, white, educated, middle-class people immersed in radical politics. It is a story of a spectrum of radicalism: radicalism by choice and radicalism by circumstance, radicalism of long duration and temporary radicalism, radicalism as defined by self and radicalism as defined by others, radicalism through politics and radicalism through lifestyle. It is a story of people with diverse histories of political activity or inactivity galvanized to support those who defied the government, people who, as the events unfolded, became more skeptical of government, even radicalized. It is a story of a time when rebellion was in the air.

The legendary Sixties did not end abruptly but spilled into the Seventies. From the seeds of the civil rights and the antiwar movements grew the women's movement and the gay and lesbian movement. Left groups of many varieties and with many splinters emerged. The younger generation was furious at the older one for sending its members to die in Vietnam, in a pointless, immoral war. With the release of the Pentagon Papers, Americans learned that their government had lied to them throughout the war. The government's reaction to antiwar activism widened the chasm between the official world and the citizenry. Interference with and surveillance of legal protest activity engendered additional mistrust of the government. The Watergate scandal, which broke in

1972, bred cynicism about the honor of politicians. Countless other episodes not as widely known fueled antigovernment sentiment within progressive movements. Fred Hampton, a leader of the Black Panthers, was gunned down in his bed by FBI agents. In 1977, *Ms.* published the results of a Freedom of Information Act request, and women learned that former FBI Director J. Edgar Hoover considered the women's movement a subversive organization and had ordered extensive surveillance of women's groups that extended even to day care centers (Braudy and Thom 1977; Pogrebin 1977). And, in the early part of the decade, many grand juries were convened to cripple the antiwar movement. Even paranoids had real enemies.

In 1970 campuses throughout the United States exploded into angry demonstrations and strikes to protest President Richard Nixon's expansion of the Vietnam War into Cambodia. That same year, Susan Saxe and Katherine Power, students at Brandeis University near Boston, became active in the National Strike Information Center which coordinated college demonstrations throughout the country ("Saxe, Power— From Honor Roll to FBI's 10-Most-Wanted List," 1975).

On September 23, 1970, Saxe and Power, along with three men, robbed a bank in Brighton, Massachusetts. During the course of the robbery, one of the men shot and killed a police officer. The three men were arrested shortly after the robbery. One was quick to inform on his partners (Harris 1976, 319). The robbery had been committed in the name of the Revolutionary Action Force, a radical group formed by the five to protest American involvement in Vietnam and Cambodia. The group had also robbed a bank in Philadelphia and had audaciously burglarized the National Guard Armory at Newburyport, Massachusetts. Classified documents obtained during the armory raid were given to an alternative newspaper in Boston, which then reported the army's contingency plans, called Operation Geronimo Bravo, for counterinsurgency operations against the civilian population of Boston (Echols 1989, 262).

Despite a massive "manhunt," Susan Saxe and Kathy Power evaded capture. Their names and pictures were added to the FBI's Most Wanted List, which, with the addition of underground leftist radicals, swelled from the traditional ten to sixteen fugitives in the early 1970s. By 1974, the FBI had captured only one radical from its list.

Four and a half years later, in Lexington, Kentucky, the search for Susan Saxe and Katherine Power resumed. The effects of the FBI's intrusive tactics and the subsequent grand jury investigation reverberated throughout Lexington and the nation. In this essay, I describe how different groups in Lexington—gay and straight; feminist, socialist and apolitical; male and female—were impacted by the FBI and grand jury investigations. Those affected came to the incident with different levels of knowledge about FBI and grand jury abuses and with different levels of political commitment. Yet, even those peripherally touched by the investigation were radicalized, whether in thought or deed, by their brush with law. Some people impacted by the investigation characterized themselves as radical. Others were branded as radical by the government. The label "radical" was used by many different people to refer to a broad range of thought and behavior.

This essay draws upon oral history interviews with more than thirty-five people involved in the Lexington FBI and grand jury investigations and with a handful of those involved in the parallel investigation in Connecticut. I interviewed Susan Saxe, but at the time I was conducting interviews, Kathy Power was still a fugitive, so I was not able to interview her. The interviews were conducted between 1986 and 1988, all over the country, and included people directly affected by the grand jury investigation, their supporters, and their attorneys.

What Happened Here?

When Lena Paley and May Kelley moved to Lexington, Kentucky, in the spring of 1974, their arrival was not remarkable. They blended easily into the community around the University of Kentucky. The two claimed to be exploring women's communities throughout the country in search of a site for the women's press they wanted to establish. They asserted that they were lesbians, and, through a shopkeeper at a bookstore near campus, they found Carlotta,[1] one of the few women in town who openly identified herself as a lesbian. Carlotta belonged to the gay liberation organization at the University of Kentucky and spoke on behalf of that organization to university classes on the subject of homosexuality.

Carlotta lived in a large house near campus with a group of lesbians, including her lover, June. She immediately invited Lena and May to move into the house and introduced them to a circle of friends and acquaintances. Carlotta and June belonged to a lesbian feminist study group, which Lena and May joined. Even when the study group was not meeting, the house was filled with women and their intense political discussions. Lena and May were enthusiastic participants.

May found a job as a secretary at a local dairy. Lena went to work as a cook at Alfalfa, a new vegetarian restaurant across the street from campus. There, Lena became known as a skilled and innovative cook. She was also known for her discourse on politics and food. The layout of the restaurant allowed for conversation between cook and patrons. In the same breath, Lena could criticize a male co-employee for being sexist while warning him about the dangers of eating saccharine. Alfalfa employees became acquainted with May, who often met Lena at the restaurant after work.

Lena and May were uncomfortable with drug use at the big house near the campus. One of the women who lived there, Etta, was a particularly heavy drug user. She was bitter about Lena's and May's criticism of her. Eventually, Lena and May moved to a new apartment on the other side of campus. One of their neighbors was a young gay man, Terry, who happened to be president of the university gay liberation organization.

In the fall, May left town. A few weeks later, Lena moved on. Lena had lived in Lexington only a few months, but, through many long evenings of talk, acquaintances had become friends, and these friends were dismayed when she refused to give them a forwarding address. She insisted that, though friendship was forever, it did not require continuity or communication. Lena's friends disagreed with her concept of friendship and were sad to lose her, but they did not challenge her decision to leave their lives so completely any more than they questioned her dyed red hair, a great incongruity for someone who espoused radical feminist politics. It was a time in which people earnestly experimented with new ways of conducting relationships and living their lives.

Not too long after Lena's departure, a man who had worked with her at Alfalfa happened to see the FBI's Most Wanted posters and came across photographs of Susan Saxe and Katherine Power. He was surprised at how much they resembled Lena and May. Soon everyone around Alfalfa was speculating about whether Lena and May were actually Susan and Kathy. The rumor reached Carlotta, June, and their friends.

To the women who had known them intimately, the possibility that Lena and May had been fugitives was confusing and frightening. It was hard to believe that the women they knew, liked, and respected could have been involved in bank robbery and murder. It was terrifying to think what might happen to them if they were found. The heiress Patty Hearst's May 1974 kidnapping by, and subsequent conversion to, the Symbionese Liberation Army (SLA) was often in the news. Patty and the SLA members William and Emily Harris were still fugitives. In May 1974 police had surrounded and apparently firebombed a house containing the other members of the Symbionese Liberation Army, killing all occupants (Hearst 1982, 28–31, 253). Friends of Lena and May imagined the two women perishing in a similar inferno.

A man from Lexington contacted the FBI in Cincinnati, Ohio, and told agents that Susan Saxe and Katherine Power might have been living in Lexington. The man was a friend of Etta. Soon, the FBI sought out Etta, who submitted to many protracted interrogations in which she revealed details about Lena, May, and mutual friends and acquaintances, whom she named. A broader FBI investigation focusing on employees of Alfalfa, lesbians, and feminist activists followed. It was January 1975.

The people at Alfalfa Restaurant cooperated with the FBI, but the experience in the women's community was more adversarial from the outset. The FBI's heavy-handed treatment of one woman, Polly, set the stage. Polly was relatively new in town. She was a feminist and a leftist and was friendly with people in both groups. One evening an FBI agent came to her door and told her that the house was surrounded by agents. He accused her of being Katherine Ann Power. Even after she produced identification, the agents persisted in questioning her. They mentioned Carlotta and June. As soon as the agents left, Polly called Carlotta and June. The lesbian community was on notice. The women had come to the attention of the FBI. They were scared.

FBI agents questioned the many women whose names they had obtained from Etta. The group included women who had come into contact with May and Lena through the study group or by visiting the house where May and Lena lived with Carlotta and June. Agents questioned women active in feminist organizations, particularly the Women's Center and the Rape Crisis Center. Their investigation extended to a lesbian bar and to women's organizations in Cincinnati.

Five women who were contacted by the FBI in Kentucky refused to talk: Carlotta and June, Wendy, Ruthie, and Dolores. Terry, Lena's and May's gay neighbor, also refused. Some of these six people had been close to Lena and May. Others were barely acquaintances. Some were quite fond of them; others disliked them. Although none of them had done anything wrong or knew where Lena and May had gone, they were steadfast in their refusal to cooperate. They were not sure that Lena and May were Susan and Kathy, and, beyond fearing for Lena's and May's safety, they came to fear for their own. To what lengths would a vindictive government go to punish people who had befriended the fugitives who had eluded the FBI for four and a half years?

As the investigation proceeded, the FBI provided additional reasons to refuse to cooperate. First there was the incident at Polly's house. Then, in an attempt to pressure Wendy to cooperate, agents obtained her long-distance telephone bill and, to try to enlist their aid, contacted all the people she had called. They told her grandmother that Wendy was a lesbian[2] and that some of her friends were members of Students for a Democratic Society, a New Left student group that had spawned subgroups, such as the Weather Underground, that advocated the use of violence. Wendy's grandmother was told that her granddaughter's friends were responsible for bombings and shootings. The six uncooperative witnesses were repeatedly approached by FBI agents. When they referred the agents to their attorney, however, the agents never contacted him. Unfamiliar cars followed the six and staked out their homes. Their mail arrived opened. Agents made inquiries about people's political beliefs and sexuality. Because of the investigation, lesbians and gay men unwillingly came out of the closet, and several of the witnesses told their parents before the FBI could. A friend's parents saw a television broadcast of a demonstration in which she participated, guessed she was a lesbian, and confronted her about it. All of these comings-out were difficult, and the repercussions were long lasting.

Robert Sedler, a University of Kentucky law professor, agreed to represent the six resisters. From him, they learned that it is not a crime to refuse to talk to an FBI agent, though it is a crime to lie to one. Since the FBI had no subpoena power, it could not force them to talk. Given these limitations, the FBI resorted to a tactic it had employed many times in the past to harass, intimidate, demoralize, silence, incapacitate, and spy on the Left. It had the United States Attorney subpoena them to appear before a grand jury. The six had then yet another reason to maintain silence, to protest this abuse of the grand jury process. The use of "political" grand juries was so rampant in the early 1970s that reform legislation was proposed in Congress; the House Judiciary subcommittee held hearings on the subject in 1973, at which Senator Edward Kennedy testified on March 13, 1973, warning that the practice was a throwback to the worst excesses of the McCarthy era.[3] After a brief respite, the use of political grand juries resumed in 1975. The extent of their reemergence is reflected by the contents of an early issue of *Quash, A Grand Jury Newsletter,* published in October 1975, which describes FBI and grand jury harassment in New York City, San Francisco, Kansas City, New Haven, Lexington, Philadelphia, and the Pine Ridge Indian reservation in South Dakota. It also reported on additional grand juries investigating the Symbionese Liberation Army, a radio station that played poetry written by women in the Weather Underground Organization, and film makers who had interviewed members of the Weather Underground. While previous grand juries had targeted leftists, the Lexington grand jury and a related one in New Haven were the first directed at lesbians and feminists.

Grand juries are shrouded in secrecy and governed by arcane procedure. If a witness provides an answer other than her name in response to any question, no matter how trivial, she may be considered to have waived any constitutional protection against answering more questions. Further, she must pick her way around these legal landmines without the presence of an attorney in the grand jury room. The best she can do is to ask the United States Attorney to excuse her after each question, dash out into the hall, and quickly confer with her attorney.

As the Lexington grand jury resisters ran in and out of the grand jury room for frenzied consultations with their attorneys,[4] their supporters lined the halls. The case followed standard procedure. After the witnesses refused to answer, asserting their Fifth Amendment and other rights, the United States Attorney asked the court to grant them immunity, which it did. The grant of immunity deprived the witnesses of any Fifth Amendment protection for their silence. The dance in and out of the grand jury room resumed. Again, the witnesses refused to testify. All six were held in contempt of court for refusing to testify and were jailed on March 8, 1975.

Although Lexington is the site of a large federal prison, the witnesses were sent in pairs to three different county jails. Wendy and June were sent to Franklin County, the state capital. Carlotta and Dolores went to Bell County, hours away in the mountains of southeastern Kentucky. Terry and Ruthie were incarcerated in Madison County, only about twenty miles from Lexington but reputed to have the worst jail in the state.

Since the witnesses were found to be in civil, rather than criminal, contempt, they could choose to end their incarceration at any time by testifying. The pressure was tremendous. Every day they were in jail, they had to decide again not to testify. Theoretically, the purpose of the incarceration for civil contempt is to coerce testimony, not to punish silence. A witness who never agrees to cooperate can be held for the duration of the grand jury, a maximum of eighteen months, after which she can be subpoenaed to a new grand jury and held another eighteen months. The potential term of coercive incarceration is endless. In this case, in addition to the possibility of indefinite incarceration for civil contempt, there loomed a threat of indictment for harboring fugitives or for a related crime, because of Lena's and May's sojourn in Lexington. The Lexington Six and their friends and supporters never believed that the purpose of the grand jury was a legitimate one, that is, to consider the appropriateness of new indictments. When challenged in court for using the grand jury improperly as an investigative tool, however, the government alluded to new indictments.

Terry and Ruthie suffered from separate confinement in the state's most miserable facility. Ruthie found the incarceration physically debilitating and was sure she knew nothing that would aid the FBI. Within days, she decided to purge herself of contempt by cooperating. She was released on March 14 and testified on March 20, 1975. On March 27 Susan Saxe was arrested in Philadelphia (Redwine 1975, 1).[5] Consequently, Terry decided to testify and was released on March 31. The remaining four witnesses decided to stay in jail until the result of their appeal became known. After they lost their appeal in May, three more witnesses, Carlotta, June, and Dolores, testified. Only Wendy remained in prison. She never testified. Her incarceration lasted fourteen months.

The Community Is Radicalized

In the manner of that time, the six grand jury resisters came to be known as the Lexington Six. The impact of their case was felt far from Lexington and by many more than six people. Geographically, the case extended to Louisville, where one of the resisters lived; to Cincinnati, to which the FBI investigation extended; to Connecticut, where the search for Susan and Kathy spawned a parallel investigation with the jailing of two grand jury resisters; to Boston and Philadelphia, where FBI investigations were commenced; to Gainesville, Florida, the home of their attorney, Judy Petersen; to New York and the Grand Jury Project; and to women's communities all over the country, which lent support, analysis, and criticism to their sisters in Lexington and which braced themselves for visits from the FBI.

In Lexington, the case most directly affected five groups: the recalcitrant grand jury witnesses (the Lexington Six); the defense committee formed to give legal, political, and personal support to the Lexington Six; the people who worked at Alfalfa Restaurant; feminists, both lesbian and heterosexual; and lesbians and gay men. At one point, supporters of the Lexington Six wore buttons proclaiming, "I am Kathy Power." Among the many meanings implied by this slogan was a fundamental one: They were as vulnerable to the government as the remaining fugitive. The button proclaimed allegiance to the radical fugitive.

Lena/Susan and May/Kathy were the prototypical radicals of this story. They willingly undertook extreme acts to further their political beliefs. They chose to live underground, relinquishing what was familiar and comfortable about their former lives. They even sacrificed their ability to do significant political work. While underground, they could not allow themselves to become too visible in any political movement or organization. Neither could they remain long enough in any place to develop deep community ties or engage in long-term projects. While in Lexington, Lena and May did not wholly avoid political life. They participated in all those political discussions at the house, in the lesbian-feminist study group, and at Alfalfa Restaurant. Sometimes, the "hunger," as Susan Saxe called it, became too great, and Lena and May risked attending a political meeting. They tried to stay in the background but could not always keep quiet. In Lexington, Lena was remembered for her comments at meetings of the Women's Center and at the support committee for the striking coal miners at the Brookside mine in Harlan County. Lena and May were far more radical than most people with whom they interacted in these Lexington venues, but they were not politically or culturally alien from them. Their differences were a matter of degree.

Within the study group, Lena and May articulated lesbian separatist politics. Unlike some separatists at the time, their indictment of patriarchy did not exclude a leftist critique of capitalism. For example, they encouraged the group to read works by the Chinese Communist leader Mao Ze-dong. The other women in the group recognized Lena and May as more radical and more knowledgeable and they liked the excitement and challenge of their ideas.

Aside from the six who went to jail, the people who had the most intimate and long-term involvement in the case were those who formed and sustained the defense committee. The group came together shortly after the first FBI inquiries but well before the first court proceedings. The composition of the group changed over time and was especially fluid in the early weeks of its existence, but, during the months of the Lexington Six's incarceration, one core solidified and endured. That core group consisted of college graduates or students in graduate or professional school and tended to be older than the grand jury resisters, who were undergraduates or recent college graduates. Most of the defense committee members had previous experience working in political groups. The law students worked on the legal defense with Bob Sedler and Judy Petersen; the rest of the committee raised money and solicited support for the grand jury resisters through public speaking, demonstrations, and media work. Once the six resisters were jailed, the defense committee added the task of satisfying their day-to-day needs, making sure they had visitors whenever they were allowed and providing them with whatever items the jails would permit them to have—books, stationery and stamps, cigarettes, games, clean clothes.

Most of the defense committee members knew each other from past political activities—antiwar organizations, the United Farm Worker's Gallo wine boycott, the Brookside coal miners strike support committee, or Friends of the Firefighters (a local group). Many of them had been members of an informal local group, the Sunday Socialists, which became a chapter of the democratic socialist New American Movement. Compared to the politics of revolutionaries like Susan and Kathy, the Weather Underground, or above-ground Marxist-Leninists, the New American Movement's gradualist politics, with its greater emphasis on electoral work, were considered tame or reformist by the more radical groups, which believed that radical political change was not possible without violence.

Many of the defense committee women had been members of the Red Star Sisters, a combination consciousness-raising, friendship, and study group that grew out of the Sunday Socialists. The group disbanded to form a broader based socialist-feminist union in preparation for the national socialist-feminist conference scheduled for the summer of 1975 in Yellow Springs, Ohio. In addition, members had participated in other women's groups, such as the Kentucky Women's Political Caucus, which worked to elect more women to office; the Lexington Women's Center, which provided a space and forum for feminist activities; the Lexington Rape Crisis Center; and Amber Moon Productions, a women's nonprofit music production organization. Overall, defense committee members within the core tended to have similar views about political issues and approaches and to count at least some of the other members among their friends.

The most difficult issue the defense committee confronted was what position to take about the five of the Lexington Six who testified before the grand jury.[6] The witnesses were confident they knew nothing that would help the FBI:

> No one here knew them [Lena Paley and May Kelley] by any other names or identities. No one knew where they went when they left Lexington. (Lexington Grand Jury Defense Committee n.d., 1)

In retrospect, it seems they were correct on this point. Although Ruthie testified before Susan Saxe was arrested, her testimony played no part in the arrest. Neither were there repercussions from the testimony of Carlotta, June, and Dolores. May/Kathy was not arrested; no new indictments were issued. Nevertheless, testifying was a complicated matter. The wisdom distilled from past grand jury investigations was: Never talk to the FBI or a grand jury, since it is impossible to anticipate how the most innocent bit of information might be used to jeopardize someone. It might provide some crucial link with which to concoct criminal conspiracy or perjury charges against the witness or someone else. Besides, the FBI was perceived as the enemy, addicted to information gathering. Why fatten FBI dossiers? The approach adopted by leftists around the country was one of noncollaboration: Anything other than complete silence was tantamount to collaboration with the government.

Carlotta, June, Ruthie, Dolores, and Terry did not feel good about testifying. They were exhausted from their ordeal in jail. Wendy was now alone and still making the daily decision to remain silent. The defense committee developed a position urging resistance rather than noncollaboration. One should maintain silence as long as possible:

> None of the people who have agreed to talk to the grand jury here have in any way changed their views on FBI harassment, grand jury abuse, their right NOT to talk to the FBI, or their view that non-cooperation (with the FBI or inquisitive media people) is the best form of resistance. They

only agreed to talk because they were unable to withstand the inhuman conditions of Kentucky county jails. Although we all understand that *anything* said to a grand jury or the FBI might possibly hurt someone, none of the six (one of whom remains in jail) felt she or he had [given] any information which led to the apprehension of Susan Saxe or could lead to the apprehension of Katherine Power.

In view of this, we of the Grand Jury Defense Fund Committee, feel sympathy and respect for these people and affirm our support for their continuing resistance. We, in no way wish to diminish the meaning of the courage and commitment [*sic*] they showed in resisting as long and as far as they could. (Lexington Grand Jury Defense Committee n.d., 2)

Those espousing noncollaboration (although they also used the term "resistance") stressed the danger of abandoning silence and implied that those who spoke were disloyal. This widely held position was expressed at a demonstration in New Haven, Connecticut, organized to protest the incarceration of grand jury resisters. The radical feminist newspaper *Off Our Backs* covered the demonstration with an article that included the position of Susan Saxe's Philadelphia supporters:

Just as Saxe had emphasized in her guilty plea statement . . . that feminism is non-collaboration, the Philadelphia women also felt there was "no room for cooperation with the FBI." They stressed this as more than just an individual tactic:

"Non-collaboration as an individual commitment is courageous and necessary, but it has little value as a tactic or a creative force in our respective communities unless the commitment to non-collaboration is community-wide. . . . We must foster and develop the sense that when one of us is called before the grand jury, we are all under attack, and when one of us goes off to jail, there are three more who come to continue her work." (Janover 1975, 4)[7]

General distrust of the government's tactics and motives intensified on March 19, 1975, when the Socialist Workers Party revealed publicly the results of its Freedom of Information Act requests, which showed that for decades the FBI had attempted to destroy the SWP through its Cointelpro program of surveillance and dirty tricks (Perkus 1975, 181).

The case of the Lexington Six attracted national attention. Those who testified were first pressured by feminists to maintain their silence, then criticized by political activists in other cities for testifying. The members of the defense committee were sensitive to criticism from big cities on the coasts, fearing that their ideas and positions would be written off as having come from a bunch of politically unsophisticated yokels. Within the committee, the issue exploded when two members wrote a letter in response to criticism from the Seattle Radical Women. While not condemning the witnesses who testified, the letter's authors expressed disagreement with their perception of the witnesses' politics, with lesbian separatism, and with the notion that it is all right to resist no further than one feels personally able. The letter criticized the defense committee for being haphazard and for weak political analysis; it also suggested a lack of cohesion within the committee, a position that surprised other members. The letter seemed to position its authors as more radical than the other defense committee members. The rift caused by the letter and its sentiments was never mended, and the letter's authors left the defense committee.

The relationship between the committee and the witnesses was a complex one. The members of the defense committee considered themselves more politically sophisticated than the witnesses. In fact, they had greater longevity in the movement, more experience as activists, and more years of political study. For the most part, the Lexington Six thought the committee did an excellent job on their behalf. "I would put my life in their hands again" was Carlotta's assessment. Ruthie was the one resister critical of the defense committee. She felt some of the members were more concerned about political principle than about the resisters. To this day, two defense committee members worry that they coerced witnesses into going to jail against their own instincts or desires and fear that they forced their more radical politics on younger and less experienced women. While not articulated by other defense committee members, a similar concern may have contributed to their protectiveness of the witnesses who testified.

Had the issues of political sophistication and coercion been presented to the witnesses, they would have disagreed and even been insulted. While most of them had little experience as activists, they saw themselves as political people, particularly because they were gay and lesbian. Their analysis of the FBI investigation and grand jury emphasized the attack on the gay and lesbian community; the defense committee concentrated on grand jury abuse. Each witness decided to resist based on her or his own combination of these reasons: S/he was furious; s/he wanted to protest the abuse of using the grand jury as an arm of the FBI; s/he was angry at the FBI's tactics and intrusion into their lives; s/he feared additional retaliation by the government; s/he liked Lena and May; s/he wanted to protect Lena and May; s/he was not sure Lena and May robbed the bank; s/he was not sure that s/he disapproved of the robbery; s/he wanted to protect Lexington's gay and lesbian community; s/he was rebellious. The only witness who mentioned pressure as a factor was Ruthie, who felt pressure from Polly, by then a defense committee member, and from Carlotta. All of the resisters interviewed said they were proud of what they did; most would do it again.

Wendy stands out from the other witnesses because she remained in jail for the balance of the grand jury term—fourteen months. According to Wendy, in some ways she was better situated than the others to remain in jail. She had finished college but had not found a job, so incarceration did not interfere with either work or school. She was not involved in an intimate relationship. She was an orphan and did not feel parental pressure and disapproval, as did some of the other witnesses. In fact, some members of her remaining family were supportive, especially her grandmother and her sisters, one of whom moved to Lexington to join the defense committee and take care of Wendy while she was in jail. Wendy also had a closer personal and political connection to the defense committee, on which all the witnesses relied during the court proceedings and incarceration. Wendy was the only member of the Six who had been active in antiwar and other left politics before the investigation. She had been an ardent antiwar activist, a Red Star Sister, and a Sunday Socialist. Wendy's long-time political activism and knowledge of past FBI and grand jury harassment and persecution strengthened her resolve. Ultimately, she remained in jail to publicize and combat grand jury abuse.

The Lexington Six were radicalized by their experience with the judicial system and Kentucky's county jails. Before the grand jury investigation they were white, middle-class students who might have critiqued government but who had little firsthand experience of how institutions wielded power. The reality was profoundly and permanently disturbing. Even with her new realizations about the workings of the system, Wendy was the only one of the five women who remained politically active after her release from jail. She moved to Washington, D.C., where she went to work for the American Civil Liberties Union's National Prison Project. She was also active in the women's and the left political communities. Over the years, however, her activism ceased as well. The only one of the six who continued to be politically active was Terry, who devoted his efforts to the gay rights movement and who organized the group wedding at the 1986 Gay and Lesbian March on Washington. His career as an activist was cut short by his death a few years later.

The Lexington Six, with the exception of Wendy, defined themselves as radical through their radical beliefs and their homosexuality more than through their activism. Similar self-definition was adopted by the other lesbians, lesbian feminists, feminists, and gay men touched by the investigation. While some were politically active in women's groups or in the campus gay organization, many were not. While some were questioned by FBI agents, many were not.[8] A few participated in the defense committee; more helped out on an occasional basis by showing up for demonstrations or visiting people in jail. Even people who never had contact with the FBI and who were not politically active in any way were affected by the investigation. They were scared and vulnerable. To put the events in Lexington in 1975 into historical perspective, it is important to note that the Stonewall Riots, a turning point in the lesbian and gay liberation movement, occurred in 1969. Yet, until 1992, gay and lesbian sexual acts were criminal in Kentucky. Any sexually active lesbian or gay man was an outlaw. The women's movement, too, was relatively new at the time of the investigation. To the Lexington Six, asserting their identity as lesbian, gay, or feminist was a revolutionary act. The statement they prepared and read in conjunction with their court appearance contained an expression of the radical nature of feminism:

> This entire [Grand Jury] procedure represents the extent of the grip that male institutions and masculine value-systems have on the lives of all of us. It is a patriarchal premise that the most effective way to relate to people is through the use of power. This male concept has proven so successful that it has been institutionalized. Our government, which purports to represent, even to "be" the people, relates to the people through power techniques and principles. It is this male concept of institutionalized power which defines people as defendants, and holds them in contempt of one male power institution as they exercise their rights guaranteed to them by another male power institution.

> Women who separate themselves from men, sexually and psychologically, pose a totally unique kind of affront to masculine power, and are likely to suffer the vengeance of the police and the courts in an especially severe way. Though everyone suffers the consequences of patriarchy, the women's movement is one of its prime targets now, for it challenges the validity—

the virility if you will—of all of its structures and definitions. For instance, as two women in Connecticut who were undergoing similar prosecution in this same investigation have noted in their statement, the legal system presently acknowledges certain "sacred" relationships in which people retain legal privacy, including that of husband and wife. We agree with the Connecticut women that the kinds of personal relationships to which we claim the same right to privacy go beyond these traditional ones. (Lexington Six n.d., 3)

The Lexington Six were also adamant in their belief that living as a lesbian or gay man was a radical act:

The male witness among us feels he would like to emphasize these positions with the following remarks: By our lifestyle, we, as gay people have effectively frightened the patriarchy to the point where the government feels it must repress us and put us away where we can no longer pose a threat to its definitions of how a person should live his/her life. Gay people are one of the most vulnerable minorities in this country today. Laws protecting us have been initiated in some cities and states, but as yet no noticeable change has come about in the majority of people's minds towards the rights of gays. Therefore, we as gay people, but more importantly as people who supposedly have rights and freedoms, seek changes in the country in which we live in to hopefully make it a less oppressive environment in which to live our lives as we damn well please, without the interference from any tool of the patriarchy. (Lexington Six n.d., 3-4)

These ideas were typical of the time; many other feminists, gay men, and lesbians shared these views.

To a lesser extent, the people at Alfalfa Restaurant also adopted a radical stance by rejecting conventional values and mores and by outlawing themselves by smoking marijuana, but these acts were rebellious rather than consciously political.

Other as Radical

Experiencing the FBI and the court system in action was a radicalizing experience for everyone connected with the case of the Lexington Six. Even the most politically seasoned of them were stunned by their encounters with the FBI and the grand jury. They might have read about police excesses against black or antiwar activists in bigger cities, but all that was distant from their own experiences. As the case progressed, they realized how they and their friends were perceived by others. Nice people, beloved people, were seen by outsiders as scary and radical. Supporters of the Lexington Six packed the courtroom for every hearing. They might have been wearing T-shirts and jeans, but they were quiet and observed courtroom decorum. Marshals stood ready to pounce on spectators for the slightest infraction of any courtroom rule, and periodically the judge sternly cautioned the audience not to be unruly, even though the spectators behaved with propriety throughout the proceedings. It was a lesson in being perceived as Other. "They made you pay for not being mainstream," observed one defense committee member. The FBI agents, the U.S. Attorney, and the judge did not care about fine distinctions between pot-smoking hippies, lesbian feminists, lesbian separatists, socialist feminists, democratic socialists, and revolutionaries. It was all the same to them. They were furious that white middle-class kids would not cooperate. The Lexington Six and their supporters were all perceived as radicals, childish yet dangerous at the same time.

It is an odious admission, but in a sense J. Edgar Hoover and his G-men were right. Every organization, from the National Organization for Women to the socialist-feminist union, from the Revolutionary Action Force to the Weather Underground to the New American Movement, was subversive. Lesbians and feminists and defiant students were all subversive. The breadth and depth of the thousands of rivulets of ideas, experiments, organizations, all feeding into the stream of a counterculture and the river of a political movement was indeed subversive of the status quo.

NOTES

Grants from the Kentucky Foundation for Women, the Kentucky Oral History Foundation, and the Money for Women Fund supported the research for this chapter.

1. With the exception of the names of the attorneys and of Susan Saxe (Lena Paley) and Katherine Power (May Kelley), all the names in this article are pseudonyms.

2. This is not the only occasion on which FBI agents used outing and contacting family members as a tactic of coercion. At the time these events were unfolding in Lexington, a similar investigation was being conducted in Connecticut, another place the FBI believed Susan and Kathy had lived while under-

ground. There, they approached the mother of one witness at work and told the sister of another that she was a lesbian (Harris 1976, 322, 346).

3. Additional discussions of earlier grand jury investigations were readily available at the time of the Lexington grand jury. For example, see Cowan 1973, Donner and Lavine 1973; and Donner and Cerruti 1972.

4. By the first grand jury appearance, Judy Petersen, an attorney from Gainesville, Florida, had joined Bob Sedler in representing the witnesses. She had previously represented leaders of the Vietnam Veterans Against the War when they were the targets of a grand jury investigation. Later in the case, Mary Emma Hixson, an attorney from Louisville, took on a substantial part of the defense work.

5. No one ever suggested that Ruthie's testimony led to Susan's arrest but, even years later, Ruthie was uncomfortable about how closely the arrest followed her testimony. The FBI never found Kathy Power. She finally surrendered in September 1993.

6. The other difficult issue arose once Susan Saxe was arrested. The committee had to adopt a public position about the bank robbery. Some committee members condemned the use of violence. Others viewed the robbery in light of the victim (a bank, part of the military-industrial complex) and the time it occurred (at the height of antiwar protests). Given a slight change of circumstance, maybe they could have been provoked to such an act. Although long and serious debate followed, the issue was not as divisive for the group because its resolution did not have an immediate or personal effect. Eventually, they devised a way to support Susan but not the robbery.

7. Italics in original.

8. Most people who were questioned by the FBI were not subpoenaed to the grand jury because they cooperated, often unwillingly, providing as little information as possible.

BIBLIOGRAPHY

Anonymous. 1975. *Quash, A Grand Jury Newsletter* (October).

Braudy, Susan, and Mary Thom, ed. 1977. "Gazette," *Ms.* (June), 69–76.

Conyers, John, Jr. 1975. "The American Inquisition," *Ramparts* (August/September), 14–16.

Cowan, Paul. 1973. "The New Grand Jury," *New York Times Magazine* (April 29), 1–7.

Donner, Frank J. 1980. *The Age of Surveillance* (New York: Knopf).

Donner, Frank J., and Eugene Cerruti. 1972. "The Grand Jury Network," *Nation* (January 3), 5–20.

Donner, Frank J., and Richard L. Lavine. 1973. "Kangaroo Grand Juries," *Nation* (November 19), 519–53.

Duberman, Martin. 1993. *Stonewall* (New York: Dutton).

Echols, Alice. 1989. *Daring to Be Bad* (Minneapolis: University of Minnesota Press).

Gitlin, Todd. 1987. *The 60s: Years of Hope, Days of Rage* (New York: Bantam).

Harris, Richard. 1976. *Freedom Spent* (Boston: Little, Brown).

Hearst, Patricia Campbell, with Alvin Moscow. 1982. *Every Secret Thing* (Garden City, N.Y.: Doubleday).

Hixson, Emmy. 1977. "Grand Jury Abuse: A Case in Point," *American Association of University Women Journal* (April), 12–15.

——— (Mary Emma Hixson). 1978. "Bringing Down the Curtain on the Absurd Drama of Entrances and Exits—Witness Representation in the Grand Jury Room," *American Criminal Law Review* 15(4): 307–35.

Janover, Madeleine. 1975. "Demonstration of Unity: Grand Jury News," *Off Our Backs* (November), 4.

Kennedy, Edward M. 1973. "Testimony of Senator Edward M. Kennedy," *Hearings on the Fort Worth Five and Grand Jury Abuse* (March 13), 1–15.

Lexington Grand Jury Defense Committee. n.d. *What Happened Here?* (leaflet).

Lexington Six. n.d. *Statement of Witnesses Subpoenaed by Lexington Federal Grand Jury* (leaflet).

Perkus, Cathy, ed. 1975. *Cointelpro, the FBI's Secret War on Political Freedom* (New York: Monad Press).

Pogrebin, Letty Cottin. 1977. "The FBI Was Watching," *Ms.* (June), 37–44.

Redwine, David S. 1975."Susan Saxe Seized in Downtown Philadelphia," *Boston Globe*, March 29, 1.

"Saxe, Power—From Honor Roll to FBI's 10-Most-Wanted List." 1975. *Boston Globe*, March 28, 3.

Chapter Three

"Something about the Word"
African American Women and Feminism

Shirley A. Jackson

African American women have been less visible than white women in most of the prominent feminist groups in the United States. This was true of women's groups in the 1970s, at the beginning of the modern feminist movement, and it is true of self-defined feminist organizations in the late 1990s. Often, this absence has been interpreted either as meaning that African American women do not sympathize with the demands of feminist politics—i.e., that feminist issues are most relevant for white women—or as indicating that African American women do not seek gender equality with the same zeal as do their white counterparts—i.e., that gender militancy has been racially segregated, practiced largely by white women.

I suggest a different route toward understanding the relationship of African American women to contemporary feminist issues and feminist organizing. I separate issues of practice and identity, suggesting that African American women often engage in practices that are similar to those used in white feminist organizations even while they shy away from the label "feminist." This way of analyzing African American women and feminism recognizes the diverse experiences, conditions, and interests of African American women (Collins 1990). It also takes into account the political complications that arise for women who are responding to oppressions based on both race and gender (Almquist 1979; Rowbotham 1992).

Beginning in December 1994, I conducted interviews with thirty African American women who were involved in African American women's organizations. Among other questions, I asked these women about their roles in the organizations, their past and present activism, the a:tivism of members of their families, and their political affiliations. Originally, I did not intend to focus on issues of feminism in this study. However, during the course of the interviews it became apparent to me that asking about the respondent's organizational and political activities necessarily raised issues about feminism. Further, it became evident that many respondents were engaging in activities that could be considered feminist.

In the early years of the modern feminist movement, young women often engaged in "rap groups," consciousness-raising sessions that brought women together to discuss their lives; through these, young women often changed their perception of themselves and society (Freeman 1979). Rap sessions also are common in African American women's organizations today, although they often are not seen as feminist processes. Rap sessions in the early modern feminist movement often excluded men for fear that they would challenge the women's solidarity with each other. In contrast, rap sessions in African American women's organizations sometimes (but not always) welcome men.

In addition, the use of "rites of passage" activities, used during the early modern women's movement (Ferree and Hess 1985), also can be found in some African American women's organizations. Rites of passage ceremonies are used in connection with efforts to revive African rituals and culture. They existed in the Black Power movement of the 1960s and are found in both women's and men's African American organizations today.

Such parallels between early modern feminist practices and the processes within African American women's organizations today prompted my interest in exploring to what extent these women had adopted personal identities as feminist through their organizational work. I found that there was a significant difference between those who chose to adopt feminist ideas as part of their identity and those who did not. Much of the variation was due to differences in age, social class, educational background, and history as an activist. These interviews suggest that some African American women are not only unwilling but also unable to claim a feminist identity. Such separation from feminism, however, reflects not so much a lack of identification with feminist principles and goals as a discomfort with the word "feminist."[1]

Contemporary African American Women and Feminism

The women in this study are all involved in African American women's organizations or in organizations that were founded by and continue to be led by African American women. These organizations deal with myriad issues: health, service, civic, advocacy, education, mentoring, and welfare. At the time of interview, the women ranged in age from twenty-six to eighty; their level of education ranged from eighth grade to master's degree. Their income ranged from an estimated $5,800 to $300,000 per year, including husband's income for married women. Some of the women interviewed were welfare recipients who had no paid employment but who were volunteers at organizations; the incomes of these women are based on what they receive from their AFDC grants. Others held paid positions as directors of their organizations. Some combined paid work in an organization with other employment, further supplementing their income.

When asked whether they considered themselves to be feminists, the women in this study responded in a variety of ways. I classify their responses into four categories: (1) unfamiliarity; (2) suspicion; (3) adamancy; and (4) fence-sitting.

Unfamiliarity is fairly straightforward. These respondents were not sure what I meant by the word "feminism" and asked me to define the term. Usually, the respondents asked, "What do you mean?," although the question often was phrased with suspicion. For example, when I asked Gloria[2] if she considered herself to be a feminist, the following interchange occurred:

> *Gloria:* What exactly . . . what is a feminist?
> *SJ:* If you understood it more completely, do you think you might then "become" a feminist?
> *Gloria:* Basically, I'm for myself.

Suspicion was expressed in tone of voice and was followed by questions that took the form of "What do you mean by *that?*" or by a hesitancy to answer. The women were also suspicious of my response to their answers. If they identified themselves as feminists, would I interpret this to mean that they were lesbian? Would I perceive them as more willing to support feminist issues than race-based issues? Would I see this as problematic?

Respondents who expressed *adamancy* about their positions, whether or not they considered themselves to be feminists, often stated their views with firmness. While some of the respondents eventually became reflective about the question, their initial response was to staunchly assert a position.

> SJ: Are you a feminist?
> Respondent: A feminist?! No.

> SJ: Do you consider yourself to be a feminist?
> Respondent: Not automatically, though. I'd have to say I did feminist work for about ten years before I would use the "f" word in relationship to myself.

In a conversation with Sandra, who claimed a feminist identification, I asked,

> SJ: Do you see yourself as a feminist?
> Sandra: Yes.
> SJ: Okay. And give me your definition of what a feminist is.
> Sandra: A feminist works on issues to promote the interests of women.

When I asked if she would be surprised if very few women in the study said they were feminists, Sandra's response was no. She commented that " 'feminist' has been made into a dirty word." I asked if she thought women in her organization would identify as feminists. She responded, "Well, if you asked them would they be interested in promoting women's interests, they'd all say yes. If you'd say, 'Are you a feminist?' most would say no."

Fence-sitting was exhibited by those respondents who said they were feminists and then changed their minds or who said they were "another kind of feminist," such as a womanist, and thus could not be neatly categorized as feminist or nonfeminist. Respondents who were unsure how to answer sometimes hedged their answers. At times, it was unclear whether the respondent simply lacked a firm opinion on whether to define herself as a feminist, whether she was suspicious of my motives or concerned about my response, or whether it was simply the term "feminist" that provoked an ambivalent reaction. For example, when I asked Anna whether or not she was a feminist, she first asked what I meant. I then responded with an answer that may have shaped her subsequent response: I explained that African Americans have been engaged in feminist activity for a long time, as workers outside the home and as caretakers in the home taking care of their children, husbands, and significant others. Anna then responded that, given my explanation, she is a feminist.

In contrast, Sharon replied that she was a feminist, but it depended on what *I* meant by the term. My definition of feminism was determinant in how she defined herself.

Laverne was a different type of fence-sitter from Anna or Sharon. She had a definite idea of her identity, but the language she used depended on her audience. Laverne made it clear that she was not dismissing the term "feminism" but that she felt that the word "womanist" best defined her as an individual.

> *SJ:* Looking at the type of organization you've actually built and this is something that is woman-centered, would you consider yourself to be a feminist?
>
> *Laverne:* Um, you know, uh, I have a . . . a . . . womanist way of viewing life because I am a woman and it's Afrocentric and female. Uh, I don't really know what the word "feminist" means. . . . What I talk about is gender-based thinking. I try to view the world through the eyes of the women that I know and I work with, and so I . . . you may define that . . . I don't reject the label [feminist] but, um . . . I rarely use that term to define myself.
>
> *SJ:* Is yours [language] womanist?
>
> *Laverne:* It would be womanist. It would be. Uh . . . the deal with it is that I have found . . . I worked with a lot of traditional feminists and I found that the women I work with are more concerned with family and community. And that kind of individualist Eurocentric thinking and the issues that for many years, the primary concerns including reproductive health and gender orientation, are not significant issues for the population that I work with [African American women].

In another interview, Claudia, age 64, responded to the question of feminism this way.

> For some things yes, and other things, no. . . . The reason that I say yes is equal pay for equal work, I'm in favor of all that. But I still like for the door to be opened for you, to pull the chair out, and for you to tip your hat.

She went on to explain,

> For some things I feel that I'm a feminist. But I mean . . . if you're doing the same job I feel like you should get paid for the same job. I feel you should have the opportunity to pursue if you want to do something. I

couldn't answer yes or no because, like I said, in some respects I am, and in some respects I'm not.

Why do these African American women have such difficulty claiming an identity as feminists? Why do they express such ambivalence about feminist militancy when they are engaged in activities in their organizations that promote the empowerment of women and that mirror many of the activities of feminist organizations? The answer lies in the complicated relationship between the modern women's movement and African American women.

The Early Years of Modern Feminism

In the early years of the contemporary women's movement, the concerns of white middle-class women were given center stage. Betty Friedan's 1963 book, *The Feminine Mystique,* is considered "the single most influential critique of women's position in contemporary society" (Ferree and Hess 1985, 35). Friedan focused on the plight of bored, middle-class housewives. Often highly educated, these women were prevented from entering the paid labor force by social pressures to find fulfillment as a wife, mother, and keeper of the home. Friedan and those who sympathized with her might have been wishing for employment outside the home, but there were plenty of working-class white, African American, Latina, and other women of color who did not have the luxury of staying at home. They worked outside the home out of necessity. They did not have the option of searching for meaningful work but found work wherever they could. As white suburban women, following the call of feminism and lured by expanding job opportunities for women in the 1960s and 1970s, found employment, it was poor and working-class women working as domestics who often picked up the slack of running their households. These women cleaned houses and cared for the children of their employers, while continuing to do unpaid housework and child care in their own homes.

Further, in the early years of the modern feminist movement, there was a persistent focus on men as a common oppressor of women. Working-class and poor women or women who suffered from racism, however, often did not want to distance themselves from men whom they saw as sharing a common oppression of race or social class. Paula

Giddings (1984), for example, argues that African American women were reluctant to embrace the modern women's movement for three reasons. First, the women who emerged as leaders in the feminist movement were largely white and middle class and were looked upon with suspicion by African American women. Second, the women's movement was growing at the same time that the civil rights movement was in decline. Some African American women felt that white women would reap the benefits of the struggles waged by African Americans. And, third, African American women objected to the idea that sexism was the major problem in the lives of women. The separatist ideology of some in the early period of the modern women's movement—the idea of women separating themselves from men and viewing men as the common oppressor—had little appeal to women who did not see sexism as the major problem in their lives (Ferree and Hess 1985). Most African American women refused to adopt a gender-separatist philosophy that they saw as central to the feminist movement because, they argued, grouping African American men along with white men as the cause of gender oppression ignored how African American men have suffered from racism at the hands of both white men and women. Further, they saw separatism as presenting African American women with an either-or choice between issues of gender and those of race.

Women involved in the women's movement were also derided by many in the African American community (and elsewhere) as lesbians, an idea that has persisted into the present (hooks 1984). The African American community has always had a strong emphasis on conventional standards of sexuality. Any movement away from these standards often is met with hostility and exclusion (see Smith 1983; Lorde 1982, 1984; Clark 1983; Collins 1990; Christian 1985; and Jordan 1981).

Feminism and the Black Power Movement

Many African American women view white women's liberation as different from their own (Polatnick 1995). During the 1960s and 1970s Black Power movement, some African American women began to question women's role in society. They were met with resistance and hostility by militant African American men and women who felt that all women's liberation efforts were part of the "reactionary white women's movement" (Polatnick 1995, 20). For African American women who chose to stand beside (or, in some cases, behind) African American men in the struggle for racial equality, there was a tension between demonstrating that racial issues were a defining factor in their lives and sympathizing with some of the goals of the women's movement. African American women who affiliated with women's movement organizations were seen as traitors and sellouts by the Black Power movement at the same time that many found women's roles in the Black Power movement increasingly uncomfortable.

The autobiography by the former Black Panther Party member Elaine Brown, *A Taste of Power* (1992), provides insight into the variety of roles that African American women played in the Black Power movement, especially the roles of woman, African American, and revolutionary. In many cases women were blocked from leadership opportunities and even derided by men in the movement who continued to view women primarily as sexual partners rather than as political comrades. Some women went along with this sexist and gendered treatment. Others refused, recognizing that while they were struggling for freedom within white male-dominated society, they also were forced to struggle as women within an African American male-dominated organization. Within the Black Panther Party, for example, the idea of revolution focused on race oppression, leaving the perception that the fight for gender equality was "a white girl's thing" (Brown 1992, 191). Men in the Party were supposed to be making decisions about the direction of the organization while women remained in the kitchen, cooking and serving food and drinks to the men before they themselves were allowed to eat. Panther men imposed a patriarchal relationship in the organization, furthering the subservient position of African American women in society. Brown herself was mentioned in an interview that I conducted with Francesca, who noted that "Elaine Brown was very respected by women in the Party. Because in fact she did do some things that did give them more power," although she also concurred that the Black Panther Party was a "very misogynistic organization."

In addition to the pressure that African American women experienced from the Black Power movement to remain within the racial movement and not be coopted by a movement based on gender, they received a similar message from a very different quarter. In a study commissioned as part of President Lyndon Johnson's "war on poverty," the sociologist (and later U.S. senator) Daniel Patrick Moynihan also argued for a change in African American women's behavior. Moynihan's report, *The*

Negro Family in America: A Case for National Action, released in 1965, implied that African American families were chronically impoverished in part because of a structure of strong women and absent fathers, i.e., that African American families were based on a pathological matriarchy. The solution appeared to be similar to what men in the Black Panthers were urging—that African American women become more passive and allow men to be in charge of politics and family life. At a time in history when white women were beginning to assert that they had the same rights as men, African American women were being persuaded to give up their rights.

The Myth of Sisterhood

In the contemporary feminist movement of the 1980s and 1990s, African American women's activism and white women's activism continue to show important differences. Even the meaning of the women's movement is different for African American women than for white women (Ferguson 1973; Lerner 1979). Of particular concern in the contemporary women's movement have been "issues of inclusion and difference" (Buechler 1990, 131). A main criticism lodged against the women's movement has been that it posited the image of a "universal woman" with gender-specific shared concerns, thus ignoring the ways that race, social class, age, and social ideologies produce differences among women. African American women committed to the Black liberation movement frequently are in agreement with the ideas of the women's liberation movement but are wary of joining a movement that does not deal directly with economic and racial concerns (Hemmons 1980). There is an underlying fear among African American women that the movement can and will abandon them (Dill 1983). In addition to African American women, Asian and Pacific women also have felt alienated by the western modern women's movement, especially when they have had to choose between alliances based on gender and those of race and nationality (Yamada 1983). Native American women have felt a similar strain over issues of racism and classism in the women's movement (Chrystos 1983).

There are several barriers that keep sisterhood among women out of reach; prominent among these are race and class (Dill 1983). From the women's suffrage movement of the late nineteenth and early twentieth centuries to the contemporary women's movement, African American women have felt forced to choose between struggling against racial barriers and battling those of gender. In response, African American women have constructed a separate feminist identity that acknowledges oppressions by race and by gender. Although African American women are not found in large numbers in the women's movement, they are involved in Black feminist organizations that share the white feminist agenda on issues such as day care, welfare, equal pay, affirmative action, and equal employment opportunities (Puryear 1980). The formal root of African American feminist thought can be traced to the beginning of the modern women's movement. In 1973 African American feminists formed the National Black Feminist Organization (Combahee River Collective 1983). Later groups continued to build Black feminist agendas by organizing African American women, largely excluding white women from their organizations. In so doing, however, they built a tradition of "Black feminism" (Tuttle 1986) that was seen as separate from the norm of white feminism. In a new manifestation of the Black feminist tradition, the writer Alice Walker has suggested that African American women's feminism is "womanist," that is, rooted in the African American folk expression that mothers use to tell their daughters that they are engaging in "outrageous, audacious, courageous, or willful behavior" (Walker 1983, xi). However commendable the idea of a "womanist" tradition, however, the term is used primarily within African American intellectual circles. Few women who are hesitant to call themselves "feminists" or "Black feminists" are aware of the alternative term "womanist."

Conclusion

The women interviewed in this study are hesitant to embrace an identity of feminism. They engage in feminist activities and processes in their organizations and they are interested in feminist issues, but they do not consider themselves feminist. In large part, this is because they think of feminists in the 1970s popular sense of the term: as antimale, male-bashing, bra-burning, white, middle-class women. They do not want to be seen as antimale, although the organizations with which they are associated are dominated by women. Many argue that, since African American women as a group had been excluded from the women's movement, there is no reason to join white women in the struggle for women's rights. Others see racial oppression as more pressing than gender oppression. As one sixty-year-old woman explained, "Well, I'll tell you . . . until Black men are free, I cannot be free."

Clearly, these women maintain negative images of what it means to be a feminist. But their alienation from the term also has to do with language. Three decades after the beginning of the modern women's movement, it is still regarded as a white movement by these women. The power of language shapes African American women's attitudes toward participation in feminist organizations, although not their commitment to many feminist goals and ideas. The terms "Black feminist" and "womanist" begin to suggest a commonality across race on issues of gender, but the history of the women's movement provides a powerful and negative lesson to African American women, suggesting that their concerns can be expendable to those of the white majority. It is important to begin by understanding the ways that African American women define their own gendered identities and goals (Moss 1995) and how this shapes their understanding of their place in the social world.

NOTES

1. This trend seems to hold for white women as well. This is not surprising given the modern backlash against social movements that began in the 1960s and 1970s (Omi and Winant, 1994).

2. This and all names are pseudonyms.

BIBLIOGRAPHY

Almquist, Elizabeth E. 1979. "Black Women and the Pursuit of Equality." In Jo Freeman (ed.), *Women: A Feminist Perspective*. Palo Alto, Calif.: Mayfield, pp. 430–50.

Brown, Elaine. 1992. *A Taste of Power: A Black Woman's Story*. New York: Pantheon.

Buechler, Steven M. 1990. *Women's Movements in the United States: Woman Suffrage, Equal Rights and Beyond*. New Brunswick, N.J.: Rutgers.

Christian, Barbara. 1985. *Black Feminist Criticism, Perspectives on Black Women Writers*. New York: Pergamon.

Chrystos. 1983. "I Don't Understand Those Who Have Turned Away From

Me." In Cherrie Moraga and Gloria Anzaldua (eds.), *This Bridge Called My Back: Writings By Radical Women of Color*. New York: Kitchen Table, pp. 68–70.

Clark, Cheryl. 1983. "The Failure to Transform: Homophobia in the Black Community." In Barbara Smith (ed.), *Home Girls: A Black Feminist Anthology*. New York: Kitchen Table, pp. 197–208.

Collins, Patricia Hill. 1990. *Black Feminist Thought: Knowledge, Consciousness, and the Politics of Empowerment*. Cambridge, Mass.: Unwin Hyman.

Combahee River Collective. 1983. "The Combahee River Collective Statement." In Barbara Smith (ed.), *Home Girls: A Black Feminist Anthology*. New York: Kitchen Table, pp. 272–82.

Dill, Bonnie Thornton. 1983. "Race, Class, and Gender: Prospects for an All-Inclusive Sisterhood." *Feminist Studies* 9 (1): 131–50.

Ferguson, Renee. 1973. "Women's Liberation Has a Different Meaning for Blacks." In Gerda Lerner (ed.), *Black Women in White America*. New York: Vintage, pp. 587–92.

Ferree, Myra Marx, and Beth B. Hess. 1985. *Controversy and Coalition: The New Feminist Movement*. Boston: Twayne.

Freeman, Jo. 1979. "The Women's Liberation Movement: Its Origins, Organizations, Activities, and Ideas." In Freeman (ed.), *Women: A Feminist Perspective*. Palo Alto, Calif.: Mayfield, pp. 557–74.

Friedan, Betty. 1963. *The Feminine Mystique*. New York: W.W. Norton.

Giddings, Paula. 1984. *When and Where I Enter: The Impact of Black Women on Race and Sex in America*. New York: William Morrow.

Hemmons, Willa Mae. 1980. "The Women's Liberation Movement: Understanding Black Women's Attitudes." In La Frances Rodgers-Rose (ed.), *The Black Woman*. Beverly Hills, Calif.: Sage, pp. 285–99.

hooks, bell. 1984. *Feminist Theory from Margin to Center*. Boston: South End.

Jordan, June. 1981. *Civil Wars*. Boston: Beacon.

Lerner, Gerda. 1979. *The Majority Finds Its Past: Placing Women in History*. New York: Oxford University Press.

Lorde, Audre. 1982. *Zami, A New Spelling of My Name*. Trumansberg, N.Y.: Crossing Press.

———. 1984. *Sister Outsider*. Trumansberg, N.Y.: Crossing Press.

Major, Reginald. 1971. *A Panther Is a Black Cat*. New York: William Morrow.

Moss, Barbara A. 1995. "African American Women's Legacy: Ambiguity, Autonomy, and Empowerment." In Kim Marie Vaz (ed.), *Black Women in America*. Thousand Oaks, Calif.: Sage, pp. 19–37.

Omi, Michael, and Howard Winant. 1994. *Racial Formation in the United States: From the 1960s to the 1990s*. New York: Routledge.

Polatnick, M. Rivka. 1995. "Poor Black Sisters Decided for Themselves: A Case

Study of 1960s Women's Liberation Activism." In Kim Marie Vaz (ed.), *Black Women in America*. Thousand Oaks, Calif.: Sage, pp. 110–30.

Puryear, Gwendolyn Randall. 1980. "The Black Woman: Liberated Or Oppressed?" In Beverly Lindsay (ed.), *Comparative Perspectives of Third World Women: The Impact of Race, Sex, and Class*. New York: Praeger, pp. 251–75.

Rowbotham, Sheila. 1992. *Women in Movement: Feminism and Social Action*. New York: Routledge.

Smith, Barbara, ed. 1983. *Home Girls: A Black Feminist Anthology*. New York: Kitchen Table.

Tuttle, Lisa. 1986. *The Encyclopedia of Feminism*. New York: Facts On File Publications.

Walker, Alice. 1983. *In Search of Our Mothers' Gardens*. New York: Harcourt Brace Jovanovich.

Yamada, Mitsuye. 1983. "Asian Pacific American Women and Feminism." In Cherrie Moraga and Gloria Anzaldua (eds.), *This Bridge Called My Back: Writings By Radical Women of Color*. New York: Kitchen Table, pp. 71–75.

Chapter Four

Winona LaDuke

Sonya Paul and Robert Perkinson

Winona LaDuke first spoke before the United Nations when she was only eighteen years old. In the nearly two decades that have passed since, she hardly has paused for a breath. Today, LaDuke is one of the most prominent Native American environmental activists in North America. She brings a burning focus to her work, which is devoted to turning society "from the synthetic reality of consumption and expendability to the natural reality of conservation and harmony."

LaDuke is an enrolled member of the Mississippi Band of Anishinabeg (also known as the Ojibwe or Chippewa), but she grew up with radical parents in East Los Angeles and Ashland, Oregon. She went to college at Harvard, then dove head-first into Indian politics while completing graduate school along the way. As a leader in the ultimately successful struggle against James Bay's hydroelectric development in the 1980s, she became an international voice for indigenous environmental concerns.

These days, LaDuke prefers to balance broader campaigns with battles closer to home. She has returned to her father's White Earth Reservation in northern Minnesota, where she lives with her two children, Waseyabin, age six, and Ajuawak, age four. As campaign director of the White Earth Land Recovery Project, LaDuke divides her time among an eclectic variety of local issues, from land restoration to organic agriculture.

Even from the backwoods, however, LaDuke remains connected to international forums. She lectures regularly at universities, serves on the board of Greenpeace, and is the environmental program officer for the Seventh Generation Fund. Last spring, she organized a national benefit tour with the Indigo Girls, raising funds for a host of grassroots organizations and thrusting the growing Indigenous Women's Network (IWN) into the national spotlight. In September, she led an IWN delegation to the World Conference on Women in Beijing.

LaDuke is also an accomplished writer, and is currently finishing a book on Native environmentalism for South End Press.

Face to face, LaDuke has a commanding presence. She has an incredible drive to get things done, and some friends call her "the Duchess." But she also exudes great personal warmth.

We spoke with her at her home on White Earth. It is an unassuming log house overlooking wild rice beds and beautiful Round Lake. Inside, the frenetic pace makes the dwelling a political office as much as a home. We sat on the deck in the sunshine, as the sounds of the children playing mingled with the calls of birds.

Q: You were born in L.A. and educated at Harvard. How did you make your way back to White Earth?

Winona LaDuke: Ever since I was little I wanted to come back and work in the Indian community. My father is from White Earth, and I never felt entirely accepted on the West Coast. As a kid, I was always the one passed over at dances and never picked for sports teams. At that age, it's easy to blame the victim—you're too dark or your hair is funny. But that's not what it's really about. It's about learned racism and classism. Eventually, I started to question what's wrong with America.

My family also had a keen sense of social responsibility. I was never told to go out and make money, but to do the right thing. Before my parents split up, they were both active in Indian politics in Los Angeles. Later, I remember my mom taking me out of school for antiwar and civil rights marches.

Q: What led you to the Ivy League?

LaDuke: I'm not sure. I certainly wanted to escape from my hometown. I also think I went to Harvard because they told me I couldn't. My guidance counselor basically said, "Don't bother. Go to vo-tech."

But once I got there it turned out to be a transformative experience. A great bunch of Indian students came and found me, and I was politicized pretty quickly. I was also very fortunate to have excellent role models. One of the first events I attended was a speech by Jimmie Durham of the International Indian Treaty Council. He talked about how there was no such thing as the "Indian Problem." He said that it was a problem with America. As a college student, I was trying to understand the world, and all of a sudden I just got it. His message of decolonization resonated with me entirely. So I asked him if I could go to work for him. From that point forward, at the age of eighteen, I worked on Native environmental campaigns all over the West and learned from people on the front lines. They laid the foundation of my political thinking.

School was different. There I learned how to utilize the resources of a major institution to benefit communities. For example, while doing environmental research on corporate practices in Indian Country, I found that more information was available to me in Cambridge, thousands of miles removed, than on the reservations themselves (which is part of the problem).

Q. How does it feel to be back home after a whirlwind month on the road with the Indigo Girls?

LaDuke: Oh my God, what a relief! We called it "the big party," but it was tremendously successful. We raised about $250,000 for local organizations and their projects. But the "Honor the Earth" tour also raised political awareness. With the Indigo Girls, the concerts drew the attention of an entirely new constituency. Their fans seemed to be mostly young women, and most of them probably had not thought much about indigenous issues. It was a great opportunity for us. We reached some 40,000 people with a message that may really challenge their thinking.

Q: Are you worried that the support you received exists only on the surface?

LaDuke: Well, I don't assume that anyone will automatically be moved toward political action, especially in an audience that largely doesn't know anything about Indian people. But before you can expect anyone to act, you have to talk to them about the issues. We tried to give the audience tangible ways to relate to the Indian community and its struggles. We had action cards, political speeches, local press conferences, and a lot of literature available. This provided an opportunity beyond buying sage or crystals or however else those folks might relate to Indians. So while only a few will start to actively support indigenous causes, I think everyone at least heard us. That's important.

Q: When you mention the "sage and crystal" scene, it brings to mind the Indigo Girls' album, *Rites of Passage*. On the cover, their faces are painted with what look like Native American designs and a lot of their lyrics have Native American themes. Do you think they have been guilty of adopting indigenous symbols disrespectfully?

LaDuke: No, in my experience they have been very respectful. Like a lot of people, they find some resonance in the Indian community, but they have their own spiritual practice. Both of them come from long Christian traditions, and they reflect that in their music. So, to me, Amy and Emily—the Indigo Girls—are not spiritual panhandlers.

Also, when they played the Indian communities on the tour, they brought something with them—their hearts. That is the essence of much indigenous thinking—balance. You only receive if you give. Those who appropriate aspects of Native cultures or merely purchase Indian products miss that essential reciprocity. As a consequence, they might read a book or own an artifact, but the meaning is lost.

Q: Do you see the Indigenous Women's Network becoming a major player in Native American politics?

LaDuke: I don't foresee it becoming a prominent national organization with its own agenda, separate from work Indian women are doing in their own communities. The women of IWN are very active and don't need a new institution. They need an interactive forum that leverages resources and empowers traditional, community-based women. In my view, national Indian organizations should not have a franchise on the "Native American perspective." Our communities have a diversity of views, and local women have a right to have their voices heard. Today they are not, and I want IWN to amplify their voices.

Q: What are some examples of IWN's work?

LaDuke: We work on a wide spectrum of concerns. In North America, we host international conferences, publish our magazine, *Indigenous Woman,* and support a growing list of local projects. Most of them are cultural and environmental, but they aren't always what you might think. For instance, when I lived at Moose Factory in James Bay, Canada, IWN supported a reservation diaper service. Moose Factory was a real Pampers community—handing money to disposable-diaper companies and creating sanitation problems in our dumps. Most babies today are in disposables. Since most women work and don't have automatic washers, a cloth diaper service made a tangible economic and environmental benefit. I'd like to start one on every reservation.

Q: How do you see IWN's participation in the World Conference on Women in Beijing? Do you think these jet-set conferences can have tangible impacts on women's lives?

LaDuke: I think you have to do political work on all levels. The United Nations is one arena, and we think there is real progress to be made. At the official governmental forum in Beijing, we're pressing on two major issues: first, we wanted the United Nations to legally acknowledge indigenous "peoples," as opposed to "populations" or "people." This would guarantee a new level of international recognition and legal rights. Secondly, we were urging governments to adopt the Declaration of the Rights of Indigenous Peoples, a comprehensive legal document drafted by indigenous organizations in Geneva over the last several years.

At the nongovernmental-organizations' forum, we wanted to begin making inroads for indigenous women. I believe grassroots women have an absolute right and need to participate on equal footing in these forums. Ours was an alternative voice to that of the central U.S. delegation. We share some common ground, but the issues of the mainstream women's movement are not always our issues. Indigenous women's concerns are more integrated with human-rights struggles. Take, for example, the feminist movement's focus on freedom of choice. It's an important issue and I am pro-choice, but I don't believe that abortion rights are the primary concern of Native women.

Q: What should the women's movement take on?

LaDuke: Issues of survival. As a woman, I think it makes sense for me to worry about whether my great-grandchildren can live here and whether indigenous communities can survive. I also think the mainstream women's movement should be more concerned about the environment. That's a women's issue. Take breast cancer, for example. Women should be rioting. Instead, the disease gets overly personalized and all of the toxic dumping and environmental destruction that cause it get ignored.

The women's movement has immense resources at its disposal, but historically it has focused on an exceedingly narrow range of concerns. It has misused its power.

Q: You mention the conflicts in Beijing between the perspectives of traditional, white feminists and indigenous women. How have you dealt with similar problems in your environmental work? You work extensively with Greenpeace, for example.

LaDuke: I've been on the board of Greenpeace since 1991 and have seen it undergo major changes. Greenpeace has grown from its "guys-on boats" reputation to being capable of working closely with communities. When I first started, Greenpeace was suing some Indians to stop their subsistence harvest. Today, we have a sovereignty policy that prevents that type of interference. Now there is a lot more collaboration and discussion with Native peoples.

My work has been to support Native campaigns, leverage resources, and challenge Greenpeace's basic political agenda. We need to revisit who gets to decide what is an important and urgent issue. This is a fundamental question that needs to be asked of these white organizations: "Who has that right?"

For certain, Greenpeace's work is light years ahead of other big environmental groups. Locally, for example, we've been battling the Nature Conservancy—a totally white organization here. They bought 400 acres of our land and gave it to the state of Minnesota. I want them to purchase land and give it to us.

Q: How do you respond to those who criticize you, a Native American environmental activist, for working within these mostly white organizations?

LaDuke: White organizations have to be pressed from within. They are not going to change on their own, and they need to be politicized and informed. Sometimes, non-Native people can spark that reorientation, but other times they need assistance from indigenous organizers.

In any case, I have a lot of respect for Greenpeace. I believe in the principle of bearing witness and direct action. I may not always agree with them, but I don't always agree with Indian organizations, either. So I'm not ashamed of my work there. Greenpeace is a proactive organization that has a significant presence in twenty-six countries. My work in Greenpeace is a battle, but it's a battle worth fighting.

Q: In the environmental movement, the word "sustainability" has become almost a cliché. How does your concept of sustainable economics and development differ from mainline understandings?

LaDuke: Native communities have an inherent advantage in understanding and creating sustainability. They have cultural cohesion and a land base, and both of these foundations are essential for any sustainable community. These days, there are a lot of New Agers creating "intentional communities," collective farms, housing, and so on, and I think it's great. But those who build community from scratch have much less going for them than we do. They have to make a community; we already have one. Indigenous peoples collectively remember who they are, and that memory creates a cultural fabric that holds us together. That's why rural, Native organizing is so vital. It can be the watershed of sustainability.

Q: How does this traditional understanding of sustainability shape your political work?

LaDuke: Take White Earth. Here we have a sustainable-communities project. Its purpose is to sort out what is useful from our culture and from Euro-American cultures in order to move forward. On our organic raspberry farm, for example, we use tractors and other technologies. We also are investigating solar and wind power in the area. Innovations don't have to be indigenous, but they should at least make sense within our cultural practice and context. The question we ask ourselves is, "Does this technology fit?" As it turns out, it's a question of fundamental importance. It's natural to ask from the perspective of indigenous values, and it speaks to the entire framework of sustainability.

But the question of whether a product should be invented at all almost never comes up in the United States. If it did, we would live in a very different world. Products that don't biodegrade might never be produced, and our economy would have an inherent base of common sense. I believe that in order to build a sustainable society overall, indigenous peoples need to reinsert this criterion into the mainstream, "If the Creator didn't make it like that, should it be here?"

Q: What doesn't fit?

LaDuke: I don't have all the answers. There are a number of factors that a community can use to decide, "How big is its impact? How will it change the land? Does it make us lazy?" Sometimes you know something doesn't fit right away. For example, some people are using air boats to harvest wild rice now. But there is widespread opposition on the reservation because wild rice is a cultural wellspring. According to our traditions, the Creator gave us wild rice as a food, and the instructions on how to harvest it didn't include an air boat.

Q: You mentioned working with this philosophy on White Earth. How has your work evolved here?

LaDuke: We founded the White Earth Land Recovery Project in 1988 after exhausting nearly all legal means to reclaim our reservation. The land dispossession we suffered was catastrophic. White Earth constituted 837,000 acres of Indian land when it was reserved under an 1867 treaty, but almost all of it has been taken away. When I moved back to White Earth after college, 93 percent of the reservation was owned by non-Indians and three-quarters of the Indian population lived off-reservation. This shows what has happened to us. It is the American process of making refugees.

Therefore, our project's goals are tied closely to this history. We want to recover the original reservation. We acquire land outright when we can, but we also negotiate transfers to the tribal council.

Q: Who controls land once it is recovered, and has this created any tension between you and the tribal government?

LaDuke: So far we have purchased about 1,000 acres, and that land is held by us. We hold it in trust like the Nature Conservancy. It's important to maintain this control because the White Earth Land Recovery Project has a specific cultural and environmental agenda. And it often runs counter to the tribal council's focus on economic development and gambling. They have been reluctant (and that's an understatement) to preserve traditional usage. When we wanted to build a ceremonial round House on the reservation, for instance, it almost took an act of Congress to get them to agree.

This is not to say we never cooperate with the council. When it comes to negotiating the transfer of government lands, we are pressing for council ownership or management. This is a practical matter, but a principled one as well. I support any form of Indian land ownership on the reservation.

Q: What impact has gambling had on White Earth?

LaDuke: I look at it somewhat pragmatically. This is the poorest county in the state. With the casino income, the council has built a housing project, renovated schools, and is building a health clinic. No one was going to do those things for us. They did it with their gambling money, and I think that's all right.

On the other hand, the casino is a giant energy-sucking machine—lights flashing twenty-four hours a day. And fundamentally, it bases our economy on service. It creates jobs but strips jobs from the land. That's not the kind of economy I want on my reservation. I don't want my community to be serving white people.

Q: Do you think expanded gaming on Indian reservations has enhanced Native sovereignty overall?

LaDuke: Not really. It seems to me that the government says a tribe is sovereign if it has a casino or a dump. But when a tribe wants to regulate pesticides or maintain water rights, its sovereignty suddenly disappears.

Q: You say that the White Earth Land Recovery Project has a cultural agenda. What specific projects does that involve?

LaDuke: It's difficult to separate "cultural" from other projects because they are so integrated. One of our most successful cultural efforts, for instance, was an economic-development initiative. In 1985, a women's marketing collective started a project to encourage the local processing and marketing of wild rice. In just a few years, it transformed an extractive industry with profits going off the reservation to an important, self-reliant base of the local economy.

We also sponsor a cutting-edge Ojibwe language program. It is called Wadison, or "nest," and it enables a small group of children and their families to become fully literate. They form the nest of fluency to sustain the more general level of knowledge carried on by everyone. Eventually, we want Ojibwe to become more popular across the board, for words and phrases in everyday speech to become cool. We also want Minnesota to recognize Ojibwe and Dakota as official state languages.

Q: A lot of nonprofits have scaled back in recent years just to survive. How do you account for the success of the White Earth Land Recovery Project and all of its programs?

LaDuke: We started out very small and I don't want to misrepresent our impact, but we have tenacity, a great sense of urgency, and our people are committed. Here, there is a local intensity that national organizations lack. This community has been through a lot, but there's an enormous amount of brilliance here. Most of all, there is no alternative. If we don't attend to our own needs, no one will. The tribal council won't preserve our language. It's almost extinct, but the council wants to wait for a federal grant to study the problem.

That's one of the reasons I always wanted to come back to the reservation and focus my political work here. Our politics emanate from cultural practice, and that helps keep me going. We hold ceremonies as well as political events. In this world it's easy to get distracted, but having spiritual and cultural cohesion helps us stay focused.

Q: What about organizing outside of your community?

LaDuke: The White Earth Land Recovery Project has been successful because we attack problems pragmatically. We know that America has to change. As a complement to rural, community-based organizing, we need to have smart, connected folks arguing on our behalf in urban areas. Our organization has hundreds of non-Indian members. A lot of them are yuppies. This helps us politically when we need to influence state leaders. We can get rich people in Minneapolis to be our advocates. They have a recognized voice that we don't. Working with nonreservation people also helps change the predator-prey relationship. We're forging ties across the divide of those who consume and those who produce.

Q: Has the country's overall shift to the right made your work more difficult?

LaDuke: My experience politically is that the further right those in power are, the more Americans wake up. In Greenpeace, for example, our revenues declined when Clinton and Gore were first elected. Everyone abdicated responsibility and thought, "good, our guys will take care of everything." That kind of thinking is totally unethical. It is an abdication of your responsibility as a human being.

Today, the insane politics in this country are making our work more clear. When I was in Alaska recently, I read that its Congressional delegation wants to change the name of the Arctic National Wildlife Refuge to the Arctic National Oil Reserve. "That's really cool," I thought. When people hear that, it wakes them up. Of course, I'm very scared for our land and our people, but the primary danger of America is its complacency. If we can keep the predator off some critical places and simultaneously spark people to consciousness, then we have a chance.

As far as White Earth is concerned, we can't get any favorable legislation in this climate. But then again, I haven't seen any type of just legislation in either Democratic or Republican eras. They say the most positive work for Indians came under the Nixon Administration. So for us, the rightward turn might not make much difference.

Q: Has there been any improvement in Indian policy under Clinton? They certainly have held a lot of conferences.

LaDuke: No, I think it's total lip service.

Q: You say that people surrendered their power to the Clinton White House. Does this occur with tribal governments as well?

LaDuke: Certainly. People think their leaders will take care of problems for them. On many reservations, it's like having the fox guard the chickens. It's dumb. This is why it's so important for a reservation-based, nonprofit sector to develop. Otherwise, tribal councils become the exclusive voice for Indian people. It is my belief that everyone has a right to determine the future equally. I should have as much responsibility for our future as my tribal chair. This type of democratization of responsibility is also more traditional. In traditional cultures everyone has responsibility. There is delegation of authority, but everyone has an important role.

Q: What would a model of traditional governance and decentralization mean for the United States as a whole?

LaDuke: It would undermine the entire structure of empire. If leadership and political power truly rested with local communities, then multinationals would find it impossible to poison their locales in the name of a "greater good." Absentee landowners would cease to exist, and small communities could preserve their distinct integrity. Cooperating on a smaller level could help everyone—Indian communities, Amish communities, urban enclaves, and so on. These can all be healthy, but they need to be nourished. As it is today, they are being technologically and culturally homogenized.

The last 400 years have been about building empires. This is not sustainable. Empires are about taking what doesn't belong to you and consuming more than you need. In order to move forward, we need to acknowledge this ongoing history. This is the fundamental paradigm of appropriation that remains unquestioned in America. We need to ask, "What right does the United States really have to this place?"

Part II

Personal and Political

Chapter Five

African American Women in the Civil Rights Movement

Spontaneity and Emotion in Social Movement Theory

Belinda Robnett

Those who have studied the history of social movements have disagreed about the conditions necessary for social movements to arise, to attract adherents, and to endure. One of the earliest social movement theories, collective behavior theory, concluded that movements were irrational, spontaneous events that tended to emerge from shared grievances and collective frustration.[1] This model has increasingly lost favor, and many social movement scholars have turned their attention to the more rational components of movements. Resource mobilization theory posits that, while grievances and frustrations may spark collective action, resources—money, persons with free time, and other such pragmatic elements—are essential for shaping those grievances into a viable social movement. This framework disavows the strategic significance of emotions and spontaneity and claims that social movements develop through rational, planned activity, just as organizations that maintain the status quo do.[2]

The political process variant of this model adds the notion that movements, while emerging out of rational choices and dependent upon resources, require political opportunity;[3] the state (i.e., its economy and institutions) must be open to challenges, or the incipient movement would be crushed. Both resource mobilization theory and its political process variant emphasize structure, strategies, and institutions.

In contrast, new social movements theory stresses the internal dynamics of social movements and focuses on the need to develop movement cultures, or shared attitudes about society, and movement identities, or personal transformations of potential movement followers. Scholars with this emphasis suggest that, in the past, these forms of movement work were less necessary because movements such as the French Revolution attracted individuals with similar social backgrounds and experiences, whereas new social movements (e.g., the peace movement) center on issues that do not necessarily draw upon a constituency with shared social characteristics and experiences. Others add that developing movement culture and identity are difficult, even when participants are all women or of the same race.[4]

Recently, within these theoretical frameworks, there has been a new wave of social movement work that emphasizes micromobilization. These theorists analyze the processes by which consensus is formed and action is mobilized. As Bert Klandermans notes, structures alone cannot mobilize individuals to act.[5] Potential constituents must be convinced of the credibility and legitimacy of participation and must be persuaded to act. Research has therefore centered on discerning the processes necessary for persuading adherents and potential constituents to join a movement.[6]

David Snow and his colleagues outline four social psychological processes central to the recruitment process. *Frame bridging* involves providing those already predisposed to one's cause with information sufficient to induce them to join the movement. The process of *frame amplification* rests on the compatibility of the movement's values and beliefs with those of the potential constituents and emphasizes efforts to convince individuals that their participation is crucial and that the movement's goals can be achieved. *Frame extension* occurs when movement adherents cast a wider recruitment net, incorporating concerns not originally part of the movement's goals but valuable as a means of expanding support for the movement. Finally, *frame transformation* is the process whereby individually held frames, or beliefs, are altered, entirely or in part, to achieve consensus with the movement's goals.

This brief discussion of recent theoretical disputes among students of social movements provides the context for the research presented in this essay. Scholarly dialogue, while valuable, has largely focused on arguing the supremacy of one set of constructs over another, obscuring the need to deepen our understanding of the concepts and assumptions within them. The present study of African American women in the civil rights movement addresses this need by focusing on three salient areas of research that I believe have received inadequate attention: social location and movement identity formation; definitions of leadership; and the dialectical flow of movement momentum.

A holistic theory ought to address both the emotional/internal motivations discussed by the collective behaviorists and the external and presumably more rational concerns over resources and political opportunities emphasized by resource mobilization theorists. Although new social movement theorists emphasize the internal factors that maintain social movements, including culture and identity, they do not provide us with an understanding of the strategic uses of emotion for micromobilization and group solidarity. Moreover, we know neither who performs these tasks or how.

Social Location and Identity

The significance of the social position of movement carriers (those who do the emotional and psychological work necessary to support the movement) within movements with both men and women participants has generally been neglected. Although identity is discussed in the context of developing collective identity, group consciousness, and solidarity,[7] an analysis of who is likely to succeed at the bridging, amplifying, extending and transforming techniques needed to persuade potential constituents to join the movement has been neglected. Consequently, the significance of who is doing what type of micromobilization for the movement is left unanalyzed. We do not yet fully understand how mobilization takes place in day-to-day community work, and we do not know who is likely to do such work.

This brings us to a second problem. Although social movement theorists often discuss movement leaders, the concept of leadership itself has generally not been analyzed. Typically, movement participants are dichotomized as leaders or followers. An analysis of race, class, gender, and culture has led me to a reconceptualization of leadership activities within social movements. In the civil rights movement, many so-called "followers" operated as what I term bridge leaders—people who utilized frame bridging, amplification, extension, and transformation to foster ties between the social movement and the community and between prefigurative strategies (strategies aimed at spurring individual change, identity, and consciousness) and political strategies (organizational tactics designed to challenge the movement's existing relationships with the state and other societal institutions).[8] Indeed, the activities of bridge leaders in the civil rights movement enabled potential followers to overcome the formidable barriers that separated their personal lives and the political life of civil rights movement organizations.

Feminist scholars, of course, have challenged the basic approaches and the theoretical underpinnings of analyses of political participation.[9] They suggest that a top-down view of political participation necessarily excludes women and ignores their significant contributions. In contrast, several studies of women's organizations have analyzed organizational hierarchies in terms of their forms of power and leadership.[10] Other feminists writing about women's organizations have approached the study of social movements through an examination of women's networks[11] or their separate subgroups within a movement.[12] Yet, the notion of bridge leaders is largely undeveloped in feminist as well as social movement theory.

This lack of acknowledgment that social movements have more than one level of leadership has led to several problems in theory development. Aside from the fact that race, class, gender, and culture shape who does what for the movement, focusing on only formal leaders has led to an overemphasis on rationality and the planned nature of movement activities.

The civil rights movement was a rebellion by Blacks seeking mainstream inclusion and equal access to social institutions. Therefore, formal Black leaders had to speak simultaneously to two opposing constituencies. While their fundamental intention was to speak for and act on behalf of all Black people, they understood that fulfilling the goals of the movement demanded that they persuade white leaders of the civic irrationality of racism and the democratic logic of desegregation. Seeking concessions from four successive administrations constrained the leaders of the formal Black movement; the white body politic would have crushed the movement entirely. Formal leaders were not out of touch with the mass of Black people, but they understood that their adherence to their constituents' desires had to be balanced with the need to gain the state's approval for change. Pushing the state too far could have been disastrous. The leaders had to appear as rational leaders in control of the activities to which they led their followers.

While formal leaders kept an eye on the state apparatus for opportunities and concessions, bridge leaders kept their fingers on the pulse of the community. The goal of bridge leaders was to gain trust, to tie the masses to the movement, and to act in accord with their constituents' desires. It was within this context that bridge leaders' actions were much less restricted. The divergence of viewpoints and goals between bridge leaders and formal leaders necessarily created a degree of conflict. Yet, ironically, this conflict also contained a symbiosis that served to sustain and strengthen the momentum of the movement. When formal leaders were reluctant to act in a particular way, bridge leaders often acted in their stead. Likewise, their affiliation with movement organizations and formal leaders gave legitimacy to the activities of bridge leaders.

Reconsidering Rationality vs. Emotion, Spontaneity vs. Planned Activities

The kind of work done by bridge leaders was a characteristic consequence of their position as the trusted representatives of the people. Many of their actions were spontaneous responses to planned activities gone awry and were motivated by the high emotions stirred up at such times. This truth requires a reconsideration of the ways in which social movement theories have depicted emotion and rationality in relation to leadership.

An Historical Perspective

Max Weber, one of the founding fathers of sociology, discerned three forms of leadership; charismatic, traditional, and legal. Traditional authority is conferred by one's rank and status in society, while legal authority is the legitimate use of force codified by law. These two types of authority are created by the position rather than by any personal characteristics of the individual. In contrast, charismatic authority remains independent of one's status or position and instead derives from one's personal qualities. Weber believed that "true charisma" tends to be short-lived, emerging during moments of crisis when the emotionally charged masses look to some extraordinary individual to lead them. Followers generally perceive the charismatic leader as one who embodies extraordinary capabilities, at times even a degree of supernatural power. The main point here is that, for Weber, the acceptability of emotion and spontaneity as leadership qualities was form-specific; these elements were not antithetical to leadership per se.

Whereas, to Weber, charismatic authority develops outside of societal institutions and organizations, Aldon Morris has argued that, in the case of the civil rights movement, charisma developed within the most central of Black institutions, African American Christianity. The Black church, he argued, demanded that ministers be charismatic, and the majority of them "claimed to have been 'called' to the ministry by God. . . ." [13] Since ministerial charisma was rooted in the Ultimate authority, church or movement members endowed these men with supernatural and extraordinary qualities. Thus, Black ministers were likely candidates for charismatic leaders.

Morris describes charisma as an outgrowth of the interactions between a minister and his followers, an interaction determined by the institution of the church and the Black culture. Such an explanation necessarily precludes the emergence of women as charismatic leaders, since within the institutional context of the Black church and within the context of the culture, they could never be viewed as such. Yet, the findings of my study suggest that women were indeed charismatic leaders and in just the context that Weber describes.

If we begin by defining charisma in relational terms, as Morris does, rather than simply in terms of personal attributes, then charisma may be defined as "the effect one individual has on a group of other individuals. Without the effect, there is no charisma." [14] The purpose of charisma is "not simply behavioral change [as one would expect from traditional or legal authority, i.e., coercive power], but a conversion of individual values and beliefs." [15] This, of course, was what Weber had in mind when he wrote that "charisma 'manifests its revolutionary power from within, from a central metanoia [change] of the follower's attitudes.' . . . Charismatic leadership can thus be defined in terms of the extent of the impact an actor has on the fundamental values and beliefs of other actors." [16]

Given this definition, I argue that women were, indeed, leaders in the civil rights movement. They emerged as short-term charismatic leaders during moments of crisis when people were emotionally charged by an incident. Women's leadership was accepted during these moments, and they made spontaneous decisions that took extraordinary courage. As bridge leaders, women did not gain their leadership positions through their participation in traditional leadership roles within or outside an institution, although some bridging activities fit the gendered division of labor traditionally found in Black churches; rather, their position as short-term charismatic leaders developed out of their interactions with followers in the cultural context of the movement.

Morris's error is to confound charisma that arises within an organization and charisma that emerges from a culturally ascribed position in society. Cultural theory suggests "that the fundamental choice made by people, from which all other decisions derive, is the way of life they embrace. An individual's preferred culture operates as a decision rule, instructing the individual what to prefer and how to behave." [17] Cultures contain hierarchies in which one's social position rests; these positions are, in turn, defined by the values society places on certain personal attributes, such as race, class, and gender.

Ministerial authority was rooted in church structure and in Black cultural traditions. There were hundreds of charismatic Black ministers. Even when jointly bestowed by the institution, authority and charisma were not enough to catapult just "any" minister into formal leadership of an entire movement. Dr. Martin Luther King Jr.'s emergence as "the charismatic leader of the civil rights movement" was decisively tied to his goodness of fit with a set of culturally prescribed attributes; Black, a man, educated, and a minister. Had any one of these constructs differed, he could not have led the movement.

Women in the civil rights movement were excluded from formal leadership positions, and they have continued to be excluded by researchers. These exclusions, however, should not be taken to mean that women were neither charismatic nor leaders. Many of my respondents characterized women as charismatic and in much the same way Weber suggests. Moreover, the emergence of such leaders reinforces my argument that emotion and spontaneity were central elements in the formation and sustenance of movement mobilization. According to Weber, "pure charisma is seen as a short-lived 'creative' force, erupting in times of 'mass emotion' and with unpredictable effect." [18] It was not the case that emotion and spontaneity were never a part of Dr. King's and other Black male formal leaders' decision making, only that these leaders had to be concerned about the impact of their actions on the state. Their legitimacy in the eyes of the state depended on their appearance as legitimate, rational leaders.

Morris also confounds legitimacy and social constructs of power. King's legitimacy and charisma derived from his traditionally prescribed authority as a minister, along with his status as an educated man. The legitimacy of women as bridge leaders, in contrast, emerged from their traditional status as community bridges to the church and from their individual acts of courage, which led their followers to trust them. For Dr. King, then, charisma derived from interactions with his followers, but these interactions were influenced by culturally prescribed social constructs, combined with his traditional authority position as a minister in the Black church. As Reinhard Bendix, in stating Weber's position, notes:

> Charismatic leadership effects an "internal" revolution of experience, in contrast to the "external" revolution that occurs when, for example, people adapt themselves to a major change in legal rules without at the same time internalizing the ideas behind it. . . . Traditional rule is characteristically permanent, however temporary may be the power of an individual patriarchal master. Charismatic leadership, on the other hand, is the product of crisis and enthusiasm.[19]

It is clear that King's charismatic appeal, coupled with his social position as an educated man and a minister, led to mass support of his formal leadership position. Morris, in describing King's rise to power, argues that charisma is a tool knowingly used by clergy to "stimulat[e], persuad[e], and influenc[e] crowds."[20] He elaborates:

> Students of charismatic leadership have persuasively argued that if individuals are to be recognized as charismatic leaders, they must personify, symbolize and articulate the goals, aspirations, and strivings of the group they aspire to lead. The ministers who were to become the charismatic leaders of the movement occupied strategic community positions which enabled them to become extremely familiar with the needs and aspirations of Blacks.[21]

The implication is that, at least for the formal leadership, charisma was a tool used in a planned, strategic, and rational manner by those in authority. Yet any discussion of the emotional use of charisma is neglected. Throughout this article I argue that women bridge leaders often acted to "personify, symbolize, and articulate the goals, aspirations, and strivings of the group they aspire to lead." This form of charismatic leadership did not emanate from institutionalized training as a charismatic leader. Yet, I argue that bridge leaders were often considered charismatic and displayed their power in planned as well as spontaneous, emotional, and rational acts of leadership. In social movement literature, the terms "emotional" and "rational" are, of course, rarely found in combination. Three examples of such interactions serve to illustrate these points.

Montgomery Bus Boycott

In 1946, for personal and political reasons, the scholar and Alabama State College professor Mary Fair Burks founded the Women's Political Council of Montgomery, Alabama. That same year, Mrs. Burks had been involved in a traffic accident with a white woman. A white on-looker had summoned the police, claiming that Mrs. Burks had cursed the white woman. Prior to the civil rights movement, accusations of this nature were taken as sufficient evidence for incarceration. It came as no surprise, therefore, when Mrs. Burks was arrested and taken to police headquarters. She was interrogated and released only after the white woman exonerated her.

This humiliating experience prompted Mary Fair Burks to begin an organization that would work within the community to educate individuals about their constitutional rights and encourage them to register to vote. This group was composed primarily of professional women. Jo Ann Gibson Robinson, a young professor at Alabama State College, joined the WPC in 1949, and she became its president one year later. Under her direction, the WPC developed chapters statewide and began to discuss ways in which some of the laws might be changed. In an interview, a WPC member, Mrs. Johnnie Carr, recalls, "People like Jo Ann Robinson, Mary Fair Burks, and Mrs. A. W. West worked very hard as leaders to get us organized. We had been working for years together." [22]

The women of the WPC had long been concerned about the segregation of public services, such as the bus lines and the public parks. Like many other women, Jo Ann Robinson suffered degrading treatment on the segregated buses. And, like Mrs. Burks, her participation in the WPC sprang from her personal experience as well as political conviction. As she recalls,

> I suffered the most humiliating experience of my life when that bus driver had ordered me off the fifth row seat from the front and threatened to strike me when I did not move fast enough. . . . I had not forgotten that ordeal. I had not told it to anybody, not even my closest friends, because I

was ashamed for anybody to know. Yet I could not rid my mind, my thoughts, my memory of it![23]

Throughout 1954 and 1955, the women of the WPC met six times with the mayor and city bus officials in an effort to negotiate better bus service, though they did not request an end to segregation. In March 1954, the women threatened a citywide boycott of the buses if their demands were not met.[24]

On December 1, 1955, Mrs. Rosa Parks refused to relinquish her seat to a white man. The previous spring, there had been a similar incident, which led to the arrest of Claudette Colvin for refusing to give up her seat on the bus. Her case was tried at the state level, and she was found guilty. The effort to press the case at the federal level was abandoned because E. D. Nixon, a highly respected community leader and the former president of the local NAACP chapter, and others believed that her character was unsuitable for a desegregation case. He felt that such a case would, most assuredly, receive press attention, and she was not only an immature teenager but pregnant as well. Another opportunity arose in October 1955, when Mary Louise Smith also refused to give up her seat on a bus. She too was arrested and found guilty under the segregation law, but again E. D. Nixon did not find her character suitable. She came from extremely impoverished surroundings, and her father was known for his bouts with alcoholism.[25]

The women of the WPC were infuriated by these decisions and felt that the emphasis should be on challenges at the local, rather than the federal, level. At the very least, they argued, pursuing these cases should entail challenging local segregation laws through confrontation with city officials. The suitability of the women's characters for a federal action, they insisted, should not preclude local leadership's pressing for change within the local government.[26] Clearly, women were pressing male leaders to act against the system of segregation long before the Montgomery Improvement Association and the Southern Christian Leadership Conference came into existence. They had continuously challenged the system on their own initiative.

On December 1, 1955, Rosa Parks refused to relinquish her seat to a white man. When Jo Ann Robinson and the women of the WPC heard of her arrest, they decided to call a bus strike. The women of the WPC had, for several years, discussed the possibility of a bus boycott, tactics like distributing flyers as a means of mass communication, and mechanisms for gaining cooperation from the black community. Mrs. Thelma Glass, an active member of the WPC recalls:

> We had all the plans and we were just waiting for the right time. We had discussed, well, every angle of it had been planned. We talked about transportation and we talked about communication and all the things that would happen when we finally decided to do this.... [A]t one of the meetings, we had asked Mr. Nixon ... to hear our plans and to talk with us. It was planned years in advance before it actually came to fruition.[27]

The women came to realize that, although they worked closely with others within their respective neighborhoods, they possessed neither the necessary legitimacy nor the institutional power within the black community to maintain support for a boycott. Some within the community did not even know of the existence of the WPC. Any successful boycott, they decided, would need a "legitimate," well-respected leader within the black community. Both Mary Fair Burks and Jo Ann Robinson also recognized that they could never be considered formal leaders or gain the support needed by the masses. A successful action, they believed, could be achieved only through the formal leadership of the ministers. They did not believe, however, that the ministers would call a boycott on their own. Of special significance is the fact that, though excluded from formal leadership, women understood their own power to move the community to action. It is this understanding that characterizes the relationship between the formal and the bridge leadership. This symbiotic or mutual exchange relationship has important implications for understanding the ways in which mobilization occurred in the civil rights movement.

Jo Ann Robinson's understanding of these relationships did not prevent her from initiating the boycott. She, along with two students, drafted and mimeographed leaflets to be distributed throughout the community.[28] Women had a full understanding of the limitations placed on their status and power. The women of the WPC were not without the knowledge or tactical skills needed for mobilization, yet they knew that as women, they could never gain community sanction to act as formal leaders. Although gender was not the only category that could unilaterally bar a woman from achieving a formal leadership position, it did override any amount of innate talent a woman might possess.

Now, after the success of the first day of the boycott, it was time for community leaders, who were mostly men clergy, to decide whether to continue the protest. The evening of the first day of the boycott, the formal leaders assembled to discuss what should happen next. Many of the ministers did not want to continue the boycott, or, if they were to support it, they wanted to do so anonymously.

> E. D. Nixon rose in anger. "How do you think you can run a bus boycott in secret? . . . Let me tell you gentlemen one thing. You ministers have lived off these wash-women for the last hundred years and ain't never done nothing for them. . . . We've worn aprons all our lives. It's time to take the aprons off. . . . If we're gonna be men, nows the time to be mens." [29]

Nixon pointed out that the women had risked arrest; now it was the time for men to step forth in support. He then threatened to tell all the parishioners of the various congregations that their preachers were cowards. With this, the ministers agreed to support a boycott and to form the Montgomery Improvement Association.

Women often acted on their own initiative to provide support for the boycott. Early on, it became clear to women such as Georgia Gilmore and Inez Ricks that financial support was critical to the operation of the carpool. They immediately organized neighborhood bake sales. These two women created local fund-raising clubs, Mrs. Gilmore's No-Name Club on the east side of town and Mrs. Ricks's Friendly Club on the west side, which competed to raise the most funds for the boycott. Each club provided about $100 per week.[30] Though considerably more money was needed and outside support would later become central to success, the initiative and the organizing skills of these women sustained the MIA in its infancy.

Later, northern organizations such as In Friendship, which was based in New York, raised money for the boycott. In Friendship was formed by Ella Baker, A. Philip Randolph, Bayard Rustin, and Stanley Levinson. Rustin was a long-time black activist, and Levinson was a Jewish New York attorney sympathetic to the movement. In Friendship raised money to support activism throughout the South; their numerous discussions with Dr. King would eventually lead to the development of the Southern Christian Leadership Conference.

In February 1956, the entire MIA was arrested and brought before a grand jury on charges of conspiracy. In addition to Dr. King and other male leaders, women such as Mrs. Rosa Parks, Mrs. A. W. West, Mrs. Gregory, and Jo Ann Robinson were arrested. City officials believed that the arrests would deter the majority of black citizens from participating in the boycott. The effect was quite the opposite, as is described by the Reverend Benjamin J. Simms. On the morning of the arrests,

> blacks had come from every section of town. Black women with bandannas on, wearing men's hats with their dresses rolled up. From the alleys they came. That is what frightened white people. Not the tie and collar crowd. I walked into there [to be indicted] and the cops were trembling.

He continues,

> I got in line behind the late Mrs. A. W. West. . . . One of the police hollered "allright you women get back." Three great big old women with their dresses rolled up over work pants told him and I will never forget their language, "We ain't going nowhere. You done arrested us preachers and we ain't moving." He put his hand on his gun and his club. They said, "I don't care what you got. If you hit one of us you'll not leave here alive." That was the thing we had to work against, keeping those blacks from killing these whites.[31]

It seems fitting here to point out that mobilization often rested on emotional appeals, whether spontaneous or planned. Not all mobilization work was organized in advance, with careful tactics and strategies. The unnamed women who led this group responded spontaneously and emotionally to a situation in which formal leaders and, in this case, even bridge leaders were unable to respond. Their actions provided the energy critical to mobilizing the people's continued commitment to acts of resistance. Without support from these women, the efforts of the MIA would have been severely weakened.

Of all those arrested, only Dr. King was indicted and found guilty. Though the state court upheld the constitutionality of segregated buses, that decision was later overturned at the federal level. The black population of Montgomery had won its first battle against the system of segregation.

It is clear that without the initiative of the women of the Women's Political Council, the Montgomery bus boycott would never have taken place. Likewise, the Council's continued efforts to mobilize and sustain popular support helped to create a stable and solidified base for the boycott. During the Montgomery Improvement Association's infancy, women utilized their community connections in order to organize financial support and to maintain the welfare of movement participants. This was the cornerstone of continued mass movement activities.

Finally, it is important to emphasize that, although these community networks provided the tool for mobilizing popular support, equally important was the extent to which spontaneity and emotion stimulated grass-roots support for the boycott. As I have pointed out, these women could empathize with the humiliation suffered by others on the buses. It was their emotional responses to inequality that provided the impetus for their initiation of and participation in the boycott. Given the context of their lives, their anger and humiliation served as the basis for their planned activities.

The assumption that emotional responses are irrational or irrelevant has obscured the symbiotic relationship between emotionalism as a tool of mobilization and planned action as a process of coordination. There were many instances of spontaneous and emotionally energizing acts by movement participants, exemplified by the Reverend Simms's description of women's vocal challenges during the arrest of the MIA leadership. These events should not be discounted or ignored because they are the by-product of emotions. Nor are they anymore irrational than planned strategies and tactics. In fact, given the reprisals meted out to leaders of the boycott, one could argue that continuing such actions was quite irrational, for they could easily result in death. The point is that the boycott was a success not only because of resources such as local funding or careful strategies and tactical planning but also because of emotional responses and spontaneous activism. Bridge leaders effectively mobilized many movement participants by appealing to their emotions and seizing on the high energy of the spontaneous. A second event serves to further illustrate these points.

The Freedom Rides

During 1961, the Congress of Racial Equality (CORE), a civil rights movement organization based in New York, began development of a project called the Freedom Rides, in which a busload of black and white activists would ride from Washington, D.C., to New Orleans and test the desegregation of local bus and transportation facilities. The goal was to force the southern states to comply with the 1960 Supreme Court decision banning segregation on interstate trains and buses. CORE was also challenging the segregated public facilities in the terminals—the restrooms and lunch counters that served the passengers. The first ride took place on May 4, 1961, and proceeded through the South without much difficulty, until it reached the Rock Hill, South Carolina, terminal. There two of the black male riders were beaten by a mob of white men for attempting to use the restrooms designated for white men only. The ride continued, however, making it safely through stops in Winnsboro, South Carolina, and Augusta, Georgia. After a stop in Atlanta, they thought it best to divide up, with half of the Freedom Riders boarding a Greyhound bus and the other half a Trailways bus. When they reached Birmingham, Alabama, a mob tore into the riders, beating them severely. Many were near death.

Eugene "Bull" Connor, Birmingham's commissioner of public safety, was known for his intolerance of black civil rights. Police were not sent to the mob scene for nearly a half hour. Though the CORE riders were unable to continue, Diane Nash, a bridge leader in the movement organization the Student Nonviolent Coordinating Committee (SNCC), phoned the Reverend Fred Shuttlesworth, a leader in Birmingham, to insist that the rides continue. She told Shuttlesworth, "The students have decided that we can't let violence overcome. We are going to come into Birmingham to continue the Freedom Ride." Shuttlesworth responded, "Young lady do you know that the Freedom Riders were almost killed?" She replied, "Yes, that's exactly why the rides must not be stopped. If they stop us with violence, the movement is dead. We're coming; we just want to know if you can meet us." [32] Spontaneous decisions were often made by women bridge leaders during moments of crisis when they were propelled into temporary formal leadership positions. Many felt that "the spontaneity was as important as being organized." [33]

Diane Nash organized a group of Nashville students to begin a ride to Birmingham. Emotions ran high as the students who volunteered contemplated the consequences of continuing the rides. Lucretia Collins, one of the volunteers, recounts her decision to join the rides:

> I could see how strongly someone would have to be dedicated because at this point we didn't know what was going to happen. We thought that some of us would be killed. We certainly thought that some of us, if not all of us, would be severely injured. At any moment I was expecting anything. I was expecting the worst and hoping for the best.[34]

Diane Nash explained high emotions of the riders:

> These people faced the probability of their own deaths before they ever left Nashville. . . . Several made out wills. A few more gave me sealed letters to be mailed if they were killed. Some told me frankly that they

were afraid, but knew this was something that they must do because freedom was worth it.[35]

Although realistically afraid and contemplating their own deaths, the students overcame their fears and continued the rides. Eight student volunteers boarded the bus but were stopped on the outskirts of Birmingham, jailed for a night, and driven by the police chief, "Bull" O'Connor, to the Tennessee border. Nash and others returned to Nashville and assembled even more students to ride to Birmingham. Ruby Doris Smith joined the group in Birmingham, and the volunteers struggled to persuade a bus driver to take them on to Montgomery. This time, the Kennedy administration convinced Alabama's Governor John Patterson to send police to escort the bus from the outskirts of Montgomery to the bus terminal. The police kept their word until the city limits were reached, then disappeared. When the bus pulled into the terminal, it was met by hundreds of angry whites brandishing clubs and baseball bats. Several Freedom Riders were severely beaten.

That evening Ralph Abernathy's First Baptist Church hosted a gathering to honor the Freedom Riders at which Dr. King, Ralph Abernathy, Diane Nash, and John Lewis, another SNCC leader, held a press conference. Though King rallied in support of the rides and supported their decision to continue, he did not join the riders as they continued to Jackson, Tennessee. James Forman in *The Making of Black Revolutionaries* states, "I recalled . . . King's statement that he was not going to take a Freedom Ride because he was then on probation and his advisors had told him it would be unwise." He continues,

> Even Diane Nash, who had strong convictions but tried not to speak evil of anyone, expressed a mixed opinion of Dr. King, "He's a good man but as a symbol of this movement, he leaves a lot to be desired. He has been affected by a lot of middle-class standards. If he wanted to, he could really do something about the South. He could go to Jackson and tell those people why they should participate in and support the Freedom Rides." [36]

Nash, as a bridge leader, was able to come to the fore when the formal leadership was either unable or unwilling to risk alienating its legitimacy in the eyes of the state. Nash, without such responsibilities, could acknowledge and build on the emotions of the masses. At that moment in time, the momentum of the movement depended on the continuation of the Freedom Rides. They had become a critical factor in mobilizing support from mainstream Americans who watched the coverage of the horrible beatings on the evening news.

Dr. King's decision, while a disappointment to those in SNCC, grew out of his concern for his image in the eyes of the state. King understood the need to remain credible. This was, after all, a movement for inclusion, and recent civil rights legislation and court decisions had indicated some support for the movement by those in power. It was critical that King not alienate his state supporters. His primary task was to maintain a balance between the needs of the movement and the judgment of the state.

An obvious strength of the bridge leadership tier was its relative autonomy. The emotions and the spontaneity so critical to movement momentum and mobilization could be harnessed by bridge leaders. Moreover, this freedom in leadership served to constantly remind the movement's formal leaders of the flesh-and-blood constituency they represented. This symbiosis between the formal and the bridge leader tiers ensured that movement momentum would not be sacrificed to governmental reluctance. Yet, the focuses of the two sets of leaders on occasion differed. Nowhere is this more clear than in the interactions between bridge and formal leaders at the 1964 Democratic National Convention in Atlanta.

The 1964 Democratic National Convention

On April 26, 1964, SNCC, whose philosophy was to build indigenous leadership within local communities throughout the deep South, organized the Mississippi Freedom Democratic Party (MFDP). The MFDP was established to counter the efforts of racist southerners who continued to prevent blacks from voting. For example, in the Second District of Mississippi, 52.4 percent of the population was black, but only 2.97 percent of the eligible black voters had been allowed to register to vote.[37] Despite increasingly violent reprisals, the MFDP succeeded in challenging the Southern Order by holding alternative elections. Having won sixty-eight delegates and elected representatives to the convention, the MFDP was well positioned to challenge the white delegates who were occupying those seats illegitimately, having won them by elections held under Jim Crow laws.

Upon their arrival in Atlantic City, the MFDP delegation was met by other black civil rights leaders, including Dr. King, Bayard Rustin, and Roy Wilkins, as well as the long-time white activist and lawyer Joseph Rauh. Rauh worked out the most promising strategies for MDFP's challenge to the white delegation. At the same time, political tension over the challenge reached the White House.

President Lyndon Johnson, who had been in office only a year, having suceeded to the presidency after the assassination of John F. Kennedy, was determined to win the nomination. He was well aware that his commitment to civil rights had alienated many southern Democrats and that he could ill afford to have his name linked to the Mississippi Freedom Democratic Party or its actions at the convention. Johnson was determined to control the MFDP challenge so that it did not endanger or overshadow his nomination.

In addition to his concern over the MFDP challenge, Johnson was cautious for another reason—his selection of Senator Hubert Humphrey as his running mate. Humphrey had already alienated many white Southerners by standing up to segregationists at the 1948 Democratic Convention. His position as a potential running mate was further weakened because he had lost the 1960 presidential nomination to John F. Kennedy. Under intense pressure to reshape his image so that he might be more palatable to southern whites and with the political stakes high, Humphrey pushed the delegation to accept a compromise in committee rather than allow the seating decision to go to the floor. Had the MDFP taken the dispute to the convention floor and had the effort been successful, the nation would have witnessed the removal of white representatives and their replacement by blacks. Humphrey and Johnson understood that this powerful imagery would have lost them the election.

To circumvent this possibility, a subcommittee to the Credentials Committee was appointed to seek a compromise. After this committee brainstormed for an entire weekend, Humphrey emerged and met with Dr. King, Rauh, MFDP chairman Aaron Henry, and Bob Moses of SNCC, urging them to accept a compromise. At a subsequent meeting called by Representative Charles Diggs of Michigan, Humphrey met with Dr. King; Mrs. Fannie Lou Hamer, vice-president of the MFDP; Aaron Henry; Joseph Rauh; a white MFDP activist, the Reverend Ed King; and Representatives Robert Kastenmeier of Wisconsin and Edith Green of Oregon. Fannie Lou Hamer, the twentieth child of sharecroppers, has been described as a charismatic leader, one who "when she sings can make a church tremble." [38] Ed King recalls Mrs. Hamer's confrontation with Humphrey, quoting her as saying,

> "Senator Humphrey, I been praying about you; and I been thinking about you, and you're a good man, and you know what's right. The trouble is, you're afraid to do what you know is right." She says, "You just want this job [as vice president], and I know a lot of people have lost their jobs, and God will take care of you, even if you lose this job. But Mr. Humphrey, if you take this job, you won't be worth anything. Mr. Humphrey, I'm going to pray for you again." [39]

The only tenable offer to come out of that meeting was presented by Representative Green, who suggested that any of the delegates willing to take a loyalty oath be seated. Mrs. Hamer consulted the MFDP delegation, which decided that the compromise was unacceptable. Mrs. Hamer's steadfast position during these negotiations, that the delegation should not accept any compromise unworthy of its cause and its constituency back home, resulted in her deliberate exclusion from future meetings.

Meanwhile, Rauh continued to lobby representatives and became increasingly aware of the power of President Johnson. While many of the convention's delegates supported the challenge, they were unwilling to publicly show their allegiance. Any support of the challenge now would be construed as a vote against the Johnson/Humphrey ticket, since the two men had so well succeeded in distancing themselves from the MFDP cause. Frustrated, and with waning support, Rauh agreed to a meeting with Walter Reuther, a union leader and negotiator, whom Johnson had persuaded to hammer out a deal.

At yet another meeting with Dr. King, Bayard Rustin, Aaron Henry, Bob Moses, and the Reverend Ed King, a final compromise was offered. The MFDP would be given two seats as at-large delegates. Even before Rauh had time to report back to the delegation, pressure to accept the compromise mounted. Walter Mondale, an aspiring politician and a legal assistant to Senator Humphrey, presented the compromise to the Credentials Committee. Rauh, recalling his experience, later stated, "I don't know if you've ever been in a lynch mob but this is one. They started hollering vote, even while I was still talking." [40]

Bowing to the atmosphere of near panic, Rauh and Mondale told reporters that a compromise had been reached. Bob Moses, meanwhile, had returned to the delegation, and the decision to accept or reject this latest compromise was debated. Some members worried that their representatives in the negotiation were too eager to surrender.

Despite the pressure exerted on the delegation, privately Dr. King did not feel satisfied with the compromise and confided to Ed King that, if he were a sharecropper, he would not have accepted the compromise. But King was swayed by Humphrey's private promise to wage war against racism in Mississippi.[41] Others, such as Roy Wilkins and Bayard Rustin, also accepted the compromise. During a heated argument, primarily with the women in the delegation, Wilkins told the women that they were ignorant of the political process, that they should listen to their leaders and just return home.

In an interview, another of the delegates, Mrs. Unita Blackwell, recalls the event. Mrs. Hamer, she remembers,

> just sat there in the back . . . and she said "Girl, I'm going to tell you the folks didn't send us up here for no two seats. When we left Mississippi, we said that we wanted all of the seats or half because we wanted to be represented in our state. . . ." So the three of us were just sitting there . . . and she said no compromise. "We been compromisin' all our life." I can feel it right now. Yes, honey, you could just feel the power of it. And, honey, they looked at us and told us we were ignorant. . . . The rumor went around that we was sixty-eight ignorant folks from Mississippi and didn't understand politics . . . and we looked at them and said, "We do understand more than you understand. We understand what we come out of." [42]

The delegation members felt betrayed. Originally, they had come to combat the Mississippi system of disenfranchisement; now they found themselves battling their own. They no longer felt the sense of optimism and empowerment that had characterized the days leading up to the challenge. Many of the leaders were claiming a moral victory, but Hamer saw it as a defeat. Later, she remembered herself saying,

> "What do you mean moral victory? We ain't getting nothing." What kind of moral victory was that, that we'd done sit up there, and they'd seen us on the television. We come on back home and go right on up the first tree that we get to because, you know, that's what they were going to do to us. What had we gained?

Unita Blackwell concurred:

> Them people had not been talking to us poor folks. They had a certain clique that they'd talk to. The big niggers talk to the big niggers, and the

little folks, they couldn't talk to nobody except themselves, you know. They just goin' to push the thing on through and have us there for showcase. But we tore that showcase down. That's for sure. We told them what we think.[43]

Despite their loss of power at the convention, the women aired their anger to other MFDP members. Hamer, in tears, made a plea to the delegates not to go along with the black formal leaders. She and Annie Devine convinced "Henry Sias, a sixty-nine-year-old farmer who was chairman of the Issaquena County Freedom Democratic Party in the western part of Mississippi," to renounce his support for the compromise. He recalls,

Now I seen Mrs. Hamer cry 'cause I got up on the floor; they wouldn't accept no two seats. . . . I changed my mind right there. Those two women just shamed me right there. When they got through talking and whoopin' and hollerin' and tellin' me what a shame it was for me to do that, I hushed right then. See, I backed off and drew way back in that corner.[44]

Through emotional and impassioned pleas, the women were able to persuade many of the delegates that they had a responsibility to their constituents at home. They continued to debate, and when the vote was taken, the delegation decided to reject the offer. However, Rauh and Mondale had already announced the unanimous acceptance of the compromise by the delegation. Hamer and others were furious. In response, she and the other women leaders, holding "guest" tickets to the convention, forced their way onto the convention floor. They all stood in a circle for two hours, in silence.

The split between the formal leaders and the women leaders of the delegation illustrates the extent to which many planned activities required spontaneous decisions that were fraught with emotion. Moreover, women, as bridge leaders, often operated semiautonomously in what Sara Evans and Harry Boyte term a "Free Space."[45] The women in the MFDP were better positioned to remain loyal to the constituents. This is not to suggest that the formal leaders were out of touch with the masses, only that the requirements of their pivotal relationship with the state necessarily shaped their decisions.

Conclusion: Emotion and Spontaneity in Social Movement Theory

Classical collective behavior theorists conceived of social movements as spontaneous events that were unplanned and irrational. In an effort to refute such ideas, researchers, most notably John McCarthy and Mayer Zald, developed a different conceptualization of movement activities.[46] They focused on the similarity between social movement activity and normal organizational activity. Social movements were not unusual events but were planned, rational activities that depended upon the availability of resources.

Both Aldon Morris and Doug McAdam, in reformulating this model, stressed the importance of preexisting organizational structures for the development of the civil rights movement. They contend that the structures and organizations of this preexisting network were essential for planned, coordinated, rational movement activity. Drawing on the work of Jo Freeman, Lewis Killian, however, criticizes resource mobilization theory in general and Morris and McAdam in particular. He suggests that not all civil rights movement activities emanated from preexisting organizations and that many activities were spontaneous. He is careful to emphasize that calling actions spontaneous in no way implies that they are irrational. In his analysis of the Tallahassee, Florida, bus boycott of 1956, he provides a convincing argument that the boycott began as an unplanned event and that civil rights movement organizations emerged after its inception. This case, Killian concludes, establishes that not all civil rights movement activities were planned in advance, as is argued by McAdam and Morris. Rather, both spontaneity and planning were essential for successful movement momentum.[47]

Freeman calls for a reformulation of social movement theory to account for "both planned and spontaneous, leader-directed and grass roots" activities.[48] In an effort to address this problem, Killian develops a model that emphasizes the need for spontaneity in the early stages of a social movement and during periods of transition. He does not, however, develop a clear interactive conceptualization to account for these seemingly diametrically opposed conceptions of movement activities.

The root of this problem lies in several problematic assumptions. First is the still commonplace but false dichotomy, common in both scientific and mainstream cultures, drawn between rationality and emotion.[49] While displaying calm rationality was an important tool used by formal civil rights leaders in order to maintain their legitimacy with the state, emotions certainly prevailed behind the scenes. Moreover, while bridge leaders displayed emotion more readily, it can not be concluded that their behavior was any more irrational than that of formal leaders. Rather, the actions of bridge leaders were determined more closely by the event of the moment than by considerations of state approval. Thus, an action that may have been interpreted by the state, by nonpartici-pants, or even by formal leaders as irrational may have been an action emotionally charged but nonetheless rationally calculated to produce a particular goal. Rationality, after all, does not have an objective reality. It is subject to individual interpretation.[50]

The second problem centers on the notion, still prevalent in social movement theory, that individual movement behavior must evince "self-interest," whatever that is, in order to be considered rational. While there may seem nothing wrong with such an assumption, in practice such a view tends to conflate emotion and irrationality. Rational choices, as conceptualized by social movement theorists, are only those choices that develop out of self-interest. Any decisions except clearly self-inter-ested ones are thought to be irrational. Notions of the collective good or social ethics are not considered as a basis for rational choices.

This utilitarian approach to social movements has, of course, been challenged extensively by social movement theorists.[51] In her argument against this approach, Jane Mansbridge states, "People often take ac-count of both individual's interests and the common good when they decide what constitutes a 'benefit' that they want to maximize."[52] More-over, as Verta Taylor notes:

> Feelings come into play in classical resource mobilization formulations only as affective ties that bind participants to challenging groups, and they are secondary to questions of strategic success in motivating activists.[53]

Taylor and others discuss emotions as an important organizing tool among already recruited participants.[54] They emphasize the emotional aspects of commitment and the development of cultural climates as critical to the sustenance of social movements. Yet these and other critics of rational choice models still fail to develop a sufficiently interactive model of social movements.[55]

I have argued that emotions and unplanned movement activities led to the successful mobilization of adherents and potential constituents of the civil rights movement. It was, in point of fact, women's extraordinary acts of courage that defined their leadership. It was precisely during these emotionally charged, courageous moments that women, despite threats to life or limb, propelled the movement forward, thereby sustaining its momentum.

Naomi Rosenthal and Michael Schwartz also support the notion that emotion and spontaneity are central, not irrational, aspects of movement mobilization. Moreover, they argue that grass-roots groups through face-to-face interactions, emotionally charged and spontaneous events, are often the "growth sector of social movements"[56] and "play a crucial role in developing movement direction."[57]

To their credit, new social movement theorists[58] and feminist theorists[59] have also questioned the neglect of emotion in resource mobilization theory and have, instead, turned the question to the relationship of the self to the community. Their research centers on consciousness, identity transformation, and solidarity, as strategies for movement formation, mobilization, and sustenance.

Through an examination of the interactions of bridge and formal leaders, this article illustrates the interactive nature of spontaneous and planned activities, as well as the importance of emotion in social movement mobilization, calling into question the need to polarize these concepts. Moreover, I argue that bridge leaders are important agents of spontaneous activities and emotional appeals during moments of crisis when formal leaders either fail or are unable to lead.

The theoretical treatment of movement mobilization has focused primarily on the mobilization of potential recruits or followers, rather than on the dialectical relationships *among* movement leaders and *between* movement leaders and followers. Movement mobilization is consequently conceptualized as taking place in a linear fashion in which leaders begin movements and mobilize the masses. As this discussion illustrates, however, leaders are often mobilized by the masses they will eventually come to lead.

Gender, race, class and culture were significant factors in the construction of the success of the civil rights movement. The strong tier of bridge leadership, where women most often flourished, provided a powerful resource for movement recruitment and mobilization. Moreover, the partnership between Black men and women as formal and bridge leaders, respectively, was constantly renegotiated in an effort to provide freedom for the Black community as a whole.

NOTES

1. See, for example, the mass society approaches of Kornhauser 1959, Fromm 1941, and Hoffer 1951; also the Chicago School theorists Turner and Killian 1957, Park 1967, and Lang and Lang 1961.

2. See for example, Zald and Ash 1966, Olson 1965, Lipsky 1968, Gamson 1975, Fireman and Gamson 1979, and McCarthy 1979, and Zald 1973.

3. See McAdam 1982.

4. See, respectively, Taylor and Whittier 1992 and Robnett 1996.

5. Klandermans and Tarrow 1988.

6. Snow et al. 1986.

7. See, for example, Snow, Zurcher, and Eckland-Olson 1980, based on race, class, gender and sexual preference.

8. See Breines 1982, Gamson 1992, Tarrow 1992.

9. See West and Blumberg 1990, 3–35; Jonasdottir 1988; Smith 1988; Siim 1988; Spender 1983.

10. E.g., Freeman 1975, 1979, Buechler 1990.

11. See Ferree and Hess 1985, 94–103.

12. Taylor and Whittier 1992.

13. Ibid., 7–8.

14. Ellis 1986, 6.

15. Ibid., 8.

16. Ibid., 8–9.

17. Ibid., 13.

18. Seligman 1994, 5.

19. Bendix 1977, 300–301.

20. Morris 1984, 8.

21. Ibid., 10.

22. Johnnie Carr—Stephen M. Millner, interviewer, in Garrow, ed., 1989.

23. Robinson 1987, 25.

24. Mary Fair Burks interview 1/22/90.

25. Branch 1988, 127.

26. I.e., Morris 1984, Garrow 1986, Branch 1988.

27. Glass, Thelma interview 2/2/90.

28. Robinson 1987, 45.

29. E. D. Nixon 1968—Transcript, 13, Spingarn Center, Howard University.

30. Hazel Gregory interview 2/15/90.

31. Millner in Garrow, ed., 1989, 485.

32. Branch 1988, 430; Morris 1984, 232.

33. Jo Ann Grant interview, 8/25–26/92.

34. Forman 1972, 151.

35. Carson 1981, 34.

36. Forman 1972, 148.

37. Zinn 1964, 258.

38. Delluth 1964.

39. Mills 1993, 125.

40. Ibid., 127–28.

41. Ibid., 129–33.

42. Unita Blackwell interview 1/30/90.

43. Mills 1993, 129.

44. Ibid., 130.

45. Evans and Boyte 1986.

46. McCarthy and Zald 1977.

47. Killian 1984, Freeman 1979.

48. Freeman 1979, 170.

49. See England 1989, Jagger 1989 for fuller discussions of this phenomenon.

50. Weber 1978, Brubaker 1984.

51. E.g., Cohen 1985, Fireman and Gamson 1979, Marwell 1982, Klandermans 1984, Ferree and Miller 1985, Ferree 1991, 1993, Gamson 1992, Taylor 1995.

52. Mansbridge 1990, x.

53. Taylor 1995, 225.

54. E.g., Hirsh and Keller 1990, Taylor and Whittier 1992, Whittier 1995.

55. Collins 1981, 1988.

56. Rosenthal and Schwartz 1989, 46; Whittier 1995.

57. Ibid., 52.

58. E.g., Pizzorno 1978, Touraine 1981, Melucci 1985, 1989, Habermas 1984, 1987, Cohen 1985.

59. E.g., Jagger 1989, Mansbridge 1990, England 1989, Ferree 1993, Rupp and Taylor 1987, Taylor 1989, 1995, Taylor and Whittier 1992.

BIBLIOGRAPHY

Bendix, Reinhard. 1977. *Max Weber: An Intellectual Portrait*. Los Angeles: University of California Press.

Blackwell, Unita. Interview. Jan. 30, 1990.

Branch, Taylor. 1988. *Parting the Waters*. New York: Simon and Schuster.

Breines, Wini. 1982. *Community and Organization in the New Left, 1962–68*. New York: Praeger.

Brubaker, Rogers. 1984. *The Limits of Rationality*. London: Allen and Unwin.

Buechler, Steven M. 1990. *Women's Movements in the United States.* New Brunswick, N.J.: Rutgers.

Burks, Mary Fair. Interview. Jan. 22, 1990.

Carr, Johnnie. Interview. Jan. 26, 1990.

Carson, Clayborne. 1981. *In Struggle: SNCC and the Black Awakening of the 1960s.* Cambridge, Mass.: Harvard University Press.

Clark, Septima. 1986. *Ready From Within,* edited by Cynthia Stokes Brown. Navarro, Calif.: Wild Tree Press.

Cohen, Jean L. 1985. "Strategy or Identity: New Theoretical Paradigms and Contemporary Social Movements." *Social Research* 52: 663–716.

Collins, Randall. 1981. "The Micro-Foundations of Macro-Sociology." *American Journal of Sociology* 86: 984–1014.

———. 1988. *Theoretical Sociology.* New York: Harcourt Brace Jovanovich.

Delluth, Jerry. 1964. "Tired of Being Sick and Tired." *Nation,* June 1.

Ellis, Richard J. 1986. "A Theory of Charismatic Leadership in Organizations." Berkeley, Calif.: Institute of Governmental Studies in Public Organization, University of California, Working Paper No. 86–2.

England, Paula. 1989. "A Feminist Critique of Rational-Choice Theories: Implications for Sociology." *American Sociologist* 20: 14–28.

Evans, Sara, and Harry Boyte. 1986. *Free Spaces.* New York: Harper and Row.

Ferree, Myra Marx. 1991–1992. "Institutionalizing Gender Equality: Feminist Politics and Equality Offices." *German Politics and Society* 24 (Winter): 53–67,

———. 1993. "The Political Context of Rationality: Rational Choice Theory and Resource Mobilization." In *Frontiers of Social Movement Theory,* edited by Aldon Morris and Carol Mueller. New Haven: Yale University Press.

Ferree, Myra Marx, and Beth Hess. 1985. *Controversy and Coalition: The New Feminist Movement.* Boston: Twayne.

Ferree, Myra Marx, and Frederick Miller. 1985. "Mobilization and Meaning: Toward an Integration of Social Psychological Resource Perspectives on Social Movements." *Sociological Inquiry* 55, no. 1: 38–61.

Fireman, Bruce, and William A. Gamson. 1979. "Utilitarian Logic in the Resource Mobilization Perspective." In *The Dynamics of Social Movements,* edited by Mayer Zald and John McCarthy. Cambridge, Mass.: Winthrop.

Forman, James. 1972. *The Making of Black Revolutionaries.* New York: Macmillan.

Freeman, Jo. 1975. *The Politics of Women's Liberation.* New York: David McKay.

———. 1979. "Resource Mobilization and Strategy: A Model for Analyzing Social Movement Organization Action." In *The Dynamics of Social Movements,* edited by Mayer Zald and John McCarthy. Cambridge, Mass.:Winthrop.

Fromm, Erich. 1941. *Escape From Freedom*. New York: Rinehart.

Gamson, William. 1975. *The Strategy of Social Protest*. Homewood, Ill.: Dorsey Press.

———. 1992. "The Social Psychology of Collective Action." In *Frontiers in Social Movement Theory*, edited by A. Morris and C. Mueller. New Haven: Yale University Press.

Garrow, David J. 1986. *Bearing the Cross*. New York: Vintage Books.

———, ed. 1989. *The Walking City: The Montgomery Bus Boycott*. Brooklyn, N.Y.: Carlson.

Glass, Thelma. Interview. Feb. 2, 1990.

Grant, Jo Ann. Interview. Aug. 25–26, 1992.

Gregory, Hazel. Interview. Feb. 15, 1990.

Habermas, Jurgen. 1984. *The Theory of Communicative Action, Reason and the Rationalization of Society*. Vol. 1. Boston: Beacon Press.

———. 1987. *The Theory of Communicative Action, Lifeworld and System: A Critique of Functionalist Reason*. Vol. 2. Boston: Beacon Press.

Hirsh, Marianne, and Evelyn Fox Keller. 1990. *Conflict in Feminism*. New York: Routledge.

Hoffer, Eric. 1951. *The True Believer: Thoughts on the Nature of Mass Movements*. New York: Mentor.

Jagger, Alison. 1989. "Love and Knowledge: Emotion in Feminist Epistemology." In *Gender/Body/Knowledge: Feminist Reconstructions of Being and Knowing*, edited by A. Jagger and S. Bordo. New Brunswick, N.J.: Rutger University Press.

Jonasdottir, Anna G. 1988. "On the Concept of Interest, Women's Interests and the Limitations of Interest Theory." In *The Political Interests of Gender*, edited by Kathleen B. Jones and Anna Jonasdottir. London: Sage.

Killian, Lewis M. 1984. "Organization, Rationality and Spontaneity in the Civil Rights Movement." *American Sociological Review* 49, no. 6: 770.

Klandermans, Bert. 1984. "Mobilization and Participation: Social-Psychological Expansions of Resource Mobilization Theory." *American Sociological Review* 49: 583–600.

———. 1986. "New Social Movements and Resource Mobilization: The European and American Approach." *Journal of Mass Emergencies and Disasters* 4: 13–37.

Klandermans, Bert, and Sidney Tarrow. 1988. "Mobilization into Social Movements: Synthesizing European and American Approaches." *International Social Movement Research. From Structure to Action: Comparing Social Movement Research Across Cultures*. Vol. 1. Greenwich, Conn.: JAI Press.

Kornhauser, William. 1959. *The Politics of Mass Society*. Glencoe, Ill.: Free Press.

Lang, Kurt, and Gladys Lang. 1961. *Collective Dynamics*. New York: Crowell.

Lipsky, Michael. 1968. "Protest as a Political Resource". *American Political Science Review* 62: 1144–58.

Mansbridge, Jane. 1990. *Beyond Self-Interest.* Chicago: University of Chicago Press.

Marwell, Gerald. 1982. "Altruism and the Problem of Collective Action." In *Cooperation and Helping Behavior: Theories and Research,* edited by Valerian J. Derlega and Janusz Grzelak. New York: Academic Press.

McAdam, Doug. 1982. *Political Process and the Development of Black Insurgency.* Chicago: University of Chicago Press.

McCarthy, John D., and Mayer N. Zald. 1973. *The Trend of Social Movements in America: Professionalism and Resource Mobilization.* Morristown, N.J.: General Learning Press.

———. 1977. "Resource Mobilization and Social Movements: A Partial Theory." *American Journal of Sociology* 82: 1212–39.

———, eds. 1979. *The Dynamics of Social Movements: Resource Mobilization, Social Control, and Tactics.* Cambridge, Mass.: Winthrop.

Melucci, Alberto. 1985. "The Symbolic Challenge of Contemporary Movements." *Social Research* 52: 781–816.

———. 1989. *Nomads of the Present: Social Movements and Individual Needs in Contemporary Society.* Philadelphia: Temple University Press.

Millner, Stephen M. 1989. "The Montgomery Bus Boycott: A Case Study in the Emergence and Career of a Social Movement." In *The Walking City: The Montgomery Bus Boycott,* edited by David J. Garrow. Brooklyn, N.Y.: Carlson.

Mills, Kay. 1993. *This Little Light of Mine: The Life of Fannie Lou Hamer.* New York: Dutton.

Morris, Aldon. 1984. *The Origins of the Civil Rights Movement.* New York: Free Press.

Nixon, E. D. 1968. Transcript. Civil Rights Documentation Projection. Spingarn Center, Howard University.

Olson, Mancur. 1965. *The Logic of Collective Action.* Cambridge, Mass.: Harvard University Press.

Park, Robert E. 1967. *On Social Control and Collective Behavior,* edited by Ralph H. Turner. Chicago: University of Chicago Press.

Pizzorno, Alessandro. 1978. "Political Science and Collective Identity in Industrial Conflict." In *The Resurgence of Class Conflict in Western Europe since 1968,* edited by C. Crouch and A. Pizzorno. New York: Holmes and Meier.

Robinson, Jo Ann Gibson. 1987. *The Montgomery Bus Boycott and the Women Who Started It.* Knoxville: University of Tennessee Press.

Robnett, Belinda. 1996. "African American Women in the Civil Rights Movement: Gender, Leadership and Micromobilization" *American Journal of Sociology* 101, no. 6: 1661–93.

Rosenthal, Naomi, and Michael Schwartz. 1989. "Spontaneity and Democracy in Social Movements." In *Organizing for United States,* edited by Bert Klandermans. *International Social Movement Research.* Vol. 2. Greenwich, Conn.: JAI Press.

Rupp, Leila, and Verta Taylor. 1987. *Survival in the Doldrums: The American Women's Rights Movement, 1945–1960s.* New York: Oxford University Press.

Seligman, Adam. 1994. *Innerworldly Individualism: Charismatic Community and Its Institutionalization.* New Brunswick, N.J.: Transaction.

Siim, Birtie. 1988. "Towards a Feminist Rethinking of the Welfare State." In *The Political Interests of Gender,* edited by Kathleen B. Jones and Anna Jonasdottir. London: Sage.

Smith, Dorothy. 1988. *The Everyday World as Problematic: A Feminist Sociology.* Boston: Northeastern University Press.

Snow, David A., Louis A. Zurcher Jr., and Sheldon Eckland-Olson. 1980. "Social Networks and Social Movements: A Microstructural Approach to Differential Recruitment." *American Sociological Review* 45, no. 5: 787–801.

Snow, David A., E. Burke Rochford Jr., Steven K. Worden, and Robert D. Benford. 1986. "Frame Alignment Processes, Micromobilization, and Movement Participation." *American Sociological Review* 51: 464–81.

Spender, Dale. 1983. *There's Always Been a Woman's Movement in this Century.* London: Pandora Press.

Tarrow, Sidney. 1992. "Mentalities, Political Cultures and Collective Action Frames: Constructing Meanings Through Action." In *Frontiers in Social Movement Theory,* edited by A. Morris and C. Mueller. New Haven: Yale University Press.

Taylor, Verta. 1989. "Social Movement Continuity: The Women's Movement in Abeyance." *American Sociological Review* 54: 761–75.

———. 1995. "Watching for Vibes: Bringing Emotions into the Study of Feminist Organizations." In *Feminist Organizations: Harvest of the New Women's Movement,* edited by Myra Marx Ferree and Patricia Yancey Martin. Philadelphia: Temple University Press.

Taylor, Verta, and Nancy Whittier. 1992. "Collective Identity in Social Movement Communities: Lesbian Feminist Mobilization." In *Frontiers in Social Movement Theory,* edited by A. Morris and C. Mueller. New Haven: Yale University Press.

Touraine, Alain. 1981. *The Voice and the Eye: An Analysis of Social Movements.* New York: Cambridge University Press.

Turner, Ralph H., and Lewis M. Killian. 1957. *Collective Behavior.* Englewood Cliffs, N.J.: Prentice-Hall.

Weber, Max. 1978. *Economy and Society.* Vol. 1. Berkeley: University of California Press.

West, Guida, and Rhoda Blumberg, eds. 1990. *Women and Social Protest*. New York: Oxford University Press.

Whittier, Nancy. 1995. "Turning It Over: Personal Change in the Columbus, Ohio, Women's Movement, 1969–1984." In *Feminist Organizations: Harvest of the New Women's Movement,* edited by Myra Marx Ferree and Patricia Yancey Martin. Philadelphia: Temple University Press.

Zald, Mayer N., and Roberta Ash. 1966. "Social Movement Organizations: Growth, Decay and Change." *Social Forces* 44, no. 3 (March): 327–41.

Zinn, Howard. 1964. *SNCC—The New Abolitionists*. Boston: Beacon Press.

Chapter Six

Goody Two-Shoes and the Hell-Raisers
Women's Activism, Women's Reputations in Little Rock

Beth Roy

"You know, this will probably be something that I made up in my head," Susan said apologetically, "but I can just remember her attitude. It was just a haughty, snotty, look-down-your-nose-at-me attitude that she had."

She was speaking of her high school classmate, Minnijean Brown. Minnijean was one of nine black students who integrated Central High School in Little Rock, Arkansas, in 1957, the year Susan was a senior. Susan's recollections of Minnijean echoed those of many of her white classmates as I talked with them about their brush with history at Central High.

Their hostility toward Minnijean was matched only by their contempt for another girl, a white junior named Sammie Dean Parker. "Who were the segregationist student leaders?" I asked Nancy, another senior that year. "Sammie Dean Parker was the only one I knew," she replied. "Sammie Dean Parker was taken to jail that day. She was kicking, spitting, scratching, and the policeman couldn't do anything with her, she was so out of control."

When Little Rock's Central High School was desegregated in 1957, I was a teenager fresh from the South, glued to a television in my northeastern college dormitory. Staunch rows of National Guardsmen sliced statically across the screen, standing militarily erect in front of the magnificent school building. Governor Orval Faubus's serious face appeared, reading earnest messages of resolution to "protect the peace" and prevent the undemocratic imposition of integration on the good citizens of his state. Network commentators, all men, read somber but excited reports of late-breaking news.

But when the cameras turned to the streets around the school, the images were quite different. Girls and women moved through the crowds. Elizabeth Eckford, a frail-looking black teenager clad in the sort of big gored skirt fashionable at the time, clutched her schoolbooks and clenched her jaw as she was turned away from the front door by the Guards. A white girl her age screamed at her, open-mouthed. The mob of women and men noisily hounded her retreat. One gray haired white woman shielded the terrified Elizabeth, turning to chastise the crowd as she accompanied the girl onto an empty bus.

Over the next months, the news media continued to report an unusual amount of activity by women: Daisy Bates headed the state NAACP, for example, and Margaret Jackson the hastily formed Mother's League of Central High, an offshoot of the Citizens Council's fight to preserve segregation. Inside the school Elizabeth Huckaby, the liberal vice principal, did daily damage control.[1] When the high schools were closed the following year, Adolphine Fletcher Terry, a doyen of Little Rock society, announced, "It is evident that the men are incapable of doing anything. I have sent for the young ladies." She formed the Women's Emergency Committee to Open Our Schools, studied the political process and helped to elect a school board and a state legislature that removed the roadblocks to integration (Ashmore 1988, 281).

That women populated the stage on which the drama of Central High was played is not a coincidence. School desegregation was a struggle that especially evoked women's activism; who else could better claim the moral authority to speak up when the site of contention was the domain of children? But the women who did speak up faced a particular set of dilemmas. It was the 1950s; the ideal of white womanhood pictured Mother in the kitchen, tending traditional values along with the home fires. To enter into public discourse was itself an act of defiance, therefore, and especially problematic for segregationist women who, by weighing in to defend the status quo, betrayed it.

These paradoxes of women's radicalism shade and inform the stories that white women graduates of Central High tell about those times. Everyone made choices about how to act during that year of crisis. What women say about their own behavior and about that of their peers tells several other stories, too: about women's lives then and now, about relations between white and black Americans in the second half of the twentieth century, about the nature of political action itself. By focusing on tales told about Sammie Dean and Minnijean by their classmates, as well as on the stories two of those classmates tell about themselves, I explore the moments when all those themes came together.

Meaning and Emotion

Over a period of three years in the early 1990s, I recorded forty oral histories of or long interviews with people, both black and white, who were involved with the integration of Central High School in Little Rock in 1957. My interviewees ranged from Governor Faubus and white adults in the mob outside the school to the African American registrar (for almost fifty years) in the black high school; from people who worked for and with the NAACP to bring about desegregation to students who chose in subsequent years to continue attending segregated black high schools when they might have enrolled in Central High. The single largest group were white students at Central High in the year of drama, 1957–58.

The good news and the bad news about my interviews is that they resulted in miles of tape and reams of transcripts, the oral historian's bane. To find my way through the tangle, I devised a method of starting from emotional "hot spots," recurring topics about which people spoke with passion. Never were the women alumnae of Central High hotter than when they spoke of their two classmates, Minnijean and Sammie Dean. What exactly did their hostility express, not so much about the women of whom they spoke, but about themselves and about the intense period of history through which they lived?

Storytelling is a political act.[2] How we portray the past, ourselves, and our fellows can defend or contest social arrangements. Often, I found "errors" in my interviewees' accounts; they placed the National Guard in the wrong place at the wrong time; insisted people were where they couldn't have been at a crucial moment; announced that one of the Nine was an "outsider" planted inside Central High for strategic reasons, while other people attested to that very person's having been born and reared right up the street.

It is precisely in these distortions of "fact" that political arguments reside (Irwin-Zarecka 1994). "Memory fails," wrote Karen Fields (1994, 89), leaving blanks, and memory collaborates with forces separate from actual past events, forces such as an individual's wishes, a group's suggestions, a moment's connotations, an environment's clues, an emotion's demands, a self's evolution, a mind's manufacture of order, and yes, even a researcher's objectives.

How memory is shaped by emotion is full of meaning, because individual emotion is linked to social life. What we think and feel, how we interpret our lived experience, is deeply informed by who we are as social creatures at a moment in time. Psychology itself, that most personal of arenas, is a social construct, because the beliefs and attitudes we learn in the course of social interaction, in which I include domestic interaction, fundamentally shape the direction of individual lives and the feelings we have along the way. The lessons we learn, especially those that appear in memory later as "truths," are not accidental. Instead, they mediate social relations of power and hierarchy with great force and constitute a concrete link between individual consciousness and social structure.

"Any mistake is meaningful," Fields (1994, 93) argues. "[M]emory 'tainted' by interest is a dead-serious party to the creation of something true. The 'mistakes' it may embody represent an imperfection only in light of the particular purposes scholarship has." Let us explore some "tainted" stories, reading between the lines the personal interests that shaped them and the social history lived by the ordinary people who told them.

Goody Two-Shoes and the Troublemakers

When school opened in the fall of 1957, Central High teemed with ordinary people, two thousand white students wishing to enjoy the dating and sports and, maybe, scholarship of their high school years and, most of all, to be left in peace by the adult world they would all too soon be joining. The latter was a wish not to be granted. For a variety of reasons, not least among them Little Rock's reputation for peaceful race relations, the school had been chosen as a prototype for desegregation. Characteristically, most of those who were students on opening day did not believe themselves to be history makers, even in the midst of mayhem. Said Helen,[3] a white woman I interviewed who was a senior that year, "I went to school, just nothing, no big deal. I didn't see if there was commotion going on up here, I didn't see it. 'Cause I came in the side door, went to my locker, did my thing. . . ." Literally sidestepping history did not constitute a position, as Helen saw it. She insisted she was neutral on the question of desegregation itself: "There was plenty of room for all of us there. Now, I'm not trying to be Goody Two-Shoes, think about it. The school was big enough to accommodate everybody, so who cares?"

But some among the students clearly did care, and they protested hard. While grownup mobs raged outside the building, inside the black students were called names, tripped, kicked, and spat upon. As the year wore on, harassment took a more organized aspect. Printed cards appeared bearing racist slogans, for instance. Helen showed me one she got after Minnijean was expelled. "One Down . . . Eight to Go," it boasted. Another sported this ditty:

> Little nigger at Central High
> Has got mighty free with his eye.
> Winks at white girls,
> Grabs their blond curls:
> Little nigger sure is anxious to die.

All my inquiries about where the cards came from were in vain. Who had brought them into the school? How had Helen come by the ones she'd carefully (but shamefacedly) preserved in her yearbook? Had anyone tried to recruit my interviewees to distribute cards or join other protests? Everybody insisted she knew nothing about it, knew nobody involved, could name no names—except one, a girl named Sammie Dean Parker.

I had first learned that Sammie existed through a series of enigmatic references in a book called *Crisis at Central High*. Written by Elizabeth Huckaby, the vice principal of the school, it is a day-by-day account that was later popularized as a made-for-TV movie starring Joanne Woodward. Responsibly protecting the student's identity throughout, Mrs. Huckaby makes reference to a "small pony-tailed girl" who irked the authorities in many ways, even riling the endlessly patient vice principal herself. As Mrs. Huckaby's account proceeds, this girl becomes "the pony-tailed segregationist leader" (Huckaby 1980, 135). Years later, when I interviewed her, Mrs. Huckaby recalled her student with better humor. But still she referred to her as "the girl who was so aggressive during all of this."

Sammie's peers shared none of Mrs. Huckaby's reticence as they reminisced about their classmate:

> *SUSAN:* Sammie Dean—this is confidential, right? Sammie Dean did not
>   have the best—how do you put that?—reputation in the world.
> *BR:* She was a segregationist activist.
> *SUSAN:* Right. And plus, she also had other, uh, unredeeming qualities.
> *BR:* Would you say what?
> *SUSAN:* Well, she was the girl about town, we'll put it that way. And I
>   was Miss Goody Two-Shoes, what can I say? Sweet sixteen and never
>   been kissed and the whole nine yards. But, anyway, on one of the
>   occasions that happened, they drug Sammie Dean kicking and scream-
>   ing out of the schoolhouse. Probably the police or the troops or who-
>   ever, but anyway, it was one of the, quote, authorities. And she went
>   kickin' and screaming out of the schoolhouse where she crawled out
>   on them and they caught her.
> *SARA MAY:* Now I didn't know her, she was pretty, she was such a little
>   doll, I remember she was *so* pretty and so cute. But they were what we
>   considered white trash, really.

Susan's reference to herself as "Goody Two-Shoes" reminded me of Helen's use of the same term. Although Helen was talking about her position on desegregation while Susan hinted at sexual matters, both expressed something similar about innocence.[4] In the stories many of these white women told me, desegregation was forced on them. They acquiesced, innocently, minding their own business and the letter of the law. Nonetheless, they were treated badly, vilified in the press, repre- sented as uncouth protesters. In fact, many claimed, the mob was made up of out-of-towners. They themselves had no beef with black people. They'd always had black people working in their homes, and folks of both races were good to each other. The trouble started, as they saw it, when the black students acted badly.

Actually, it was only one student who acted badly, as they remem- bered it: Minnijean Brown. The rest were fine, quiet, respectful, demure. If only Minnijean had stayed in her place, there'd have been no trouble. Not everyone blamed the Nine for the trouble; some placed responsibil- ity on the NAACP, Govenor Faubus, the school authorities, or that mythic "outsider" who appears so regularly as a character in dramas of social contention. But many of the students did blame their black class-mates, and those who did universally focused on Minnijean.

Said Susan:

> I remember, uh, what was that girl's name? Big girl, Minnijean. She had an attitude, it was like, Okay white folks, here I am. [...]

> You know this will probably be something that I made up in my head, that I'm making up in my head now, but I can just remember her attitude. . . . I can't recall words that happened, it was just a haughty, snotty, look-down-your-nose-at-me attitude that she had.

Joyce spoke of Minnijean with more camaraderie, but in similar terms:

> Physically, Minnijean was a large girl. I was a large girl at the time; I've always been overweight. And Minnijean had, I think, more of a presence physically than the other girls did. I also think Minnijean had more, she exuded more of a sense of herself than I remember the other girls' doing. It was a confidence-slash-arrogance. The segregationists probably per-ceived it as arrogance, which they didn't like; I perceived it as confidence in herself, self-assuredness.

Martha was one of very few Central High grads who went on to a professional career. She theorized about her classmates'—and her own—view of Minnijean:

> I would describe her unlike all the rest of the blacks. I'd put it in class terms. First of all, she was overweight, so that made her more—what?— easy to tease. She was a stereotype of a Mammy, a young Mammy by white standards. Remember how there used to be the Mammy with the . . . [sketches big belly with her hands]? Okay? Because she was big and she was overweight, and she was more challenging, more asserting, she was more set. Whereas the others were very almost docile.

Mammy and White Trash: Troublemakers Disavowed

What do these descriptions of Sammie Dean and Minnijean tell us about the women who spoke them and about women's activism in the Central High struggle? Although Minnijean is cast as the problem, Sammie Dean, too, is held responsible. Minnijean may have behaved provoca-tively, but the women of Central High saw Sammie Dean's response as unacceptable, a way of acting that they themselves eschewed. Taken together, these two assessments defined black womanhood and white trash and communicated a thick bundle of beliefs about what it was to be white women in Little Rock in the 1950s, as well as challenges to those beliefs. Three aspects of the women's accounts are especially vivid expressions of underlying meaning: their references to physicality, sexuality, and class.

Right along with the person herself, memories of both Sammie Dean and Minnijean are pinned to body size. Minnijean is large, Sammie Dean small. So central were physical images that they sometimes were the hook for fishing up the controversial classmate's name itself: "What was that girl's name? Big girl, Minnijean." Sammie Dean was small, cute, pony-tailed. Minnijean was large, overweight, Mammy-like. Both girls acted in the physical world and in that respect both challenged rules of femininity. Despite herself, neither one could avoid confrontation. Sammie tangled with policemen, fellow students, and vice principals. Minnijean talked back, pushed back, and eventually dropped a bowl of chili on the lap of a white boy who had tormented her once too often. Both girls were ultimately expelled, Minnijean for the chili incident, Sammie for distributing the cards after Minnijean left, saying, "One down, eight to go." [5] Both young women were formidable.

Right along with descriptions of physical bearing were references to their sexuality, sometimes overt ("she was the girl about town"), sometimes subtle ("she was *so* pretty and so cute"). Several people claimed Minnijean left school because she became pregnant: "She also had a baby in May, or right after graduation," insisted Sara May. "We knew a nurse that was there, she *did* have a baby." Both the tone and the context in which these comments were made implied that Sammie Dean's and Minnijean's sexuality explained away the significance of their activism.

Class appeared in the almost universal description of Sammie Dean as "white trash." What that meant was elaborated in an exchange between Sara May and her friend Helen: "They were what we considered white trash, really," said Sara May, and Helen responded: "I don't know why. They were extremely well-heeled. He was a big railroad man. They had money." Said Sara May, "Well, probably because of the way she acted and the way her mother acted." Class was equated with women's behavior. Minnijean, too, was considered déclassé—"a more working-class, less educated type of black woman, a young Mammy by white standards." Let us look more closely at each of these attributions.

That Sammie Dean's and Minnijean's body sizes were noteworthy speaks of an experience familiar to most women in America. How big we are, how thin or fat, tall or short, compels our consciousness, because physical characteristics are closely bound up with how our femininity is viewed and how, in consequence, we evaluate our own sense of worth. When people told me that Sammie Dean was small and cute, they conveyed indirectly a particularly damning critique of her behavior. How striking it was to them that someone who fit the physical standard for American female approval should act in so unwomanly a manner—kicking and screaming and putting herself in the way of being dragged out of the schoolhouse.

Identifying Minnijean as big and overweight similarly served to discredit her, although in this case very directly. Big women are figures of fun, and she was "easy to tease." Mammy carries a particular weight. She is one of the few black characters in American racial mythology who is forgiven for being overbearing, because she dominates in the service of motherhood. She can be allowed to dominate, because, unlike a "real" (read white) mother whose power might be genuinely threatening, Mammy's power is ultimately none at all—she is a slave. All the comfort of forceful mothering is therefore at the service of her white charges, who are nonetheless securely in charge. Indeed, they are in the ultimate control. If mothering is constructed as a natural instinct, the designation of Mammy has succeeded in subverting that instinct, severing servant from the mothering service of her own offspring and reconstructing her "natural" instincts to the benefit of her white masters. Unlike their biological mothers, she has no choice but to be unambivalently theirs (hooks 1981).

But Minnijean could not be tamed by the label "Mammy." Her defiance was not confined; it spilled over to become a force in a fierce contest of realities. One white interviewee, searching for a way to explain her hatred for Minnijean, finally burst out, "She walked the halls as if she belonged there."

"There was plenty of room for all of us there," Helen said, more reasonably. "The school was big enough to accommodate everybody, so who cares?" But the implication was strong that it was fine for "them" to come to "our" school. The problem arose if "they" acted like they were there by right, not by generosity.

My white interviewees commonly expressed this idea by reference to concepts of "place":

MARTHA: With Minnijean, I remember not feeling very empathetic that she left. Sort of, stereotypically, that she asked for it, [that she] didn't know her place, do you know what I'm saying? That kind of feeling.

BARBARA: I just felt that she was different. . . . I felt she was probably one of the most out-of-place people in the whole school.

"Place" was an important concept in the South of that time. Segregation represented an ordering of the universe, a way of naming social hierarchies and the location within them of every individual, whether black or white. Comments about Minnijean's person and attitude, definitions of her as an individual, combine with comments about her "place" to consign her forcefully to a social position.

What place was that, exactly? Overtly, "place" was, and still is, a euphemism for racial dominance. But there is another sense in which the notion appears in my interviews, and that is about class. Significantly, just as often as her white classmates expressed animosity toward Minnijean in terms of her deviance from racial proprieties, they talked contemptuously of Sammie Dean in class terms. One clue to the link between those two conceptions is contained in things people said about their families' personal relations with black people. Helen identified her family as working class, with dignity: "If you want to say a railroad track, I lived on the wrong side of town, so to speak, in that town's way of talking. But that didn't make us trash or anything. We just lived in the older homes." Were there any black people in her life? I asked.

At one time we did have a maid, Odessa. Now, although we were middle to lower class, people had maids, right? They came in and they did the heavy work and they did the ironing.

I was always taught to respect my elders, and Mother didn't differentiate between black and white.

Many people emphasized to me how well their parents treated the family servant. "We had a maid, Lucy," said Sara May. "She was the best ole nigger-Mammy, is what she was. I mean she was wonderful. We had her almost until she died. She took care of me, she loved me, I loved her." But however much Sara May loved Lucy, she was not confused about injunctions against socializing with blacks:

SARA MAY: I don't remember any particular thing my parents said. I was just brought up to know you didn't associate with them.

Our maid was wonderful, and my mother took, we took Christmas
food and clothing and everything to them every year at Christmas.
HELEN: We took care of them.
SARA MAY: We took care of them and all that, but, you know, they were
inferior. That's all there is to it.

Back then it was okay. Now, I look back, and I do feel sorry for them.
I think it's a shame it has to be that way, but it is and it still is, for the
most part.

Sara May and Helen's stories contained a number of strategic layers.
On the one hand, they were presenting themselves in a good light,
arguing that white people in their South were benevolent, not "trash."
But at the same time, in tone and posture, they also expressed discomfort
with the southernness of their attitudes back then. "They were inferior.
That's all there is to it," said Sara May in such a way as to suggest that
their view back then was not their view now but that they should be
excused for what they thought back then, even though the consequences
of what they thought had mostly not yet changed. When she used the
phrase "nigger-Mammy" she spoke with a certain self-consciousness,
mocking herself, but also defying my condemnation. Often people said,
"That's just the way it was" in one breath and in the next defined
nuances of their culpability in "the way it was." "I never used the word
nigger in all my youth," Susan told me. "If I did I would have had my
teeth knocked down my throat; my parents wouldn't have stood for it."
Unwittingly damning herself with faint praise, Helen told me how upset
she'd been when her father said "nigger" in front of her son:

He doesn't say Negro, he says nigger. And my son, that beautiful little
blond-headed, blue-eyed boy, I can remember the first time he said it, it
just killed me. And I said, "Daddy! Don't teach him to say that. He's going
to have to be around them, and I don't want you teaching him that word."

But at the same time Helen and Sara May and Susan defined with
specificity the degrees of their own racism ("I never thought I was a
racist, but . . ." Helen said, breathing noisily through her lips in perplex-
ity, "I still haven't thought about that yet. I don't know if I am or not"),
they argued implicitly that the arrangement back then worked. Black
and white people got along fine before desegregation, they suggested,
remembering how they themselves got along with Odessa or Lucy. These
asymmetrical relationships between white families and black servants,
often the only interpersonal contact white children had with black peo-

ple, were central in constructing a certain ideology about the racial order in the South: The proper arrangement of power was white dominance (in the most benign version, as employers); the proper role for whites was gentility and for blacks service; the proper site for interaction between the races was on white domestic territory. Finally, bolstering this ideology was a prevalent myth: that these relations were equally agreeable to both blacks and whites ("She loved me, I loved her").

Taken all in all, this set of ideas described a social hierarchy and justified punitive acts against black people who failed to play their assigned role, who expressed dissatisfaction with the status quo, for instance, by enrolling in Central High—and acting as if they belonged there. The other side of the coin, however, was the way in which this prescribed racial order helped to construct a certain moral control of the behavior of disadvantaged whites as well. The very proprieties of white people's treatment of blacks—from generosity toward those who served domestically to intolerance for a lack of deference in return, from sexual prohibitions against miscegenation to tacit acceptance of the sexual exploitation of black women by white men—contained within them an underlying set of rules that demarcated class among whites. One qualified for "superior" status vis-à-vis black people if—and only if—one acted with gentility. That these white families "took care of" their black servants (that fact associating them with a thick packet of social and ethical standards clustering around acts of generosity) in one sweep both defined black people as inferior and themselves as having standing on the white class ladder. They were "middle to lower class" whites, not white trash. White trash behavior—rowdiness in public, loose sexual mores, the behavior on which Sammie's classmates commented in their very first evocations of her—constituted a set of rules that my white interviewees recognized clearly and debated, obeyed and contested in very fine gradations. It is not insignificant that the everyday behaviors out of which the categories were constructed occurred on domestic terrain and were performed by women—an example of how acts at home enforce public power relations, which in turn dictate domestic dynamics. When racial change hit the "normalcy" of Central High, the white women students, for the first time, found themselves on a public stage in which to demonstrate their acceptance or resistance of the old behavioral standards through the medium of taking positions, passively or actively, about changes in the racial order. How they put the two together, whether they acted as ladies or as white trash as they expressed their attitudes toward desegregation, constituted a rough sketch of their personal life plans, which were actively challenged at that moment in history.

Minnijean signaled that challenge when she betrayed the rules by which her racial "place" had traditionally been assigned—not so much to remain segregated as to remain grateful. At the same time, Sammie Dean challenged the social order, paradoxically, as she sought to uphold it in the form of segregation. It was not that she protested that was most significant but how she protested—without gentility:

> NANCY: Sammie Dean Parker was taken to jail that day. She was kicking, spitting, scratching, and the policeman couldn't do anything with her, she was so out of control.
>
> She came out the front entrance, the main entrance, and she was screaming at these black students as they were being led away. That they could not enter school. A policeman had walked up to her—I don't know what she was screaming, but she was screaming at them. I don't know what she had in her hand; she was throwing something. But nevertheless, he told her, you know, she had to stop and calm down and everything. Well, she kicked him. He grabbed her by the shoulders trying to calm her down, and she cussed him out. And then she started spitting on him and things of that nature, and he couldn't do anything with her, so he just took her and took her to jail.

She spit and fought and cussed; she attacked policemen and got arrested. The old class and race order was continually reproduced through daily acts of gratitude by black people and gentility by whites. Minnijean's behavior stood squarely outside that paradigm. Sammie Dean's both defied and, paradoxically, fit it. By all her physical acts of defiance, Sammie Dean confirmed the caricature of "white trash" behavior at the same time that she demonstrated that what always had stood behind gentility was force, in the form first of legalities and ultimately of violence. When the law failed, people resorted, as they historically had, to physical acts of resistance, as did Sammie. That unpleasant task was traditionally left to "poor white trash," allowing the higher classes to keep untarnished the distinguishing customs of generosity and niceness.

Somehow, though, that old design didn't work in 1957. Sammie Dean cut close to her women classmate's bone. Yes, she was acting as white trash is known to act. Yet to describe it that way did not resolve a certain discomfort. People talked about her too frequently, with too much contempt, telling thereby another story within their story. Familiar acts in changing times take on new meanings. Why else did the women of Central High focus so contemptuously and universally on Sammie Dean's behavior?

If the social order was constructed in part through certain acts, it is noteworthy that the acts I've noted were performed by women. Indeed, gentility was a deeply gendered act; men could be rough-and-tumble while women carried the torch of right behavior. In Arkansas as in many other cultures, power relations in society were signified and transmitted by the actions of women,[6] in ways very similar to the construction of white social life through the control of black people's behavior.[7] From the most charged (sexuality) to the most assumed (race relations) to the most banal (salutations), white women's behavior was minutely judged because how they behaved was a measure of the social standing of their families.

All through judgments of the women's behavior, in references both to body size and to class, is laced commentary on their sexuality. How big or small they were is spoken of descriptively; their class status is analyzed in terms of observable behavior. But sexuality falls into the realm of reputation, which is an amalgam of perception, hearsay, and imagination. Of all the arbiters of social status, women's sexuality is the most potent, at the same time that it is often the most fictionalized. Sammie Dean's peers disavowed her activism by slandering her reputation. "Sammie Dean did not have the best—how do you put that?—reputation in the world. . . . Well, she was the girl about town, we'll put it that way." Markers of sexual doubtfulness go way beyond sexual behavior itself, many of them looping around to supply implicit meaning to comments about appearance and class: "She was such a little doll, I remember she was so pretty and so cute. But they were what we considered white trash, really."

It was not insignificant that Minnijean was large, Sammie Dean small. Mammy is the essence of a desexualized black woman. Black women, in the classic southern construction (and its descendants today), are either asexual matrons or supersexual wantons. Their sexuality is denied or demeaned. Minnijean's sexuality was referenced only in terms of illegitimate motherhood. On the other hand, sexuality (at least heterosexuality) is sanctified for white women if they belong to certain classes and behave certain ways. White-trash woman is like thin black woman; she smacks of sexuality, but of a cheap kind.

There are many indications that Minnijean did not have a baby right out of high school (for one thing, she graduated in New York, not Little Rock, and a year later than Helen and Sara May), and Sammie Dean married the boyfriend with whom she had gone steady throughout that time. Their classmates may have known something less obvious about them; rumor generally has some kernel of truth to it, however distorted. But it seems likely that the personal reputations assigned to Sammie Dean and Minnijean served metaphoric purposes. Susan and Helen contrasted their own behavior and status with their classmates', construing themselves as Goody Two-Shoes, the opposite of troublemakers. At the same time that the aspersions cast on Sammie Dean and Minnijean's sexual lives served to contain and trivialize the credibility of their actions in the social world, those same expressions of disapproval also defined the speakers as not-out-of-control, not-rebels.

Raising Hell while Avoiding Trouble

Female sexuality, controlled, serves social functions; uncontrolled, it is trouble, whispering of a social order out of order. Unbridled sexuality is a mark of male vitality, not troubling, perhaps even relieving. Boys will be boys, after all, and isn't it better that they blow off steam that way than some others? Gendered double standards are, of course, endemic throughout history, and they are often carried and enforced by women. That other women were the carriers of Sammie Dean's and Minnijean's reputations is an example of the paradox of internalized oppression.[8] Any well-functioning society implants social control in the hearts and spirits of those it seeks to control.

A prime implement for doing so is the complex web of ideas with which we define the world and our own place in it, our identity. Constructed early in life and elaborated throughout it, this internalized ideology is commonly drawn from three sources: a theoretical understanding of a moment in history, a set of beliefs formed through social discourse, and conclusions drawn from personally lived experience.[9] Ideas derived in these three arenas may confirm or contradict each other. Taken together, they serve to construct particular acts of protest, as well as the self-conscious perception of those acts by the perpetrator. Moments of protest thus serve as a magnifying lens through which to view the linkage between individual consciousness and social structure. Out of our lived experience we form conclusions about how life works and who we are. We internalize these ideas and forget they are learned, not revealed, truths. But in truth, they are ideologies, reflecting fundamental aspects of social structure that in turn influence our actions in public arenas in ways that protect and reproduce those structures. Private relations thus mediate social ones, giving rise to psychological patterns with political bearing.

If women's bodies are the markers of social standing, women's minds are the parchment on which those markers are written. Stories, injunctions to behave in such-and-such a way, fears, and maternal anxieties are means by which they are communicated and thereby made functional. That level of the drama of Central High becomes clearer still when we look at the actions of those who derided the activism of Minnijean and Sammie Dean.

For despite their identification as "arch-radicals," the two girls were in fact not alone in acting. Political activism is not a category but a range. Helen acted significantly by "going in the side door." To refuse to answer a heated question is to express an opinion. Innocent everyday acts in times of trouble convey resistance and protest (e.g., Sacks and Remy 1984). Minnijean and Sammie Dean's classmates responded to the crisis in measured ways, sometimes gaily, sometimes secretly, but always significantly. Take, for example, Nancy.

Nancy came from a Little Rock family that typified gendered cultures of docility and troublemaking. Her mother came from a religious family. "There was never any disruption in their household," said Nancy. "I mean, it just ran very smoothly and properly." But Nancy's father was a different sort:

My dad was a hell-raiser. My dad did everything he could possibly do. He smoked, he drank, he ran around with women. He went to the racetrack every time he could possibly get there. Even snuck me in over there when I was thirteen years old, just because I looked mature enough to fit in. Which I did, and it just thrilled him to death to get by with it.

I never heard my mother use a cuss word in my life. My dad—it was just something that came natural to him, it was every other word. Unfortunately, I'm the same way and I don't do it to shock, it's just there. You know, I never did it around my mother until I was married and one day a word slipped out and she, when a word slipped out, she used my full name, you know.

I had a lot of fun with [my dad]. But I also have a lot of resentments against him for a lot of the things that he did.

If Nancy's parents typified the contrast between a proper woman and a hell-raising man, her own choices in the Central High drama wove a complex tapestry of both traditions:

The summer before we started in September there was just a buzz around town, you know, just a buzz around town that these Nine were going to be brought in to Central.

The only thing really I remember my mother saying was, "I'm very worried about this because I'm afraid there's going to be trouble." To tell you the truth, at the time I didn't think too much about it. I really didn't dwell on it. My dad didn't really say too much that summer.

Then when we did go to school, they did bring them in and, I mean, all hell broke loose. . . . It just went from bad to worse. Mother was actually afraid for me to go to school. And I was going to go, I wasn't going to miss anything, you know.

But the day that they brought them in, this is the way I remember it: There were so many people out in front of the school, raising hell. And it was parents, it was mainly parents. So I didn't know what was going to take place, no one else did either, and some friends and I left the school.

I went downtown to try to find my dad and I couldn't find him. He was probably in a pool hall or something, you know. I don't know where he was, but anyway I couldn't find him. I just wanted to let him know that I had left school.

Many parents had instructed their kids to leave the school if the black students came in, either because of fears for their safety or to express opposition to desegregation. I wondered if Nancy had acted independently when she left or whether she was obeying orders:

BR: Had your father wanted you to leave school? I know some parents had instructed their children to leave.
NANCY: Yes. My dad had told me to just get up and walk out.
BR: Is that because he was worried about you, or was that a protest?
NANCY: That was a protest on his part. My mother didn't want me to go; it was fear. You know, she was afraid of danger, something was going to happen. She did not want me to go that day at all. But it was left to be my decision. And like I said, I was just dying to get over there because I wanted to see what was going to happen, you know.

But nevertheless, several friends, we left and went down looking for my dad, couldn't find him, and I decided to . . . I didn't go by mom's shop to mention it to mother that I left school because—I don't know why. I just didn't.

It was interesting to me that Nancy grappled (however cursorily) with the reasons she didn't go to tell her mother that she'd left. It was her own decision, but in its aftermath her impulse was to check in with her hell-raising father, not her proper (and frightened) mother. Failing to do either, she carried on in the flow of her crowd's enthusiasms:

Anyway, in the meantime, we kind of organized. We had stopped at 15th and Main—it was a little place called Sweet-n-Cream. We had all stopped down there and several cars came pulling up, and I don't even remember who said it but someone said, "Let's have a parade." So we went to the drugstore, bought several bottles of white shoe polish and we put on the cars "Two, Four, Six, Eight. We Ain't Gonna Integrate." There were about fifteen, sixteen cars. We left 15th and Main and went downtown.

We were shouting this "Two, Four, Six, Eight. We Ain't Gonna Integrate." And we went across the bridge into North Little Rock. Went to North Little Rock High School.

North Little Rock is an independent city across the Arkansas River from Little Rock. It is a more industrial and working-class community. I asked Nancy why they'd chosen to go there:

We had no place else to go, I suppose. We didn't want to head over to Central because there was already so much trouble going on over there. We weren't actually seeking trouble. I think it was just mischief, you know, more than anything else.

We were met there by the North Little Rock Police Department. They told us that they could sympathize with us but we had no business being over there and they were going to escort us back across the bridge. As long as we did not try to get out of our cars or cause any kind of disturbance, then we were all right.

So we left. We were not trying to make trouble. You know, it was just, I think, something to do in a manner of protest. So as we came back across, I remember one of the guys—his father was a mortician—and his dad saw him. And you could tell he was furious. When we passed mom's shop, I would not look to see if my mother was on the sidewalk.

Well, we got back to our little hangout place, which was a drugstore where a lot of us congregated in the afternoon—before and after school, actually, and then on Saturdays. There was a juke box in there and (you know, kids used to have places to go. They don't anymore. But we did, fortunately) we went to the drugstore and as I walked in the door the owner said, "Nancy, your mother just called. She said that if you showed up here I was to keep you here. You're not allowed to leave." I said, "Okay."

So I went to the pay phone and I called mother. And this is what she said. She said, "I am so ashamed of you I don't know what to do." She said, "You have besmirched my name and I'm very, very upset. I'm very embarrassed and I'm very disappointed." [. . .]

We were all sitting around talking . . . and having a Coke and my dad came in and picked us all up. He was so proud of us, he didn't know what to do. He gave us money for the juke box. So it was just split. I had told him, I said, "Mother called here and I was told to stay here." And he said, "Well, you can go home with me. I'm headed home."

So I went home with my dad. My mother got off at 5:30. She came in, she would not even look at me. I mean, she was just furious. She was absolutely furious.

But that's the first day that I remember it starting.

Despite the fact that the "parade" made quite a stir in the community ("We did make the national news," Nancy said with some pride, "and that was one of the things that really upset my mother"), Nancy's story is organized around the theme of innocence. "We were not trying to make trouble," she said more than once. She carefully named the action a parade, not a demonstration, suggesting it was lighthearted, mischief, not a serious action. Their target was North Little Rock, not Central High, where "there was already so much trouble going on."

On the other hand, "it was something to do in a manner of protest." I suspected that statement applied to two domains, one public, the other private. When Nancy joined the parade, she also took a position in the politics of her family. By leaving the school, she might have satisfied both her mother's fears and her father's protest. By taking part in the demonstration, she allied herself squarely with her father:

When I was in that parade I didn't see anything wrong with that. I told my mother, I said, "I don't think I've done anything wrong. I don't want to go to school with them either. So what's wrong with me protesting? I didn't hurt anyone." So that was my answer.

Women's activism always challenges domestic as well as public power relations, because by the very act of taking a position in the public domain women violate their patriarchal assignment to domesticity.[10] If Nancy's position was aimed at both spheres, how much was she influenced by an alliance with her father and how much by her own attitude toward desegregation? Seeking insight into her views about race, I asked what her relations with black people had been before that year:

> NANCY: We had all been brought up that the blacks stayed on one end of town and we stayed on the other. Well, to me, that was not our fault. That was the way it was at that time, you know. We came to believe that, that's the way we lived, that's the way we were brought up. I don't ever remember being unkind to any black person, because I never was close enough to one. I mean, we walked on the sidewalk, and if they met us, they got off the sidewalk and walked in the street. And that's actually what it was like.
>
> BR: Do you remember what you thought about that at the time?
>
> NANCY: I thought it was normal. I thought it was normal. I thought it was normal that they sat in the back of the bus because that's the way it had always been. I'd never seen it done any other way. So to me it was normal.

Like her white classmates, Nancy defined Jim Crow as normalcy in the past and thereby justified her participation. To participate without culpability, however, her protest had to walk a very narrow edge between trouble and mischief. That her footing slipped from time to time was made evident by another detail she reported, this one overlooked by the written histories of the time. She had described the scene of Sammie Dean's arrest earlier in our conversation, ending up with the statement, "She was so out of control." Nonetheless, Sammie's arrest galvanized Nancy and her crowd:

> NANCY: We all decided that we would go get Sammie Dean out of jail.
>
> BR: Did you know Sammie Dean before this?
>
> NANCY: Yes.
>
> BR: What did you think about her? You made a little bit of a face when you mentioned her name. What does that mean?
>
> NANCY: Well, I would say Sammie Dean was an instigator. Her father was one of the top-notch segregationists in Little Rock. He was very outspoken. And, therefore, Sammie Dean was. That's what she had been taught. Nevertheless, she was kind of a troublemaker. She was a very cunning person, you know. She could just almost charm the socks

off of anyone in order to get her way. You know? She was a beautiful young girl. She was. Very attractive.

But anyway, she was taken to jail. I don't know why, I don't know who decided to do this—I did not run around with Sammie Dean, I simply knew her. We all decided we would go down there and try to get her out of jail. And we went down there and they told us that she could only be released to her parents. And that her father had already been called and he was on the way. So we left.

BR: Were you supportive of what she had done?

NANCY: I don't think it was support. I don't think I would define it as support. Like I said, I think it was just the fact that they had taken her to jail and we didn't think that any of us should be put in jail. At that age you just think, Well, this is someone I go to school with and how dare they be arrested. Even though she was kicking and cussing and you know, having a little fit and all. We just decided she didn't deserve being put in jail.

Normalcy is a good description of assumed and invisible social structures, and in this case its evocation revealed Nancy's assumptions about the world she lived in. But her story also expressed some subtle tensions contained within her assumptions. She both sympathized with and condemned Sammie's segregationist prominence. She assumed that Sammie's position was a natural reflection of her father's, that she was merely doing what comes naturally to dutiful daughters. "Nevertheless, she was kind of a troublemaker." The word "nevertheless" suggested that duty did not altogether justify the way in which Sammie Dean followed her father's political lead. She was a troublemaker. Her very act of obedience to her father caused her to betray her feminine role. Not only did she cause trouble; she caused it by using female attributes: her charm, a product of her most gendered quality, attractiveness, became a weapon of cunning. Nancy made that observation in a tone at once shocked and admiring. More than most of her classmates, she felt a certain sympathy with Sammie Dean, evidenced by her joining the trek to the police station to free her. But for the very reason that she herself was suspect in the female world of propriety, that she had allied herself with her father, not her mother, she was also careful to distinguish herself from Sammie. Both girls protested, but Sammie caused trouble, while Nancy protested innocently. Nonetheless, both took a stand in two closely interlinked struggles: one to contest desegregation's challenge to white dominance, the other to contest white society's cooptation of their female behavior as a signifier of their family's status. In doing so they engaged a set of social relations that transcended status. Their choices to obey or break the gender rules defined by their mothers expressed a position (and were an active factor) in redefining both race and gender for their generation. At the same time those redefinitions were going on, so were others—of the relationship of state and individual, of the rights of individuals to self-determination, of the proper relationship of older to younger generations.

What ultimately justified her act of support for Sammie was the intrusion of police force into their innocent teen-age world. It was at that point that a question of rights arose. Whatever Sammie had done, "she didn't deserve being put in jail." Resisting force was a common explanation given by my interviewees for their antipathy to desegregation. At its core, they claimed, it wasn't about going to school with black children. It was that change had been forced on them:

> Everyone was saying, and my dad was one of them, that the government was forcing something down our throats that shouldn't have taken place. I really did not want to go to school with them. I would not have welcomed them, but I would not have mistreated them either. I could have gone to school and gone about my business, had it been that simple. But it wasn't. It just was not that simple.

For white people to construe resistance to civil rights as a response to unjust coercion was to write their own character as Victim. It is not that I have perpetrated a wrong that deserves righting, they implicitly argued. I simply, innocently, did that which seemed "normal." What is not normal, what is not right, is that the government is forcing something down our throats. Nancy's statement that she would not have welcomed the black students to the school but also would not have mistreated them was echoed frequently by other white alumni I interviewed. Yet when she witnessed her peers "mistreating them," she did not protest; instead, she voiced yet another complaint, this one about the disruption to her own life:

> Central's a very large school, and I was coming downstairs from a class and one of the black girls was maybe four or five people ahead of me descending the staircase. I don't remember if it was Minnijean or not, but I think it was Minnijean Brown. She was going down the stairs and

someone—it was a guy—he tripped her. She fell from maybe the second to the bottom step, dropped all of her books. Someone else came and kicked them across the hall.

Well, there were hundreds of kids out in the hall trying to change classes, you know. And the things that they would holler at her. It was very disruptive. You could then go to class and you could hear a big ruckus taking place out in the hall. Teacher would get up and shut the door. It was just very disruptive, you know.

I became very disenchanted with the whole thing. I just kept thinking, This is my senior year and this is not what I was looking forward to. This is just unfair.

The main reason I guess that I resented it so is because it was our senior year, it messed up everything for our senior year. Everybody aspired to get to Central, you know, because it was the only high school and it was such a beautiful school. It's supposed to be the most beautiful high school in the United States, and the largest. So it was just something to get out of the ninth grade and get to Central. My brother, of course, was in Central ahead of me, and seeing all the things that he did and got to do and the fun and everything—well, that's what I was looking forward to in my senior year.

Well, it didn't happen. See, we had all this disruption. [. . .] So I just felt like it was unfair that it was done the way that it was done because it could have been done a better way.

Throughout her narrative, Nancy gave clear voice to her several grievances: her community had been coerced into making unwelcome changes; her classmate had been (shockingly) arrested; her prized senior year had been irreparably disrupted. So when at the end of our conversation I asked her to reflect back on all that ruckus and tell me what in retrospect she thought the upset was most about, she took me by surprise:

I don't really know exactly what it was other than I do know that everyone I was around at that time, they were talking about violence, there would be violence. When I look back on it now—I didn't think this then—but when I look back on it now I have a feeling that [the parents' fear] probably was that it would be the beginning of interracial marriage. That's the only thing I can come up with. The only thing I can come up with.

It was a stunning and meaningful non sequitur. Having complained about coercion, unjust arrests, disruption of her senior year, in the end it came back around to the realm of sexuality. Nancy might challenge her own role as woman-symbol. She might negotiate a complex balance between her duty to uphold certain standards and her desire to defy them. But when it came down to it, she joined her elders in collapsing race and sexuality as a means to describe resentments that were, it soon turned out, in some part about class. Having told me that her daughter's most adored teacher was an African American woman (a story that seemed intended to point out to me her own changes of heart over the years), Nancy then described an event at her workplace that for her was the other side of the coin:

> NANCY: [A black woman] came and made an application for a job and the salary she asked for to begin with most of us weren't even making at that time and we had been there for years. So we resented that. Just things, you know, like that.
>
> But more and more, you would see more and more of them shopping, more and more of them downtown than ever before. Then, of course, they stopped sitting in the back of the bus and things like that. To me, it was just get along in this world, you know. This is it.
>
> But I didn't want my daughter to marry one. I still don't. I still feel that way.
>
> BR: Why is that?
>
> NANCY: I guess just simply because of my background, the way that I was raised. I told Alice that. "You're to be nice to them. Respect them. But I don't want you bringing them home to play, and I don't want you to marry one." And I guess that's just because that's the way I was raised. The only reason I can come up with.
>
> BR: Did Alice ever ask for an explanation of why you didn't want her to bring black children home to play?
>
> NANCY: No, she didn't. And I don't know why she didn't, but she never did.

"I don't know why she didn't, but she never did." Long after our talk, those words looped round and round my mind. I believed her; Nancy really didn't know why her daughter never asked the single most critical question: "Why?" That she didn't seemed to me to say so much about the causes of white racism, and about its injuries to the white people who perpetrate it. Nancy is an intelligent and strong person. Why, I wondered, could she not ask that critical question? Perhaps because to question her racial assumptions was to challenge at a deeper level than she was willing assumptions about her role as woman and her place in a class order.

Questioning the Alternatives

Joyce did question what she saw happening at Central High, and she was led then to question much, much more. I met with Joyce at the social welfare agency where she works. Round and welcoming, she sat behind her cluttered desk, apologizing for the scrape, scrape, scrape of a workman preparing the building's exterior for painting. Quickly she began to tell me what had clearly been for her the defining moment of that year, when she was a junior at Central High:

> JOYCE: One of the things that happened at Central had to do with a *very* close friend of mine. She and I were just like sisters. We spent the night at each other's house. We walked to school together. We studied together. We went to church together. I would go home with them for chicken dinner after church on Sunday. She'd come home with me. I mean we were very, very, very close.
>
> I remember one time—have you had a chance to go by Central? Of course people have seen it in pictures and everything. Well, if you recall, the front of the school that faces on Park Street has stairs that go down, and there used to be a fish pond down there that was full of water and had goldfish in it, and so forth. And I remember one day, my friend (her name was Lydia) and another friend of ours, a mutual friend, Joanna, the three of us were walking down those stairs and I was between Joanna and Lydia.
>
> And I don't even remember what brought the conversation to a start or anything, but I made the comment that I just, using the language of the day, I said, "Well, I don't see what's wrong with going to school with colored kids." And Lydia and Joanna both, and Lydia predominantly, got behind me and physically shoved me all the way down the stairs and right to the edge of the fishpond and I honest-to-God thought at that moment they were going to shove me into that fishpond. And they stopped right there.

I don't remember whether the lesson came to me immediately. I think some kernel of it did, but it has grown over the years to the point that I realize that if you take a stand, if you believe in something that is not popularly accepted, if something like that is in your mind, then you either do one of two things: You either keep your mouth shut, or you be prepared to stand your ground. Because something's gonna happen. And that was a real shocking lesson to me, that even people you consider friends would take something like that so personally and focus so much anger on someone very close to them. That's the lesson I got from that.

BR: What did you do?

JOYCE: I think I kept my mouth shut for the rest of the school year with my friends.

Joyce kept her mouth shut with her friends, but she anguished over what she saw going on at school. I asked her if it had been hard, if she'd had to struggle to stay quiet, and she replied:

JOYCE: Yeah, I think I did. As a matter of fact, there were two other things that happened, one that I did sort of as my way of saying something without confronting the issue directly locally, and the other was an event that happened to somebody else that really made another deep impression on me. I'll tell you the latter first.

I remember, as I said, in September, Central was not air conditioned then, and the windows would be open in September 'cause it'd still be very, very warm. My homeroom—the front of Central faces Park Street, and as you look at it head on, my homeroom was on the lefthand end of that front part, and the desks all faced in that direction and the windows were to our left.

Every morning, they'd come over the loudspeaker and we'd all stand up and say the Pledge of Allegiance and they'd probably have bible scripture, I'm sure we did at that time, and announcements or whatever. Well, I remember the mobs had been there every day, and I'll admit, I used some of that as an excuse to check out of school, calling my mother saying, I'm scared to be here, and then go off with my friends downtown to mess around. Because every day there were the mobs out across Park Street, they were kept across Park Street and into Park Street sometimes, but they were not allowed on the campus. You could hear them out there and everything.

Well, one day we were standing there and I had my hand on my heart saying the Pledge of Allegiance and I could hear the mob, the sound escalating from what it normally was. And as I was saying the words, I turned and looked out the window, and I saw this mob of people chasing what to a sixteen-year-old girl was an elderly black man. I've since found out it was a New York *Times* reporter who was probably forty-five, something like that. I was looking and saying the Pledge of Allegiance, and I was watching them chase him across the yards on that side of the street, and I knew, I really believed that if they caught him they would kill him.

In that moment, while I'm watching this, saying the Pledge of Allegiance, hand on my heart, I'm thinking, There's something wrong here. How can this be happening in a country that we're pledging allegiance to? What's wrong with this picture? And that left an indelible—I can see it today, I will never, ever forget that. I think that, along with my parents' quasi-liberalism, and the experience with my friends, that helped to water the seeds that my parents had planted earlier on about believing in right things and trying to do what was right.

The other thing that I did was after the incident with Lydia and Joanna, and after this had happened and the mobs were still going on day after day after day, I wrote a letter to President Eisenhower and said, Do something to make this stop. All I want is my education.

Which was a fairly selfish thing to write about, but as I think back on it, I think it was a fairly activist thing to do at that time, given the fact that I had never done anything before in my life, and to write a letter to the President!

And I got a canned response; I've actually got it framed in my office at home. I got a canned response from some aide, who said, The President's happy to hear from you. We agree with you that the solution has to be found blah-blah-blah-blah-blah-blah. And I remember the day my mother encouraged me to write that letter.

I walked home from school; we lived about eight blocks from school, I guess. And as I got within sight of my house, my mother was out on the front porch waving this letter and telling me to hurry up, that the President in the White House had written me, you know. She was really, really proud, and that memory stays with me.

BR: Did other students know that you had written that letter?

JOYCE: You know, I don't remember, I sort of doubt it. I really doubt it, I doubt that I said anything to anybody. And I think that was probably hard, too, because I was so proud, and who could I tell?

Why had Joyce drawn such different lessons from the experiences at Central High she'd shared with Nancy and the others? Her family, like Nancy's, was not affluent. Her father came from a small cotton-growing Arkansas town:

> He picked cotton until he got sick of it, and then he lied about his age and took his older brother's name and enlisted in the army. You know, a little bit of a mover and shaker in a way of looking at it.

He was ambitious, rising as high as he could manage in the army. "We traveled a lot," Joyce told me, "had the experience of a lot of different cultures and places and all of that kind of thing." He also married a woman originally from the midwest. Was her mother an integrationist? I asked:

> It's hard for me to know how to characterize my mother. I don't feel totally comfortable saying that she was a liberal. But I don't feel totally comfortable saying that she was not a liberal. I don't know whether she was or not. But my memory of my mother was in some ways sort of the stereotypical, if not integrationist, moderate on the issue, who says, Some of my best friends are colored people, you know.

Like Nancy, Joyce approached the events at Central High from the point of view of her own needs. "I didn't think of myself as someone who was pushing for integration," she said. "I did think of myself as not having a problem." She echoed Nancy in harboring ongoing resentment about the injuries to her own high school experience, and especially the loss of the year after the drama when the high schools were all closed. I interviewed Joyce shortly before going to talk with Govenor Faubus. "Is there any message you'd like me to carry to the governor?" I asked her. "He won't know who the hell I am," she replied, "but tell him I still resent the fact that he cheated me out of my senior year at Central High School."

But, after the fact, Joyce made very different choices in her life, attributing their roots to the incidents she'd described to me. Her parents' "quasi-liberalism"—"trying to do what's right" while keeping quiet—was no longer an option. She became an activist on behalf of poor people, "making trouble" in a good cause and standing up very publicly, in exactly the way she had failed to do as a junior at Central High, to promote and defend her beliefs. "You either keep your mouth shut, or you be prepared to stand your ground. Because something's gonna happen." Today, Joyce firmly stands her ground, and what has happened is that she has become a radical, advocating very fundamental change in the social order of America.

Broken Promises/Promising Breaks

Looking back over my interviews, it seems to me that Joyce's classmates also took a stand. Sensing something about the close interweaving of racial change, changes in the roles of women, and changes in their prospects for economic opportunity, they took a stand for a future they believed was owed them. For most of the white students at Central High, greater educational opportunity for black children was not a very active threat. The times were booming in Little Rock. There was a sense, very present in my interviews, that the world was an oyster for these high schoolers to open. They did not represent themselves as fearful that black graduates from "their" school would become a greater competitive force: "To me, it was just get along in this world."

What they did resent and fear was the intrusion of coercive force into their seemingly predictable 1950s world. Central High itself typified all that was best in that world. "It was the only high school[11] and it was such a beautiful school. It's supposed to be the most beautiful high school in the United States, and the largest." It was also a place of uniformity, of seeming classlessness, and therefore of hope, well described by a man who graduated several years before the desegregation struggle:

> It was really kind of a wonderful, idyllic, Andy Hardy kind of high school. Very good musical programs. Fine athletic teams, which people in that part of the country tend to measure their schools by. Every year there were dozens of scholarships, always several scholarships to the Ivy League schools. People did very well.[12]

Again and again, people emphasized to me how they had rubbed shoulders with fellow students from affluent families and from poor ones, how everyone had equal rights and equal opportunities. It was not that the students didn't recognize differences. They used obvious codes (neighborhood, father's occupation, whether or not mother worked, and so on) to tell fine-grained stories of class distinctions. But the point was that they deeply believed those differences didn't matter, not, at least, so long as they all faced forward toward the future from the idyllic present of Central High.

In the context of that consensus, Central High not only defined the white students' world—"one big happy family," lacking divisions, friendly and familiar—but also defined their world view. At the time Central High was desegregated, young white people believed the world was a place without impermeable divisions where everyone had an equal chance at the good life. Beliefs about the nature of the social world are communicated in many ways, direct and indirect. In the South of the 1950s, relations between white and black people were a highly communicative system of entitlement. The typical white mother, however poor herself, gave her maid old clothing and food, and that generosity implied both her power to be generous and a direction of largesse that in turn implied her superior standing in the community and her daughter's superior prospects in the world.

To be sure, it was a world changing profoundly, a fact prophesied by nothing so ominously as desegregation itself. But the changes impending went well beyond race relations. Corporatization presented youths with the prospect of working in huge, bureaucratized structures wholly unlike the personalized work settings their parents had known, both scary and promising because they offered such new possibilities for success. Domestic migration and suburbanization meant that young women would need to leave the communities in which their families had put down strong roots, both a loss and a prospect of liberation.

White teenagers in the fifties were reared to see their places in society in very clear definition perhaps precisely because the world was in such flux. They would, they believed, probably go to college, certainly marry, join corporations if they were boys and work for them forever, follow their husbands around the country and probably not take jobs themselves if they were girls, and raise children as happy helpmates. This was the "Andy Hardy type of vision" promoted by the "Andy Hardy type of school." Although it was a vision of a prototypic middle-class life, it was precisely the life for which these students, whatever the class status of their families of birth, were certain they were destined.

The presence of the black students in that world shook their certainties; the behavior of Minnijean shattered them. Not only did Minnijean act entitled to the largesse her white classmates might otherwise have been inclined to concede her, but she was a woman—a large woman—who felt entitled to defend and assert herself. In this she was similar to

Sammie Dean, a small woman of diminished class status who nonetheless commanded center stage in the drama that was transforming the ideal world of Central High.

Desegregation was a harbinger of a multifaceted set of alterations in the world as they knew it. A decade after the end of the war and the redomestication of Rosie the Riveter, the division between women who worked for wages and those who worked at home seemed stark. Unquestionably in the first category were women of color. Both they and the white world assumed the necessity, not to mention the propriety, of their employment as domestic, agricultural, or light industrial workers. White working-class women very often worked for wages also, but that fact was frequently questioned and contested in their families. By the postwar period, the illusion of gendered divisions of labor were far-reaching; the wives of white working men often saw their own jobs as "temporary," filling a financial need for the moment despite their husbands' shame about that necessity. The ideal type of domestic life was actively constructed by media and policy to be a one-earner family (May 1988). White women were encouraged to go to college, not so that they might get a job but in order to contract a more affluent marriage. Airline work offered a similar trajectory for girls from families who could not afford college (and sometimes also for those who could). In the popular imagination, stewardesses got to have adventures, see the world, and meet prosperous prospective mates, all while being paid well for a glamorous job.[13]

Alongside those forces that promoted a neat separation of economic and domestic life, however, other, contradictory developments were simultaneously taking shape. As it turned out, the promise of marriage as a refuge proved false; life in the labor force was not so temporary after all. Over the decades between then and now, service industries, which depend on women's labor, grew monumentally in the United States, as industrial manufacturing, employing mostly men, declined. One-earner families became a nostalgic memory of the past (and for many Americans a memory that never happened) (Rifkin 1995).[14] However unimagined those transformations may have been at the moment Nancy painted slogans on her classmates' cars, she nonetheless paraded straight into a period of historic change and became entangled in all the contradictions thereof.

Presentiment is a risky basis for sociological analysis, but I nonetheless hazard the dangers of this particularly thin and slippery ice and defend the inclusion of intuition and fear in the category of empirical data to be unpacked and deciphered. We commonly craft behavior in the present under the influence of fears about the future; those fears always contain some kernel of truth, some accurate intuition about changes brewing, however ephemeral at the moment and however much inaccuracy and distortion our fears may also contain.[15] Because political behavior is often informed by such intangibles, it can appear to be irrational if we do not articulate the unspoken airs that may in fact form its underlying heat.

More than who attended which school, desegregation represented the dismantling and re-creation of a life vision for both blacks and whites. The white coeds were supposed to be in control of their world, even if that control was won at the price of adapting to a certain definition of femininity. So long as they conformed, they were certain they had all the world to gain. But their hatred of Minnijean and Sammie Dean speaks of the tenuousness of that certainty. In reality, they could not control their small world, their high school; armed force imposed on them changes they did not wish. They could not control members of their own group; Sammie Dean scrapped and tangled with authority. They could not control the black students whom, in the tradition of graceful southern defeat, they were prepared to "allow" as guests in their school. Minnijean "walked the halls as if she belonged there."

Perhaps on a deeper level they were particularly unforgiving of these two particular women because they challenged the very means by which women in general had been told they could win some measure of control in their lives. As women, they had internalized and accepted as "truth" notions of appropriate behavior for girls and women. Sammie Dean's family were "white trash," Helen argued, because of the way their womenfolk behaved. "Mother would have died for shame if her daughter's name had been put in the paper, or if I'd gotten in any type of trouble," Helen told me. "While we had our beliefs and our opinions, you didn't voice them to the public. You just didn't do that."

In return for "not doing that," girls gained the promise of a feminine place in an idealized type of society. They also accepted a role in constructing just such a society, a white society with little room for genuine black equality. When Sammie Dean broke the rules for women, she challenged implicit promises of a rosy future because she challenged her peers to "do that," to act on their beliefs in public. Minnijean broke rules governing both women's and black people's behavior, and for that she was doubly hated.

The women of Central High recounted their memories of Minnijean's and Sammie Dean's transgressions with all the vigor of their disapproval back then, even though we met in very different times. Presentiment had become the present; indeed, for many of these women, it was fast becoming the past. Nancy had moved more times than she could count, following her husband's corporate career from pillar to post, until at last he found himself "downsized" in his fifties. Helen also had reluctantly relocated for the sake of her husband's better prospects. Nonetheless, it had been necessary for her to hold a job, too, and now she counted the days until retirement and complained about the injustices of affirmative action. Martha achieved a satisfying career in broadcasting, but disappointments dotted her personal life. In her middle years, she struggled with ambivalence about her childlessness and worried about mistakes she'd made as a stepmother in her second marriage.

Throughout our conversation, Martha had been warmly honest about her feelings and beliefs. As our interview ended, while I packed up my tape paraphernalia, she generously pulled old clippings from her files to give me, pointing out photos of people whose names had come up in our conversation. Suddenly, she gasped and grew silent. I looked up from my wires. She was weeping, her eyes transfixed on a faded photograph on a yellowed page. It was a picture of the Nine, and Minnijean stood to one side, tall and stately—not overweight. On her face was a self-conscious smile; she seemed shy, chin tucked down, perhaps unsure of herself in front of the camera. She seemed very much a fifties sort of teenager, and very vulnerable.

"She was nothing like a Mammy," Martha moaned. "How could I have remembered her that way?"

"Memory fails," wrote Karen Fields, "and memory collaborates with forces separate from actual past events. . . ." Martha's memory collaborated with a reputation she'd helped to construct. All that talk among the girls had in fact constituted a political act of protest against Minnijean's disturbance of normalcy, against the implied threat to their place in a promised class order. To be sure, that place held them, too, in place, in gendered roles they both embraced and resisted.

"How could I have remembered her that way?" Martha lamented. Participating actively in the construction and defense of their Andy Hardy world, the women of Central High also felt its injuries and rebelled. Lacking clarity on the sources of their own discomfort and hope, they blamed Minnijean and Sammie Dean. In a moment of historic social change, they chose up sides, like Nancy's daughter never asking why. Only later could they begin to glimpse their own misperceptions. But they still defended untenable positions of long ago, still were tangled in webs of gender, race, class, of domesticity and political opinion, of ambivalence about their lives, their peers, and their world.

NOTES

1. The literature on Central High is blessed with a number of firsthand accounts: Bates (1986/62); Huckaby (1980); Blossom (1959); Beals (1994).

2. What we choose to tell and to omit is often an act of consent to power relations or of resistance. For an excellent discussion of this aspect of storytelling, see Ewick and Silbey (1995). I also find useful James Scott's (1990) formulation of hidden transcripts, those stories people tell only among themselves.

3. All names of Minnijean's and Sammie's classmates have been changed.

4. According to a hard-to-track citation on the World Wide Web, the term Goody Two-Shoes derives from an anonymous allegory published in 1766 and entitled "The history of little Goody Two-Shoes: Otherwise called, Mrs. Margery Two-Shoes." It reads: "With the means by which she acquired her learning and wisdom, Set forth at large for the benefit of those, Who from a state of rags and care, And having shoes but half a pair; Their fortunes and their fame would fix, And gallop in a coach and six." Paradoxically, the women of Little Rock dropped the connotation of "do-gooder" but maintained the slight air of self-derision suggested by the original as they used the term to suggest that they *were* good.

5. Sammie Dean and her parents energetically challenged Sammie's expulsion and, with the help of segregationist leaders, succeeded in getting her reinstated. Minnijean was placed in a private school in New York, where she finished out her high school years.

6. There is an extensive literature on the link between women's ways and class status, both in the American South and in many other cultures around the world. For two examples, see Blee (1991) and Rozario (1992).

7. I deal more extensively with both racial and class components to the construction (and reconstruction in the fifties) of white social relations in *Bitters* (forthcoming).

8. I draw here on many formulations of the concept of internalized oppression, especially how the site of activity is a factor in constructing social systems and the ideologies that mediate them. For some particular angles on this discussion, see Freitag (1989) and Scott (1985).

9. This formulation draws on George Rudé (1980). I have elaborated it in more detail in Roy (1994).

10. This quality of contradictory rebelliousness is a not uncommon characteristic of conservative politics in general. "Right-wing movements hold mixed stances toward prevailing power structures," writes Sara Diamond (1995) in her fine study: "They are partially *oppositional* and partially . . . *system-supportive*" (p. 6). If conservatism contains within itself this paradoxical quality, so all the more does conservative women's activism, because it is performed in two distinct domains, one public, the other private, and both sites elicit ambivalent attitudes. Like the state, the family too is a power structure that conservative women both defend theoretically and, often, resist in practice. The two dramas, one public, the other private, intertwine, supporting and contradicting each other to weave a tapestry peculiarly gendered and revealingly political.

11. In fact, it was not the only high school. Dunbar High School had been built for black students at the same time as Central in the 1920s, using a very similar blueprint. It, too, was a renowned institution, celebrated for the excellence of its scholarship. Nancy demonstrates a familiar ethnocentrism when she disappears the black school. Two new high schools were opened in 1957, Hall for white students in the newly developing white suburbs in the western part of the city and Horace Mann in the traditionally black neighborhood to the east. Much resentment by working-class white people focused on the fact that Central was integrated while Hall was left all white for a number of years afterward.

12. Andy Hardy was a character in a long series of movies spanning the thirties, forties, and fifties. The son of a poor but upstanding judge in a typical midwestern town, Andy Hardy was the ideal of white middle-class America struggling through the Depression and achieving respect and solidity in the decades following.

13. Of course, not everyone was eligible for this bountiful experience, only women who met certain standards of size and beauty, another clear example of the phenomenon of "looksism." See Chernin (1981) and Bordo (1993).

14. The influx of white women into the job market was to coincide with the demise of jobs for African American men in the failing industries of the North, an important factor in the coincidence of gender and race in reshaping social relations in recent decades.

15. And those "distortions" are, again, coded expressions of a deeper accuracy. A "middle-class" white girl myself at the time, I remember a startled recognition that I could have, indeed might have to have, a career of my own, and my ambivalence about it.

BIBLIOGRAPHY

Ashmore, Harry. 1988. *Hearts and Minds: A Personal Chronicle of Race in America* (Cabin John, Md.: Seven Locks Press).

Bates, Daisy. 1986/1962. *The Long Shadow of Little Rock* (Fayetteville: University of Arkansas Press).

Beals, Melba Pattillo. 1994. *Warriors Don't Cry* (New York: Pocket Books).

Blee, Kathleen. 1991. *Women of the Klan: Racism and Gender in the 1920s* (Berkeley: University of California Press).

Blossom, Virgil T. 1959. *It Has Happened Here* (New York: Harper & Brothers).

Bordo, Susan. 1993. *Unbearable Weight: Feminism, Western Culture, and the Body* (Berkeley: University of California Press).

Chernin, Kim. 1981. *The Obsession: Reflections on the Tyranny of Slenderness* (New York: Harper & Row).

Diamond, Sara. 1995. *Roads to Dominion: Right-Wing Movements and Political Power in the United State* (New York: Guilford Press).

Ewick, Patricia, and Susan S. Silbey. 1995. "Subversive Stories and Hegemonic Tales: Toward a Sociology of Narrative," in *Law & Society Review* 29: 2.

Fields, Karen E. 1994. "What One Cannot Remember Mistakenly," in Jaclyn Jeffrey and Glenace Edwall (eds.), *Memory and History: Essays on Recalling and Interpreting Experience* (Lanham, Md.: University Press of America).

Freitag, Sandria. 1989. *Collective Action and Community: Public Arenas and the Emergence of Communalism in North India* (Berkeley: University of California Press).

hooks, bell. 1981. *Ain't I a Woman* (Boston: South End Press).

Huckaby, Elizabeth. 1980. *Crisis at Central High: Little Rock 1957–58* (Baton Rouge: Louisiana State University Press).

Irwin-Zarecka, Iwona. 1994. *Frames of Remembrance: The Dynamics of Collective Memory* (New Brunswick, N.J.: Transaction Publishers).

May, Elaine Tyler. 1988. *Homeward Bound: American Families in the Cold War Era* (New York: Basic Books).

Rifkin, Jeremy. 1995. *The End of Work: The Decline of the Global Labor Force and the Dawn of the Post-Market Era* (New York: G. P. Putnam's Sons).

Roy, Beth. forthcoming. *Bitters in the Honey: Tales of Race and Resentment from Little Rock*.

———. 1994. *Some Trouble with Cows: Making Sense of Social Conflict* (Berkeley: University of California Press).

Rozario, Santi. 1992. *Purity and Communal Boundaries: Women and Social Change in a Bangladeshi Village* (London: Zed).

Rudé, George. 1980. *Ideology and Popular Protest* (New York: Pantheon Books).

Sacks, Karen Brodkin, and Dorothy Remy (eds.). 1984. *My Troubles Are*

Going to Have Trouble with Me (New Brunswick, N.J.: Rutgers University Press).

Scott, James C. 1990. *Domination and the Arts of Resistance* (New Haven: Yale University Press).

———. 1985. *Weapons of the Weak: Everyday Forms of Peasant Resistance* (New Haven: Yale University Press).

Chapter Seven

Reflections of an AIM Activist
Has It All Been Worth It?

Karren Baird-Olson

Several times when I have served on a panel discussing gender or racial role expectations, the moderator has introduced me by asking the audience to guess which one of the panel members is a member of the American Indian Movement (AIM). If no one knows me, no one chooses me. I am the small, strawberry blonde, blue-eyed, middle-aged woman wearing a black, dressed-for-success suit accessorized with (fake) pearl earrings and choker. Appearances can also be deceptive where social groups are involved. For example, the view that some people hold of AIM as a violent organization and the belief that its actions are nonproductive or even counterproductive serve as more examples of faulty perception based on stereotypes.

The argument I will make in the next pages is based on personal experience and is not meant to be a comprehensive sociological treatise, albeit sociology is my professional area and certainly has shaped my personal view of the world. In addition, I grew up in Montana and, as a twenty-one-year-old bride, moved to the Fort Peck Assiniboine and Sioux Reservation in 1958. My home is still there. My son and my ex-husband still live there. Thus, both my professional training and my almost forty years of firsthand experience of reservation life have shaped my personal analysis of the impact of AIM. Based on this grounded perspective, I will argue that AIM was a primary facilitator in bringing rapid change as well as empowerment to many native people and communities. Until AIM was established, change in many areas of Indian Country[1] had moved at such a slow pace that improvements in social conditions and alleviation of human suffering were, for all intents and purposes, nonexistent to both its residents and to the general public's eye. AIM created a broad-based public awareness that helped to open long-closed doors and enabled major personal and institutional change.

My first purpose for writing this paper is to correct at least a few of the myths surrounding AIM. Specifically, I will catalog five contributions AIM has made to the well-being of the First Peoples as well as to those who share this land with us. My second purpose is to tell the story of an illustrative incident of U.S. government misconduct that occurred in Washington, D.C., in July 1976—an incident that has not been discussed in the social science literature. By recounting this incident, I hope to achieve two goals: (1) to identify some of the unsung heroines and heroes of the 1970s' native activist period of American history that followed the occupation of Alcatraz Island, and (2) to point out the personal, social, and economic price that has been paid by many AIM activists, both women and men alike; sometimes the price has been a bitter one, especially in light of the denunciations and misrepresentations of some about their goals and tactics. I will begin this analysis and testimony by turning back the pages of my own life, and the life of AIM, first to the late 1960s and early 1970s and then to late June 1976.

My Introduction To AIM

Shortly after my children and I moved from Montana to Chicago in November 1969, we met Phyllis Fast Wolf and her family. We were both Plains Indian families from northwestern reservations with similar cultures, ties that helped strengthen the rapport our families immediately felt for each other. Phyllis, her husband, Frank, her daughter, Pat, and her sons not only helped us adapt to the urban world but also introduced us to the activities of a newly formed grassroots group of people who called themselves AIM (American Indian Movement). Honoring their invitations, I joined them at one of the first sit-ins at an archeological dig and later at the sit-in at Belmont Harbor.

In the early fall of 1972, I returned to Missoula, Montana, where Myrna Boyd, a dear friend who had moved to Missoula from the Fort Peck Assiniboine and Sioux Reservation, found me. She told me that she had had a dream that I would be coming back to Montana. She told me about the most recent activities of AIM. This time I was invited to join an activity called "the Trail of Broken Treaties." Because of my respect for her, because I had already learned that freedom does not come without some danger, and because of other, more personal reasons, I accepted the invitation.

Since my children were in school, they remained with my parents in Lewistown, Montana. Myrna's nine children were going to make the cross-country trek; as their "auntie," I would help tutor them. On a lovely fall day, several carloads of AIM supporters (I also took my car) headed southeast to the Northern Cheyenne Reservation, where we would meet the main group. Collecting more people as we traveled, we would then head through the Dakotas, go on to Minnesota, and finally reach Washington, D.C., in October. This trip would change the complete direction of my life.

Although there needs to be much more written from the perspectives of the participants in the Trail of Broken Treaties, the objective of this paper is not to describe that historically significant event. My focus is on a telling event that occurred four years later during the 1976 reunion, an incident I will use as a pedagogical device to illustrate my continuing commitment to the American Indian Movement.

The 1976 Incident: Harassing and Arresting the Innocent

I do not remember when it was decided that as many as possible of the 1972 Trail of Broken Treaties participants would return to Washington, D.C., during America's Bicentennial activities. As I sit here at my computer in Kansas, I find it hard to believe that it has been more than two decades since the Trail and nearly twenty years since the harassment and arrest of the innocent in 1976. I have promised that I would write about both times, but I always thought I would do it when I became an elder, because I thought my life would slow up a bit as I grew older. That has not happened. However, the time has come for us who were actually there to tell our own stories. I have asked some friends and family members to help me remember some of the things that went on that summer in D.C. Thus, the following account of the 1976 incident is based not only on my own remembrance, but also on the recollections of others—my children Shawn, John, and Nolee; Caleb Shield; Theresa McKey; Laurie Whitright and Ruby Whitright Fowler.[2]

I do remember that, as soon as my children heard about the plans for the 1976 gathering, they said they were going; they refused to be left behind in Montana again, as they had been when I traveled with the Trail of Broken Treaties Caravan to Washington, D.C., in 1972. In 1976, because of my job, my three children and I could not leave with the Montana contingent, so I told the Fort Peck group that we would meet them at the American University campsite no later than July 4.

Our preparations for the trip began during the spring of 1976. We planned to drive to Washington, D.C., camping and sightseeing along the way, and after the work was done, we would travel until we had just enough money to return home. The trip would provide three lessons for my children: (1) active participation in the creation of governmental policies; (2) visits to important historical sites; and (3) an appreciation of the diversity of this land and its peoples. Another reason for the trip, and certainly not the least important, was that it would be one of our last family activities before my older daughter left for college.

The unaware have often expressed amazement that a single woman would travel with three children across the country, as well as take an active part in protesting against the abuses of the U.S. government. In the first place, I was used to driving across the country by myself, but during this trip I was not alone. Three responsible young people—two teenagers (one seventeen and one sixteen) and a preteenager of twelve— were with me. More importantly, I wanted my children to know that they did not have to be passive victims, that they could make positive changes not only in their own lives but also in the lives of others if they had the courage to take action, to do something.

So one day in late June, we headed east. Our 1967 four-door Chevy Impala sedan was filled with camping gear, clothes, food, a U.S. map, a AAA trip plan, a journal, a camera, books, a short mother, and three long-legged children. The tent poles were tied to the side of the car, and John Mike's GI Joe, dressed like Custer, was strapped to the hood ornament. We arrived in Washington, D.C., in time for the Fourth of July activities, joining the 320 American Indians from all over the country who camped on the sports field of American University in the summer of 1976.

During one of our camp meetings, it was decided that we should take the children and young people to visit the Bureau of Indian Affairs (BIA) building where we had been surrounded and put under siege in 1972. Considering that the government had overreacted to our presence in 1972, we were not sure how officials would respond to our attempts to visit our "embassy" this time around. We were a peaceful group, but, in case the government tried to surround us again, we decided to take mostly older children and young people—forty youngsters in all—for the first trip. Ten adults were chosen to go as chaperons and tour guides for the first tour. Among that group were eleven of us from Fort Peck: Myrna Boyd and three of her children, Laurie, Chauncey, and Donald; Caleb Shields; David Campbell; the two McKey girls; and my two daughters—Shawn and Nolee—and me. My son, John Mike, would be among those who would remain at camp as a security guard. He was to go on the next tour.

The morning of our first tour was sunny and warm. In anticipation of a typical, sultry Washington, D.C., summer day, we did not take jackets. We wore Levis, summer tops, and sandals or cowboy boots. A few of us had cameras and small purses. Someone had loaned us a big yellow school bus. After telling John Mike that we would see him that afternoon, I climbed into the bus. I joked with Myrna about how I always seemed to end up chaperoning a bunch of kids on bumpy rides in buses that made me carsick. I had no idea that being carsick would be the least of my concerns.

As we drove from the American University to the BIA building, those of us who had been to D.C. before pointed out various historical sites to the kids. We laughed, we sang, and we veterans of 1972 told the others stories about how we were surrounded in the BIA building and how the government overreacted to a group of people who had come to stay in their embassy. Someone wondered if it would happen again. We agreed that this was the Bicentennial; this was obviously a tour group of youngsters and a few adults; ergo, we would be given the opportunity to have a peaceful visit. Everyone relaxed. It was a nice day.

We arrived at the BIA building in the late morning. The bus driver let us off on the sidewalk leading to the front entrance with the large, double metal doors. As the group walked toward the doors, we old-timers pointed out remembered landmarks. We came up the steps and found that the doors had been locked. We were denied access to our own embassy! For a few minutes we stood dazed. Then we regrouped. We decided to sit down, sing, and pray until the doors were opened.

Shortly thereafter, several expensively dressed white men came out to tell us that they were afraid we were carrying weapons and were going to take over the BIA building. We were told that if we agreed to be searched and to go in groups of ten or fewer at a time, we would be admitted. This was a flimsy excuse, since our summer clothing would have made it very difficult, if not impossible, for any of us to conceal the types of weapons necessary to take over the building. Also, it would have been extremely difficult to supervise so many children and young people during such an action.

The sun began to reach high noon; those of us from the semiarid plains of northeastern Montana began to notice the humidity. Someone found a water faucet on one side of the U-shaped building. Our stomachs began to tell us that we had not eaten since early that morning. Still we sat, and still we prayed and sang.

Then they came: dozens of black-helmeted men wearing black clothing and riding dark motorcycles, coming in lines down the avenue. I remember feeling sick to my stomach. Déjà vu. But this time my two daughters and other young people were with me. I told Nolee and Shawn that I wanted them to leave. I knew they could find their way back to the university campsite. But they would not leave without me, nor would they leave with me. So I stayed with them.

The group agreed that we would continue our peaceful protest; that we would not initiate nor respond with violence. We told the children that, whatever happened to us adults, they were not to fight back. I kept my daughters close to me. Shawn understood that if something happened to me, she was responsible for her twelve-year-old sister, Nolee. All of us who had long hair braided it.[3]

The goon squad began to move in file across the lawn. We moved around the building into the inner rectangular-shaped courtyard of the building. Beyond the sidewalk, a grassy knoll rose slightly above us. We sat in a close circle, praying and singing. People had begun to gather on the knoll to watch the event. Others were watching from the windows of the BIA building. Television crews arrived. Someone came out of the building and turned off the water faucet. We were sweating so heavily we had no need for bathrooms.

I realized it must be close to mid-afternoon. The storm troopers had moved in so closely that their boots touched our bottoms where we sat on the cement. Nolee looked up at a Black man, younger and even taller than the other troopers, who was standing behind her. She asked him why he was doing this. She wondered why, since his people had been so mistreated, he was not joining us. I was impressed by her insights. I looked up at the man and was heartened by the painful expression on his face. He had heard her.

Minutes after this encounter between a Native American child and a young Black man, someone in our group cried out. She had been struck with a trooper's club. I pushed my daughters into the center of the circle and reminded them to remain flat on their stomachs. I felt my back being hit. I lowered my head. And then I felt myself being lifted into the air. I knew that two men had hold of me. I was lifted above their heads and then dashed to the cement. The seconds in air were like flying.

There must have been pain when the flying ended. Part of the metal figurines on my Western belt buckle were ripped off. I have snapshots of bruises on my arms and torso and face, but I don't remember feeling pain from the impact. Nor do I remember pain when my face was ground into the cement after I lifted my head to call out reassurances to Nolee. I had heard her cry out when I was manhandled, and I did not want her to try to come to my rescue.

I figured out how to move my head ever so slightly so I could watch what was happening to the children. I saw Nolee being held against the wall. I could not see Shawn. Later we were told that the children were roughly grabbed out of the middle of the circle and slammed up against the wall of the building. A young, Black trooper had broken out of the line and would not participate in the violence. I like to believe he was the man Nolee questioned.

At least three paddy wagons arrived. We were handcuffed with plastic cuffs and thrown into the vehicles. I was in one with the other adult women. The cuffs cut into our wrists. But I quickly discovered that, if I pulled against the plastic straps, they tightened. I realized that, if I could keep from straining against them and if I continued to sweat in the oppressive heat, I probably could slide at least one hand out of the handcuffs once I was out of official scrutiny. The doors of the wagon were barely closed and it had hardly begun to move before I was out of my handcuffs and removing the cuffs from the other women. We prayed.

My daughters later told me that one of our Fort Peck girls was cut badly by her cuffs. The children were separated from the adults. We were all taken to a Washington, D.C., jail, where we were questioned and booked. We women were in a holding pen where we could hear our men. We asked about the children. The officials would not tell us anything. I prayed silently. A peace came to me. I was later to come to understand that it was an experience similar to what Christians call "a peace beyond all understanding." Once again, as a group but in separate cells, we women and men sang and prayed until we were ordered to stop.

One by one we were taken out to be booked. While I was being photographed, I joked with Myrna that this experience was a bit like being in beauty queen line-ups for contestant photo sessions. My humor was not appreciated by the jail officers.

Each of us women was questioned separately by plainclothes police who looked and sounded suspiciously like FBI agents. My interrogator asked me, "Why are you involved in all of this?" He then asked me why did not I help them (law enforcement agents) fight for higher wages? My response to the first question was that they knew so much about me that it was obvious the query was purely rhetorical. The agent had enough grace to look somewhat embarrassed. My initial response to his second question was amazement. I replied that he probably made more in one year than several hard-working Fort Peck people could make together in the same time.

Later we compared notes and found that we had been asked basically the same questions. The questioners seemed to think that three of us— Myrna, a woman from the state of Washington, and I—were "ringleaders." They would not tell us where our children were.

The women's section of the jail was full. Recently, the city's prostitutes had been rounded up to keep them out of sight during the Bicentennial. We were taken to the jail library. Bare mattresses were thrown on the floor. I don't remember if we were given blankets. I do remember that I was glad my clothes had dried out while we were in the holding tank and during the questioning and booking, because the room was very cold from the air conditioning. A kindly Black woman brought us baloney and "boughten" white bread sandwiches. I was so hungry they almost tasted good. Still wearing my sweaty clothes, I sank onto the bare mattress and looked over at Myrna. The last things I remember before falling asleep were her smile and her quiet chuckle when I whispered, "I have been in some real fixes with you. But this takes the cake!"

We were awakened before dawn. I cannot remember if we were given showers. I think not. We were taken to a cafeteria warmed by the comforting smells of bacon, sausage, eggs, grits, biscuits, and coffee. Black women behind the counters encouraged us to eat heartily and praised us for our courage. "Right on, sisters!" they said. The other female inmates told us this was a highly unusual breakfast. They were pleased because they, too, had benefited from our activism.

However, as I talked later in the holding pen with several young women who were being detained for prostitution, they did not understand how we could risk so much for no immediate payback. Incarceration was part of the package that came with working on the streets. Our incarceration was not part of an immediate economic package. One young woman was supporting a child and taking classes part time to be a dentist. I talked with her about the various forms of oppression that both women and racial minorities experience. I like to think that she heard me.

The lawyers for the street women came to see them. We AIM women waited, sitting against the wall. I had just leaned my head against the wall and closed my eyes when I heard my name called. Another expensively dressed white male was at the bars of the cage, asking if there were a Karren Baird-Olson in there. Startled, I replied, "Yes, I am Karren." He beckoned me over to the bars. He was obviously upset. Talking in a low voice, he told me that taking a message to an inmate in this manner was highly unusual. But he had been instructed "from higher-up" to tell me that my girls were OK, that they and the other youngsters were being well taken care of. And word had come from my mother in Montana that if the girls and I were not released by noon, my sister, who lived in New York City, would fly down to get the girls out.

Later, I found out what had happened. When we were surrounded and taken off to jail, observers contacted the other campers at the American University. The camp leaders called our families. By the next morning, my mother had reached at least one of Montana's congressional representatives, who found out where we were. She never would tell me just how she had managed to do so much in such a short time. But then she always was a woman of action. She did say that if I wanted to stay in jail that was my business, but her granddaughters were not going to remain in such a place. (How I miss her!)

It was after eleven a.m. when we were taken from the tank to appear before a judge. Dozens of onlookers, including media people, were milling around outside of the courtroom. I caught a glimpse of the children. I could see the back of Shawn's head, and I knew that Nolee had to be close by. Several women and men approached us while we were waiting to enter the court chambers. They were lawyers who had come to assist us for no charge. One woman who had graduated from an Ivy League college told me that she had been talking with my daughters. She reported that Myrna's daughter Laurie, a boy named Sugar Frank, and Shawn had taken charge of the other young people. They had protected, reassured, and comforted them. The lawyer was so impressed with Shawn that she encouraged me to have Shawn apply to her alma mater, Bryn Mawr College.

We were taken into the courtroom, where we waited again until a white judge and lawyers entered. We women were called to stand before the judge, sitting behind his desk on the elevated platform. He looked down and told us that if we would sign an agreement stating we would never return again to Washington, D.C., he would let us all go immediately. I remember being amazed at his nerve. I knew that we had done nothing wrong, and his "solution" was unconstitutional. I remember saying something terse such as "no way" and moving back to the court benches. The other women followed. I remember the anger on his and the other men's faces. All of the lawyers—the prosecutors as well as our newly found defense counsel—disappeared behind closed doors.

We waited again. A short time later, we were told that all charges had been dropped. We were escorted outside into the bright sunlight, where we found the rest of our group and where I tried to duck away from the photographers and reporters. I do not remember how we were returned to the campsite. I think someone paid for taxis. Much to my joy, I finally could hold my girls. They told me that a Black matron had washed their clothes, allowed them to shower, fed them very well, and kept praising them for their courage. "Right on!" she said over and over.

I remember the pain and outrage on my son's face when he saw the bruises on my face and arms. He held me and his sisters and then helped me to find a shower and clean clothes.

As I write this, I realize that I am weeping over this incident for the first time. I cry not for myself but for the children who must be subjected to such experiences in order to be able to grow up in a world where all human beings are treated with respect.

AIM's Contributions

There are those, both American Indians and non-Indians, who criticize AIM, who say AIM created more problems than solutions. I cannot speak for every position that has been taken against AIM, but it has been my experience that there are four types of people who take such a stance. The first are the ignorant, those who do not know what AIM was all about. They heard about or saw only the reactive, short-term violence and/or the hangers-on who claimed to be AIM and used the movement as an excuse for doing their own violent things. The second type are the people who have been so colonized that they passively accept their own subjugation. The third group are those who are fearful. They fear change unless it is very slow, and/or they fear the danger that comes with freedom. The fourth group are those who have something to gain from the continued oppression of American Indians and/or the misrepresentation of AIM.

It is not the purpose of this paper to the discuss internal conflicts in AIM nor to address the strengths and shortcomings of AIM's organizational structure. However, I will note that all organizations have internal disagreements. No group has perfect harmony. Since American Indian groups are like all other human organizations, there are disagreements from time to time, but AIM's internal problems are no worse than those of other groups.

Overall, I believe that the social structure of the movement has been one of its greatest strengths. Why? The lack of a formal structure has been an extremely valuable strategic force. Members come to whatever activities they can participate in, not because someone has coerced them but because of individual, internalized motivation and commitment. Just as traditional warriors went in and out of battle as they were able, so have traditional AIM people given of themselves to the goal of sovereignty. Bureaucrats, such as BIA officials, and paramilitary professionals, such as law enforcement agents—including the FBI—like to see lists of members and officers and organizational charts. Such information makes their job easier when they are trying to determine accountability. Also, these data make the task of neutralizing members' effectiveness much easier. It is difficult to accomplish such an ignoble objective when there are no lists and when every member is respected and honored. If leaders are killed or silenced, there are always others to replace them. The movement does not die.

In addition to providing an alternative organizational model, the American Indian Movement has made at least six primary contributions, not only to native individuals but also to urban and reservation communities. AIM provided courageous role models; refuted racist myths and stereotypes about Indian people; created a national network of visible activists; initiated major institutional changes; enforced personal and institutional respect; and renewed hope for the future.

Role Models

I have been around long enough to remember when there were signs that read, "No Indians nor dogs allowed." I remember people saying, "A good Indian is a dead Indian." I remember my paternal grandfather wanting to talk about being part-Indian and my grandmother hushing him. I remember my oldest daughter being given an "F" in first grade for coloring children brown. I remember my husband being afraid that, if I protested the grade, she would be hurt more.

The American Indian Movement brought an unprecedented number of the courageous, the wise, the honest, the generous, and the spiritual together. We came from all parts of Indian Country, urban and rural. United, we said, we no longer have to be silent. We can ask for respect. In a spiritual and sophisticated manner, we learned how to beat the white man at his own game; how to challenge the apples; and how to renew the traditional roles of strong women. AIM members gave of themselves and provided role models for their communities.

Refutation of Racist Myths and Stereotypes

Although some efforts had been made in the past to challenge prejudice and discrimination against American Indians, for the most part this had been neither on a national scale nor on a widespread basis. AIM destroyed and/or seriously undermined dangerous prejudices about the First Peoples and provided new choices and alternate paths for Indians all across the country. American Indians were given an alternative to the pervasive image of the silent, apathetic, helpless, dumb, pagan Indian to emulate.

Major Institutional Changes

I have seen more broad, sweeping changes in the last two decades since the late 1970s than I have seen or heard about since the formation of the Plains reservations in the late 1800s. There had always been caring individuals in education, in the criminal justice system, in the churches, in welfare programs, and in other social institutions. But they were not united and they had little power. After AIM came into the public eye, fearful bureaucrats began to make much-needed changes. For example, I have seen major reforms in education. I have taught in reservation schools and in urban schools with American Indian students. My own children have gone to both types of schools. I have seen the damage of undisguised racism as well as the effects of culturally insensitive policies; both results have driven children and teenagers out of the schools. To give only one specific example of the changes brought by AIM, when a Fort Peck Reservation math teacher made a derogatory remark about my younger daughter Nolee's American Indian heritage and then said that "C" was a good grade in math for an Indian student, the school, fearful of my AIM connections, took my promise of a civil suit seriously. Nolee received a public apology. She was given the "A"s and "B"s she had earned.

Network of Grass roots Activists: Rural and Urban

Many of the original AIM members had lived both on and off their reservations. Their urban experiences had taught them how to deal with all types of white people. In addition, in the urban settings, people from the various tribes and nations were able to compare stories. Out of this shared knowledge came what is sometimes called the concept of Pan-Indianness. AIM provided an organized mode of expression, a constructive outlet for frustration and anger, a social network or community of doers, people who walked their talk.

Personal and Institutional Respect

The American Indian Movement also brought a new sense of respect, not only for oneself but from others as well. For example, during the 1972 Caravan and during the 1976 trek, I saw so-called winos and alkies become sober, responsible members of our mobile communities. If they had withdrawal symptoms, I never heard any complaints. They had something to work for. They had been given hope for the future.

One of my favorite examples of changed views of native people in the non-Indian community occurred about a year after we had returned to Montana after the Trail of Broken Treaties. Because it was winter, my AIM friends had left me at the door of the college hangout so I would not have to walk with them in the thirty-below-zero weather from the parking lot.

I walked up the stairs and into the lounge. Much to my disgust, I recognized three "rednecks" sitting at a table to my right. I tried to ignore their raucous laughter and lewd remarks. "Hey, baby, where are all your bucks?" "Let me show you how a real man screws!"

Just as I turned to go find my companions, they came up the stairs into full view of the ignorant men. My friends carried themselves proudly. Two of them braided their hair in the traditional manner. Like me, they wore beaded jewelry and ribbon shirts. There was no doubt that the men were also AIM. My three brothers looked at me. They looked at the white men behind me. They understood what had been happening. They began moving toward them. For the first time in my life, I saw Montana racists shut their filthy mouths. They literally slumped down into their seats and then quickly sneaked out the back door.

Hope

As seen earlier, AIM brought hope: For some, it was the first time; for others, it was a renewed vision for the future; for still others, a new definition. And, most importantly, the accomplishments of those often turbulent years insure that there is hope for future generations. This is not to say that all the doors have been opened. They have not. But the ceilings of opportunity are a little higher.

My children tell me that my activism as well as theirs has taught them that they do not have to keep silent about injustice, as so many of our ancestors were forced to do. They have learned that individuals can make a difference, and a united people can make an even bigger difference in insuring a world where equity is given more than lip service.

The Sacrifices of Activists

What has happened to the role models—those early activists who broke the trails? Because I am familiar mostly with the lives of the activists from my home, I will look only at the Fort Peck group. We have all made at least one major sacrifice for our activism, for our courage, and we have often paid with blood.

Murder

Two of the young Fort Peck men who were with us in 1976 have been murdered. When my three-year-old granddaughter Shelena Sky, Shawn's younger daughter, was beaten and kidnapped in 1985, the FBI did not help with our search for her. Within days after her death, a young agent told me that they would have intervened earlier if I had not been involved with AIM and ERA "stuff."

Unresolved Grief, Posttraumatic Stress Syndrome, and Alcohol Abuse

All of us have been victims of violent crime. We have been traumatized by rape or attempted rape and/or verbal and physical attacks designed to "put us in our place." The spirits of three of our Fort Peck women have been broken not only from the overreaction of whites to their peaceful activism but also from the "apples" and the fearful members of our own tribes. The three women have turned to alcohol to numb themselves or to commit slow suicide. For many of the same reasons, two of the young men also misuse alcohol.

Unemployment or Underemployment

Because we are regarded as troublemakers, we have been denied certain employment opportunities. To give just one example, during the late 1970s, I occasionally worked part-time for *The Herald News,* a reservation area weekly newspaper owned by a non-Indian family, and I became friendly with a young editor who was a newcomer to the area and was not tied into the local power structure. He told me that, during meetings of local leaders that he covered for his news beat, the "good ol' boys" openly talked about preventing me from working in order to force me to leave the reservation.

Denial of Personal/Professional Opportunities

All of us have experienced this type of backlash. Some of the most dramatic examples have occurred when conservative people have penalized our children because of our activism. For example, the judges in the 1982 Northeastern Montana Miss America Pageant, held in Wolf Point on the Fort Peck Reservation, conspired not to give my younger daughter the title because they feared her views would reflect mine. Again, a newcomer to the area who was not tied into the non-Indian power structure provided us with the documentation. Although several lawyers who were friends of mine volunteered to handle the case pro bono, Nolee eventually decided not to go to court because of the notoriety it would bring her.

Personal Loneliness

Today, in general, older heterosexual women experience difficulty in finding supportive male partners. Considering the experiences of the AIM women I know, I believe we have suffered even greater loneliness than the average older woman.

Until recently, if asked what type of woman I am, I would have said I am an average, college-educated woman who grew up in the 1940s and 1950s and, like countless other aware women, became an activist in the 1960s and 1970s. I have come to realize, however, that I, like all of the other early AIM women, am not average. We are exceptional women; we are trail blazers. But nearly all of us have paid dearly for that, not only in terms of general social acceptance but also in terms of finding supportive and lasting personal companionship. Based on my own experience and the experiences of other AIM women over the years, I have noticed four types of men who come "sniffing around" AIM women.[4] These categories are not mutually exclusive.

First, there have been the proper, established men who find us exotic, but not proper enough for long-term commitment or marriage. At first these men appear very sincere. Then, as the novelty wears off, we find that they want to keep us on a shelf like sports trophies, out of sight and out of mind, until they want a little vicarious excitement in their lives.

Second are the weak and dependent men who want to be taken care of rather than to be help-mates. A number of these men are chemically dependent. The majority of the men in this category are over forty years of age and want to be center stage in their women's lives. They are not secure enough to be able to wait; they want immediate attention. These men want young "poodles" who unquestioningly serve their masters, or they want sexual companions who will also take emotional and financial care of them.

A third category are the younger men, sometimes young enough to be our sons, who respect what we have accomplished. They want to be with us, but they have little to offer us. If we accept young men into our lives, we find that we are spending a good amount of time and energy attempting to educate them so we can communicate more easily. Often they are willing to learn, but the only men we want to rear are our sons and grandsons.

Rarely are there men in the fourth category. They are the ones whose strength and courage match ours. One of the strong men who came into my life during the 1970s died a mysterious death while he was organizing against environmental pollution in the Southwest. Often, however, even the most courageous feel threatened by our strength. And, on the other hand, when we weep, when we are fearful, when we show our vulnerability, they disappear, literally or figuratively. Most of all, although they expect us to understand their commitment to human rights, they are jealous of our dedication to others and our love affair with the search for justice.

So most of us older AIM women have resigned ourselves to unsatisfying relationships with men; those who are not resigned are alone. And being alone is not easy. If we are separated from our indigenous communities, it is even harder. At least we know that most of our daughters have strong men beside them. At least most of our sons stand beside their women. But this is only partial comfort, for we do not live just for our children and grandchildren. We try not to give up hope for finding companionship. In the meantime, we keep so busy that we are too exhausted when night comes to notice how empty and lonely our beds are.

Conclusion

Would I do it all over again? Yes. The only other choices were silent resignation, bitterness, and/or self-destruction, all of which would have doomed not only me but also my children and grandchildren. Thorough housecleaning is always messy for a time, but the ultimate result is worth the temporary upheaval.

The results of our housecleaning—the reorganization of reservation social institutions and our personal lives that began in the late 1960s— were most apparent during the 1970s. Contrary to the claims of its detractors and enemies, AIM did not die during the 1980s. Individuals as well as the movement have been busy integrating all that was accomplished. The bright young butterflies of hope of the 1960s and 1970s who turned to the elders and medicine people for guidance are now elders themselves—including me. In addition to being traditional, we are lawyers, writers, professors, movie stars, musicians, and politicians. And some of us are medicine people.

Our youthful activism brought us a respect that many of us never expected. We were fighting for respect for our children and grandchildren and never imagined that we would also receive respectful recognition. In my own life today, hardly a month goes by without at least one person calling or writing to say "thank you" for doing what I did or for being a role model.

Leonard Peltier has honored me by allowing me to speak officially on his behalf. Almost every semester, Leonard and I speak for a few minutes when I take my Kansas State University (KSU) corrections class students to Leavenworth Penitentiary. Despite the wary watch of the guards and tour guides, he sometimes gives me a brief hug. Few words are needed. We are still alive. There are so many of us who now walk in the spirit world.

Russell Means has honored the KSU Indian students twice in the last five years by serving as our keynote speaker during our annual Native American Heritage Month. Two years ago, when he came for the second time, we gave each other a spontaneous, long hug. There were tears in our eyes. What could words say?

So much has happened since Leonard, Russell, and I first met that fall of 1972. Who would have guessed that Leonard would become internationally known for his ongoing sacrifice, that Russell would become a movie star, making socially significant movies, and that I would become a university professor?

We are more than old war horses reliving our days of glory. We have been given the gift of a second rebirth. During the first rebirth, we emerged out of a cocoon of darkness, oppression, and hopelessness: the prison of colonization. We were shiny, fragile, gloriously beautiful silver creatures reaching for Father Sky, the stars, the moon, and the sun. Today, in our second incarnation, we are benefiting from the world we helped create during the early days of our activism. We helped build the ideological shelters whereby the doors to education and employment could be opened more easily and the old spiritual ways could be followed more openly. This time, our wings are sturdy gold, and we move more easily between Father Sky and Mother Earth.

Once again we are redefining *community*. We have learned how to use Euro-American technology to help us communicate through media such as this. We are not abandoning the richness of oral tradition; we have only added to it. We do this because we know that we all—white, red, black, and yellow peoples—share this earth. We are all related. We know that we are all in danger. If other peoples are unable or unwilling to learn how to communicate with and respect all life forms, then we will have to help lead the way to healing, or we will all go down together. Mother Earth can do without us; we cannot do without her. *Mitakuye Oyasin*

NOTES

1. Joanna Grey gives a clear definition of Indian Country in her paper "White Law in Indian Country": "Indian country once was the term used for a specific geographical area, the place where Indians lived. It had clear and definite jurisdictional overtones. Indian country today has a much more ambiguous definition (except where federal criminal jurisdiction applies) much the same as the fictional 'Marlboro Country.' It is an image, a sociological phenomenon." See Joanna Grey's forthcoming paper "White Law in Indian Country" (Albuquerque: University of New Mexico, Department of Sociology), 5.

2. We were part of the group of twenty-six people who came from the Fort Peck Assiniboine and Sioux Reservation, located in the northeast corner of Montana. In addition to me and my children Shawn, John Mike, and Nolee, there were Myrna Boyd; Myrna's nine children—Theresa, Anita, Jackie, Chauncey, Laurie, Donald, Boyd, Ruby, and Myrna (Porky); Myrna's two grandchildren—one-and-one-half-year-old Tanya and six-month-old Althea; Theresa McKey and her two daughters Iris and Patti; David Campbell; George (Fish) Redstone; Lyn Birthmark; and Pearl Nation and three of her children who made, at our expense, the long trek across the country.

3. We knew that there was a very real danger of being attacked by the Swat Squad. If that happened, long, flowing hair makes a handy thing to grab and to pull. Braids are more difficult to grab. Also, braids are cooler on a hot, humid day.

4. The first time I heard the term *sniffing around* was in 1958 when my husband and I had gone home to the reservation during Montana State University's spring break. He and his friends were talking about the attention some of the reservation men were giving me. One of my husband's friends used the term, thereby comparing the men to dogs. The use is an example of Indian humor.

Part III

The Ties That Bind

Chapter Eight

Rattle on the Right
Bridge Labor in Antifeminist Organizations

Susan E. Marshall

The New Right coalition that emerged as a major force in U.S. politics in the final decades of the twentieth century has been credited with influencing election outcomes, passing state abortion restrictions, and leading the backlash against social welfare spending and affirmative action programs to aid disadvantaged groups. Self-labeled the "profamily" movement since the 1970s, the New Right emphasizes social traditionalism over economic libertarianism and militant anticommunism, the other defining issues of U.S. conservative ideology (Himmelstein 1983, 1990). Somewhat ironically, given the right-wing crusade for "family values," women activists receive greatest attention as single-issue protesters against abortion (Ginsburg 1989; Luker 1984) and the Equal Rights Amendment (Boles 1979; Mansbridge 1986). Antifeminist organizations such as Phyllis Schlafly's Eagle Forum (EF) and Beverly LaHaye's Concerned Women for America (CWA) receive brief mention as defenders of traditional womanhood, but men are the primary focus of attention—the so-called "thunder on the right"—from Jerry Falwell's Moral Majority of the 1980s to later media fascination with the Christian Coalition (Crawford 1980; Liebman and Wuthnow 1983; Sigelman, Wilcox, and Buell 1987; Wirls 1986).

This study reassesses the contributions of antifeminist organizations to contemporary New Right politics, in light of recent advances in social movements scholarship that highlight the usefulness of women's participation and gender ideology to movement development (Blee 1991; Koonz 1987; Marshall 1997). It identifies women as a key constituency of right-wing activism and contends that antifeminist organizations interpret social issues in ways that serve as a bridge to women's activism for the broader conservative agenda. I further propose that these women's organizations target protests to normalize and legitimate the reactionary politics of the New Right coalition. Women function as standardbearers of opposition to policies that promote gender equity, a strategy that deflects criticism by pitting women against women and by using gender as a socially acceptable proxy for race. These findings, based on analyses of publications and of correspondence of the two largest women's organizations in the New Right coalition, offer a revised view of antifeminist organizations not merely as agents for the interests of traditional womanhood but as able exploiters of women's vulnerable position in society in order to advance their own political agenda. More generally, they suggest a gendered division of labor among organizations in conservative political movements.

The Rise of the New Right

While most students of the U.S. conservative movement have located its origins in grievances formed against the New Deal policies of President Franklin D. Roosevelt, the New Right's emergence also reflects a regional shift in political power that followed the growth of the Sun Belt and the breakup of Democratic Party hegemony in the southern states. A significant moment in its ascendancy was the presidential candidacy of Senator Barry Goldwater in 1964, although another decade passed before the establishment of autonomous New Right organizations and publications financed with the help of wealthy corporate benefactors (Crawford 1980, 3–41; Himmelstein 1990, 17–94). Political linkage to a nationally organized religious right was another important step in its development. The televangelist Jerry Falwell cofounded the Moral Majority in 1979, generating considerable attention from pundits and scholars alike, although after a few years he withdrew from politics and ultimately disbanded the organization in 1989 (Walker 1989). Pat Robertson, a presidential contender, stepped into the void and established the Christian Coalition that same year, quietly building a grassroots organization with an estimated two million members. The Christian Coalition has acquired substantial influence at the state levels of the Republican Party (Blumenthal 1994; Conason 1992; Doerr 1995; Himmelstein 1983). The group's political success is widely attributed to its ability to increase the turnout of evangelical Christian voters, who are most likely to support profamily issues—against abortion, homosexual rights, and sex education, and for school prayer (Wall 1995; Young et al. 1995). Perhaps learning from the experiences of his predecessors, Robertson has receded to a less prominent leadership role within the Christian Coalition as it has become more visible, authoring controversial books like *The New World Order* (1991), in which he charged that Satan had infiltrated the government. The Coalition's executive director, Ralph Reed Jr., served until 1997 as its spokesperson, and his press statements and policy initiatives were clearly intended to give the organization a more ecumenical and moderate public image (Barrett 1993; DeParle 1996a; Reed 1995). Often described as a skilled political operative, Reed was a supreme pragmatist, articulating stealth as an electoral strategy and endorsing competitive candidates over those who exhibited ideological purity as a way to gain Coalition leverage at the highest levels of power (Conason 1992; Wall 1995).

Women have been mentioned only peripherally in overviews of the Christian Coalition and of the New Right more generally. This omission has limited our appreciation of the strategic functions of female activists and of social issues within the conservative coalition. For example, women are more likely than men to attend church regularly and to be followers of evangelical Christianity, both of which are associated with profamily values (Hertel and Hughes 1987; Smidt 1987). Moreover, morality and family issues have historically been the most acceptable routes for female entrance into the public world of politics well before U.S. women won the vote (Cott 1977; Epstein 1981), and churches today are a source of political cues as well as a key network for recruiting conservative women into political activism (Jelen 1992; Staggenborg 1987). I suggest that the decade of the 1970s presented a political opportunity for the mass recruitment of women into conservative politics in response to the feminist movement and the concomitant emergence of personal issues onto the public stage.

The importance of the feminist movement as an incentive for the activation of conservative women is sometimes acknowledged, but its inspiration is viewed as largely negative—as responsible for altering gender roles and generating grievances among traditional women (Himmelstein 1990). I propose that, beyond arousing defensiveness among conservatives, feminism also contributed more positively to mass political mobilization. For example, young feminist activists of the 1960s and

1970s, borrowing from the rhetoric of the New Left, declared that "the personal is political" (Evans 1979). This popular slogan increased the saliency of social issues such as sexuality and reproduction and also legitimated public debate on topics previously regarded as the province of religious and medical establishments (Piven 1985; Rossi 1983). Beyond its specific message, the feminist movement eroded taboos against female protest, and its successes increased political knowledge, interest, and efficacy, making more women available for mobilization (Baxter and Lansing 1980, 41–51).

Other social movements during this period also influenced the political activation of conservative women. Civil rights leaders from the Reverend Dr. Martin Luther King Jr. to Malcolm X demonstrated the effectiveness of religion as an inspiration for political mobilization and the power of moral claims on the public conscience (Morris 1984). Riding on the legislative coattails of the civil rights movement, feminists demanded federal intervention to end discrimination against women and to create equal opportunity; constitutional amendments, Supreme Court decisions, federal legislation, and executive orders mandating affirmative action became mechanisms for the achievement of feminist goals and made the state a primary locus of conflict among contesting groups of women (Boles 1979; Freeman 1975). In the churning political culture of party realignments and emerging new constituencies that followed a decade of political activism, right-wing organizations seized an opportunity to use social issues to attract new members.

While political party organizations were slow to appreciate the political potential of conservative women, two astute political entrepreneurs possessed the leadership skills and interpersonal networks to organize this relatively untapped constituency. They are Phyllis Schlafly, founder of Eagle Forum, and Beverly LaHaye of Concerned Women for America, two early New Right organizations that have outlasted more celebrated conservative groups such as the Moral Majority. These antifeminist associations, one formed from within the Republican Party and the other with stronger roots in evangelical Christianity, reiterate the evolution of the New Right coalition. Beyond this difference, both associations built organizations with a predominantly female staff and membership, and both demonstrated early expertise at the grass-roots mobilization that would become a hallmark of the New Right.

Phyllis Schlafly, a speechwriter for Goldwater in the 1964 presidential campaign, has a long record of activism in the conservative wing of the

Republican Party and is the author of several books about national security and defense issues (see Felsenthal 1981; Marshall 1991; Schlafly and Ward 1976). She previously made unsuccessful bids for the presidency of the National Federation of Republican Women and for election to the U.S. Congress. Based in the St. Louis area, Schlafly began publishing her monthly *Report* in the 1960s and declares Eagle Forum "a leader in the profamily movement since 1972," the year the ERA passed Congress. Also a prolife advocate, Schlafly made defeat of the ERA her central mission during the 1970s and continues to remobilize her STOP ERA organization as needed to oppose ratification of equal rights amendments at the state and federal levels; to this end, she operates a well-funded political action committee as well as an education and legal defense fund (*Phyllis Schlafly Report* 1993h; EF, Schlafly letter to membership, February 1996). Eagle Forum espouses the full agenda of social conservatism, opposing sex education, homosexual rights, and affirmative action, and Schlafly's daily radio commentaries address primarily educational themes. Schlafly has elaborated a female counterimage to feminism that asserts the power of the "Positive Woman" devoted to Christian values (Schlafly 1977, 1981). But the monthly *Phyllis Schlafly Report* devotes more than half its contents to conservative political and economic issues such as military preparedness and opposition to "Big Government," and Eagle Forum even raised money for the legal defense of the court-martialed serviceman who refused to wear the United Nations uniform (EF, Schlafly letter to membership, November 1995; Marshall 1996). Eagle Forum has no membership dues, no elaborate management structure, and no formal procedures for individual input into organizational policy; yet Schlafly's charismatic leadership sustains the association, and the monthly report is her personal communiqué to supporters. Schlafly inspires her followers at an annual leadership conference and bestows Eagle and Super Eagle Awards for exceptional service to its conservative causes (Felsenthal 1981, pp. 260–63).

Beverly LaHaye, in contrast, came to politics through her husband's evangelical ministry based in San Diego (see Marshall 1991, 57–58). With Tim LaHaye, cofounder of the Moral Majority, she published books and taught seminars on Christian marriage in which she upheld husbands' headship before founding Concerned Women for America in 1979 explicitly to fight feminism and the ERA (see McNamara 1988). Now based in Washington, D.C., where it regularly lobbies Congress and submits legal briefs to the U.S. Supreme Court, CWA has recently advocated both religious liberties and student prayer amendments to the U.S. Constitution, and it maintains stronger church ties than Eagle Forum. The CWA advises ministers about legal means of political activism and guides members to "prayer, praise, and action" in its monthly magazine, *Family Voice*. To a far greater extent than the *Phyllis Schlafly Report, Family Voice* focuses on social issues, and more than half the contents of recent volumes concern prolife issues, media immorality, and homosexuality (Marshall 1996). CWA is critical of "humanist curricula" in the public schools, aims to abolish the federal Department of Education, and sponsors an annual essay contest, awarding the winners scholarships to conservative Christian colleges. Although it has a more complex bureaucratic structure than Eagle Forum, CWA remains firmly under the control of its popular "chairman," and there is no formal mechanism for the transfer of power. Annual conventions honor women's activism with Family Freedom Awards and reward political allies, such as Senator Jesse Helms, with its American Patriot Award, while local networks of prayer chapters and state conferences maintain grassroots commitment. LaHaye also hosts a daily radio show, and in 1993 she began a cable television show, "Putting Families First!" (*Family Voice* 1994c).

National survey results suggest that female anti-ERA mobilization contributed to a backlash of public opinion against feminism. In the first heady years of feminist activity, the percentage of U.S. women who rejected both the women's liberation movement and equal roles for women in society declined slightly. As antifeminist organizations began to reverse the momentum of the ERA drive by the mid-1970s, however, the share of nonfeminist women held steady at about 50 percent. Perhaps more significant, support for the ERA among nonfeminist women declined by almost one half, from 70 percent in 1976 to 43 percent in 1980, underscoring the effectiveness of opposition arguments against ratification (Cook 1989). Part of the difference between feminists and nonfeminists is overall political ideology and acceptance of gender stereotypes, with nonfeminist women far more likely to hold the individual, rather than social structure, responsible for disparities in employment outcomes. Nonfeminist women were twice as likely as feminists to believe that men were more reliable and more ambitious than women and almost four times as likely to believe that society does not discriminate against women (Cook 1989). Including men in the analysis reveals a gender gap on women's issues; nonfeminist women are more conservative on abortion and gender-equality issues than are nonfeminist men, while the gap is reversed among potential feminists and feminists (Cook and Wilcox 1991). On broader social issues, opposition to government social welfare spending increased for both sexes between 1975 and 1980, although men's opposition correlated more strongly with party identification, while women's attitudes were more closely linked to their position on feminist issues such as the Equal Rights Amendment (Deitch 1988).

The greater salience of social issues among conservative women has not escaped either LaHaye or Schlafly, who have each attempted to enhance their own political capital by attributing electoral victories to their mobilization efforts among women. Both organizations have claimed credit for the 1994 conservative Republican takeover of Congress. Phyllis Schlafly advised readers that "cultural issues" are "where the votes are," and Beverly LaHaye predicted that the new Congress would "restore the moral foundation that made this country great" (*Phyllis Schlafly Report* 1995a; CWA, LaHaye letter to membership, February 1995). Both Eagle Forum and CWA maintain alliances with the Christian Coalition. Schlafly has reportedly attended strategy conferences at the Coalition's Virginia Beach headquarters, while CWA has featured Reed and Robertson at annual conventions and distributed voter guides that are similar to the materials prepared by the Christian Coalition (Conason 1992; *Family Voice* 1994b, 1994c). Their grassroots strategies mobilize conservative women for lobbying on issues endorsed by the Coalition. In contrast to feminist groups like the National Organization for Women, monthly mailings to Eagle Forum and CWA contributors include a personalized letter from LaHaye or Schlafly that details the conservative issue of the moment and often a prepared petition with mailing instructions.

Women's participation in protest movements is a small but increasingly recognized dimension of political activism across the ideological spectrum that offers some useful insights for examination of the New Right. Revisionist historical accounts of the civil rights (Barnett 1993; Crawford, Rouse, and Woods 1990) and the antiwar movements (Evans 1979), as well as of the Ku Klux Klan (Blee 1991) and the Nazi Party (Koonz 1987), identify the contributions of female activists. Gender emerges as an important social category that differentiates routes of individual recruitment (McAdam 1992), grass roots mobilization (Bookman and Morgen 1988; McCourt 1977), and movement leadership

(Barnett 1993; Robnett 1996). Paradoxically, gender inequality may create a niche for female leadership that bridges the gap between the individual and social movement organizations (Robnett 1996). Historical studies of radical groups have found that reliance on traditional gender ideologies furthered reactionary political agendas by recruiting women with promises of elevated power and social status and by emphasizing women's role as family guardian or societal conscience to put a romanticized veneer on goals at odds with dominant cultural values (Blee 1991; Koonz 1987).

The conceptual framework guiding the present study builds on this developing exposition of women's activism in broader political movements. It shifts the unit of analysis from individual women (see Klatch 1987) to social movement organizations, examining the contributions of antifeminist associations within the New Right coalition. Social movement organizations connect individuals to the larger movement by constructing meaning, organizing experience, and guiding action (Snow et al. 1986; Lofland 1985). I propose that women's social and political marginality facilitated the work of antifeminist organizations in bridging the gap between traditional female issues and the larger conservative agenda. The strategic responses of conservative women's organizations included not just behavioral accommodation and conformity to stereotypes to enhance their own power but also more negative forms—the exploitation of female vulnerability to target the opposition and the denial of gender consciousness among their own constituency. By attacking feminism as a symbol for all that is wrong with liberalism and by using antifeminism as a bridge for female mobilization to other right-wing issues, women's associations function according to Ralph Reed's stealth strategy—not as thunder, but as a rattle on the right.

The Antifeminist Issue Base

The antifeminist agendas of both CWA and Eagle Forum extend well beyond opposition to the Equal Rights Amendment. Phyllis Schlafly testified before Congress against the Family and Medical Leave Act, claiming that it was "highly discriminatory in favor of highly paid, two-earner yuppie couples who . . . would be the only ones able to benefit"

(*Phyllis Schlafly Report* 1987). Both associations oppose the integration of women into the military and supported the refusal of the Virginia Military Institute (VMI) to admit female students (*Phyllis Schlafly Report* 1991b, 1992b; *Family Voice* 1994j; CWA, LaHaye letter to membership, January 1996). Policies of gender equity symbolize to them the errant power of Big Government. They are against comparable worth ("feminist wage control"), affirmative action, and attempts to eradicate the "glass ceiling," the goals of which are "not equal opportunity, but 'power' for feminists and the displacement of men from power" (*Phyllis Schlafly Report* 1990, 1991a). Alleged Schlafly, "Glass Ceiling is the code word for affirmative action quotas for executive women, just as 'civil rights' has become the code word for affirmative action quotas for minorities" (*Phyllis Schlafly Report* 1991a). This comment is unusual for its explicit reference to racial issues, but it reveals a common grievance against minority group power and governmental intervention to benefit all disadvantaged persons.

The frontline battle against feminism is a major contribution of women's organizations to the conservative coalition. The antifeminist campaign is more complex than is generally appreciated, however; for one thing, feminism serves as a socially acceptable symbol for other issues, consistent with Ralph Reed's intention to present a more moderate New Right image for public consumption. The results of public opinion polls demonstrate that "gender-role traditionalism"—a benign term for a belief structure in which females are judged inferior to males and perceived as better suited to domestic confinement than to full participation in public life—remains common among Americans, while its counterpart, expressions of what might be called "old-fashioned racism," are deemed so socially unacceptable that they have just about died out (Kluegel and Smith 1986, 239). This is not to argue that racism is less virulent or extensive than sexism but to suggest that there is greater disapprobation for public expressions of the former, partly because of a more unified group response by African Americans. In addition, although the Bible has little to say about ethnicity, its pronouncements on women are a strong cultural sanction for continuing the status quo of gender inequality (Peek and Brown 1980). By targeting women instead of racial and ethnic minorities, therefore, the New Right is able to oppose policies that benefit both groups with minimal political controversy.

Using members of the same social category as spokespersons against group rights is also a strategy to blunt criticism, and the dearth of minority participation in the New Right coalition further necessitates women's visible role as opponents of policies to achieve equal opportunity (Crawford 1980). A recent illustrative lesson was the 1992 Republican National Convention, where Patrick Buchanan's address announcing a "culture war" within America, which included harsh attacks on Hillary Rodham Clinton, was widely blamed for frightening voters and furthering the eventual Republican defeat. At the same convention, however, a speech by Marilyn Quayle, the wife of the vice president, which likewise took dead aim at Mrs. Clinton as a radical feminist, largely escaped public censure (see Marshall 1996). Whereas male opposition appears unchivalrous to some and raises others' suspicions of their motives, such as whether they stand to gain from women's continued disadvantage, female protests against women's rights undermine feminist appeals to social justice and shift the debate from moral issues to competing interests among a divided constituency (see Boles 1979). Antifeminism is a low-risk position for right-wing women's groups because national surveys consistently show that women, unlike minorities, have low group consciousness (Gurin 1985; Gurin and Townsend 1986; Sears and Huddy 1990). Women and men manifest little divergence on gender issues, in contrast to the wide split on racial issues between whites and African Americans. This dearth of group solidarity not only permits opposition to feminism but allows conservative groups to go further and reject the very concept of women's issues.

Eagle Forum and CWA oppose state intervention to achieve equal employment opportunity; both associations also discount the importance of violence against women as a social problem. Schlafly has lobbied to defund the Violence against Women Act, arguing that it used "false and dishonest statistics" to "put feminist activists on the public payroll" (*Phyllis Schlafly Report* 1995a). Concerned Women for America opposed Washington state's sexual harassment policy for public schools, predicting that it would encourage children "to spy and snitch on each other" (*Family Voice* 1995m). Eagle Forum denounced the resignations of U.S. naval officers in the wake of the infamous Tailhook incident as a "feminist lynching" made possible by "a bunch of wimps" among the military leadership (*Phyllis Schlafly Report* 1993f, 1995b). Phyllis Schlafly offered the following assessment of the "radical feminist" agenda:

Want to punish your boss for some remarks you didn't like? The Sexual Harassment gestapo will give him a hard time. . . . Want to punish your husband? The Violence Against Women agency will give you free housing while you accuse your husband of spousal 'rape' and the local prosecutor will believe your story without corroboration. (*Phyllis Schlafly Report* 1994e)

As these comments indicate, both associations reject almost every notion proffered by the women's movement, contending that female victimization is largely a myth, while male victims of feminist excesses abound. They depict feminist ideology as "sterile," its spokespersons as "bitter," and they identify as feminism's principal legacy a divorce epidemic that bequeaths only "the cold empty loneliness of hard-fought 'equality' " (*Phyllis Schlafly Report* 1994e; *Family Voice* 1995e). Their scrutiny of the feminist movement seeks signs of capitulation, from Jane Fonda's retirement from show business to spend more time with her millionaire husband, Ted Turner, to poll results that chart an increase in women's disaffection with employment (*Family Voice* 1994m, 1995b).

The right-wing disagreement with feminism extends to the very notion of women's issues. This position is somewhat paradoxical, because it is feminists who minimize differences between the sexes that, their opponents believe, justify continued segregation. It also contradicts the common perception that antifeminist organizations defend the interests of traditional homemakers. Nonetheless, antifeminist groups dismiss the notion of distinctly female political interests as antithetical to the self-sacrificing nature of true womanhood, tarring feminists for both selfishness and unattractive grousing. But their position is more complex. At the 1992 CWA convention, Marilyn Quayle ridiculed women's issues as a "policy ghetto," suggesting that the political influence of conservative women will not be circumscribed by traditional domestic concerns (see Marshall 1996). This explicit appeal to female political self-interest is greatly at odds with the traditional image cultivated by antifeminist organizations and was generally overlooked by observers. On the day of Bill Clinton's first presidential inauguration, CWA prepared an open letter of eleven demands for his administration, not one of which specifically mentioned women (*Family Voice* 1994d). Four years later, Concerned Women for America funded a national poll of American women to demonstrate that women's concerns are just like men's—crime and the economy topped the list, while abortion ranked almost dead last (Stearns 1996, in CWA promotional packet).

Conservative groups also capitalize on female social marginality and weak gender consciousness to attack prominent women office holders as proxies for the liberal opposition. Eagle Forum vetted the U.S. Supreme Court nominee Ruth Bader Ginsburg and pronounced her a "radical, doctrinaire feminist, far out of the mainstream" (*Phyllis Schlafly Report* 1993c). It derided "Hillary," as Mrs. Clinton is typically called, for advancing adolescent views on the "politics of meaning" and for stocking the government with her feminist cronies, amassing a "ruling clique" (*Phyllis Schlafly Report* 1993b, 1993e). Schlafly also traced the 1994 Republican takeover of Congress to public rejection of "Hillary Rodham Clinton, Janet Reno, Donna Shalala, Ruth Bader Ginsburg, and Joycelyn Elders," curiously omitting President Clinton (*Phyllis Schlafly Report* 1994e). Democratic women are not the only targets of disapprobation; Supreme Court Justice Sandra Day O'Connor, a Reagan appointee who voted prochoice on several important abortion rights cases, was chastised for "whining" about sex discrimination and for expressing views "20 years behind the times in mouthing the feminist 'oppression' rhetoric of the '70s" (*Phyllis Schlafly Report* 1990).

As both organizations have matured, their attention to feminism has waned somewhat. CWA dropped its monthly "Feminist Follies" feature from *Family Voice* in the summer of 1993, followed two years later by elimination of the "Time Out for Moms" and "A Word for Dads" columns. Eagle Forum reduced its coverage of feminist issues as well; during 1991, for example, five monthly issues of the *Phyllis Schlafly Report* focused on feminism or women's issues, compared to two in 1992 and one in each of the three succeeding years. This may be due partly to discouragement over prolife defeats in the courts and in Congress, which severely restricted protests at abortion clinics; Beverly La-Haye has noted with disappointment a decreasing zeal among abortion opponents (*Family Voice* 1995l). The election of a Democratic president, one labeled a dangerous liberal, also energized the right-wing opposition and may have provoked a shift in issue emphasis by women's organizations to aid the larger conservative effort of regaining political power. Opposition to feminism continues to be important, however, as a launching pad for women's mobilization to an expanded range of New Right domestic and foreign policy issues.

Antifeminism as Bridge Labor

A common perception of organized antifeminism is that its primary focus is the defense of the traditional homemaker against the gender-role changes advocated by the feminist movement. The rhetoric of these preeminent antifeminist associations suggests otherwise. Both groups express sympathy for the reduced status of the stay-at-home mom as a "second-class choice" (*Family Voice* 1995d), and Eagle Forum bestows an annual Fulltime Homemaker Award, but their typical policy solutions reflect mainstream conservatism, including tax reforms to benefit single-earner households and individual retirement accounts for nonemployed women. Their "profamily" message is likewise aimed more generically at conservative parents than at women. It emphasizes parental control over the contents of children's education, decries attacks on traditional family values by the entertainment industry, and locates the root cause of most social problems in liberal policies that have weakened family structure. Neither group regards women's employment as the source of family dysfunction, probably because many conservative women work outside the home. It is fathers' absence and the erosion of male authority that both organizations identify as the cause of most of America's social ills, and feminists are held responsible for both disturbing trends. Both organizations emphasize the importance of fathers as "heroic" role models needed to instill character and discipline in children (*Family Voice* 1995g, 1995o).

The ideological bridge from antifeminism to the larger conservative agenda rests also on the belief that feminists are not merely bitter women but also dangerous and untrustworthy. This depiction is effective because it is compatible with gender stereotypes and also because feminism is a liberal ideology; "radical feminism" is the preferred term for the women's movement in most right-wing tracts. As their search for prominent turncoats like Jane Fonda suggests, a primary discrediting strategy claims that feminists are not what they appear; they are political infiltrators whose aim is to effect a socialist revolution in the United States. Even their ostensible goal of personal freedom is a ruse tinged with suspect political goals; Schlafly warns, "Don't believe their demands for independence! In fact, the feminists who proclaim their liberation from men always run to Big Brother Government as a replacement" (*Phyllis Schlafly Report* 1994e).

In the aftermath of the Cold War, the search for communist foes has increasingly turned inward. Feminists are easy targets of suspicion; like communists, they are said to arrogantly advocate a social experiment at odds with human nature and the Bible. Eagle Forum charged that the premise of feminism is that "God goofed in making us in two different sexes, and our laws should remedy His mistake" (*Phyllis Schlafly Report* 1994e). Antifeminism is easily transformed into a moral crusade because sexual liberation and reproductive freedom are inextricably associated with the women's movement. According to CWA, the sexual revolution turned morality on its head by rejecting the blessings of God along with motherhood (*Family Voice* 1995e). These are not radical views, but they substantiate a divisive rhetoric on social issues that demonizes the opposition as antireligion and encourages conspiratorial explanations of political disputes.

New Right rhetoric transforms almost every social issue into a moral question derived from an errant feminist agenda. Crime could be eradicated with better moral teachings in the home; the solution is two-parent families and a firm paternal hand (*Family Voice* 1994h). Welfare is wrong because it encourages illegitimacy and makes husbands dispensable; it is the "prime example of the Irreligious Left imposing its lack of morals on the rest of society" (*Family Voice* 1994l; *Phyllis Schlafly Report* 1996a). The media, controlled by "moral perverts in Hollywood and Broadway," promote carnality among the young, and even the federal government encourages recreational sexual activity in television condom advertisements, spewing its "toxic message into our living room" (*Family Voice* 1994f, 1994g). The social changes set in motion by the countercultural movements of the 1960s have created a "moral holocaust," and our nation's leaders are ruling with "godless principles" (*Family Voice* 1994n, 1994p). Nowhere is this more evident than in education, a perfect focus for women's intervention since it falls well within the traditional female domain.

The right opposes all federal intrusion into public schools. Eagle Forum denounces national standards as an elitist idea and views the movement for national standards as an insult to parents and children alike, who are reduced to "guinea pigs in a vast social experiment" (*Phyllis Schlafly Report* 1993a, 1995c). The Department of Education is a totalitarian "Big Brother" and should be abolished, along with the "extremist" National Education Association, which endorses the "entire feminist agenda" and "is not just out to restructure education; the NEA is out to restructure society" (*Family Voice* 1994q; *Phyllis Schlafly*

Report 1995d, 1995e). They fear the proliferation of hidden coercive messages in subjects from bilingual education to antidrug programs and caution parents to be vigilant, lest their children be "trampled underfoot by pagan philosophies, strangled by situational ethics, bombarded by revisionist history, demoralized by outcome-based education, and stripped of their innocence in sex education classes" (*Family Voice* 1995n; *Phyllis Schlafly Report* 1995g). If, as they contend, "people who hate America are now writing school curricula" and "militant secularists have taken over school boards and city councils," colleges fare no better in their assessment, as university curricula are "dumbed down" to accommodate multicultural and women's studies courses and "60s-era radicals who now have tenure" brainwash students with "Political Cor-rectness" (*Family Voice* 1994r; *Phyllis Schlafly Report* 1994a, 1996c; EF, Schlafly letter to membership, March 1995, April 1996).

The moral divide is most clearly drawn on issues of sexuality, in which the government, in their view, promotes values antithetical to Christian principles. Organizational rhetoric rises commensurately and explains a large part of the antipathy against the NEA and the Department of Education, both of which have supported sex education curricula. Eagle Forum declared that "the schools are going to tell primary schoolchildren all about how to engage in sex and with what devices," and CWA advised its members that taxpayer-financed programs countenance pedophilia, tell innocent children to "indulge in promiscuity," and show eight-year-olds how to use a condom (*Phyllis Schlafly Report* 1993d; CWA, LaHaye letter to membership, October 1995, March 1996). They object to HIV-prevention programs that lie about supposedly "safe sex" and present graphically female sexual activity, demonstrating to their satisfaction that the government "champions a new morality of serial monogamy" (*Family Voice* 1995c). Homosexuality is the most heinous moral result of the sexual revolution, and the gay movement is perceived as a conspiracy—"a nationwide assault on the Body of Christ and the traditional family"—that is pushing to "take over our culture, step-by-step," infiltrating businesses, the media, the schools, and even churches. Borrowing imagery from science fiction, one CWA "expert" advises that gays have devised a plan to "breed a counterculture" by marrying and having children, and homosexuals who do not participate in this "eugenics experiment" get revenge by recruiting children inside the schools (*Family Voice* 1994i; CWA, LaHaye letter to membership, August 1995). Needless to say, these organizations

support state antigay constitutional amendments and proposed legislation to bar gay teachers from the classroom as well as the federal Defense
of Marriage Act (*Family Voice* 1995k).

The pro-life issue, which proved so effective in the political mobilization of antifeminist women in the 1970s, lies just below the surface of
many other social concerns. It functions as both a rallying cry and a
litmus test for other issues. Beverly LaHaye told CWA members that the
VMI lawsuit on sex segregation in public colleges could be the "Roe v.
Wade of the radical feminist political agenda" and warned that a favorable decision for the Clinton Justice Department could empower the
federal courts to eliminate tax exemptions for churches with an all-male
ministry, drastically alter family laws on marriage and child custody, and
mandate taxpayer-funded abortions as a constitutional right (CWA,
LaHaye letter to membership, February 1996). Juvenile crime has sky-
rocketed, they reason, because the major societal institutions, by failing
to emphasize the value of life, have served as poor role models for the
nation's youth (*Family Voice* 1995a). Opposition to health care reform
is justified in part because the proposed plan of the "Clintonistas"
included abortion services under basic coverage, and "true" welfare
reform must balance a cap on benefits for additional children with a ban
on government abortion funding (*Family Voice* 1994a, 1994l; *Phyllis
Schlafly Report* 1993g).

From the perspective of these antifeminist organizations, the devaluing
of America began with the *Roe v. Wade* decision legalizing abortion, and
feminists bear the blame for teaching "an entire generation of children
that life can be tossed aside when it is inconvenient" (*Family Voice*
1994k). Despite lobbying efforts and, in the case of CWA, the filing of
supporting briefs to the court as well as lawsuits against the U.S. attorney
general, recent court decisions have upheld the right of the Justice Department to charge prolife protesters under federal antiracketeering laws and
the legality of the federal Freedom of Access to Clinic Entrances Act
(FACE). CWA spokespersons have predicted that these acts will unleash a
"courthouse reign of terror" against prolife movement leaders (*Family
Voice* 1994e, 1994n). In the wake of the FACE Act, described by CWA
as the "only federal statute targeted against one group of people," both
organizations have denounced the religious persecution of Christians in
the United States and paradoxically likened their cause to the civil rights
movement of a despised era (*Family Voice* 1994s; *Phyllis Schlafly Report*
1994c; CWA, LaHaye letter to membership, May 1995, February 1996).

For Beverly LaHaye, these events confirmed scriptural prophesy that "the days are evil" (*Family Voice* 1995p).

With the dissolution of the "evil empire" of the Soviet Union, New Right international policy has increasingly focused on the United Nations as the greatest foreign threat to America. According to Schlafly, the U.N. is a "Trojan Horse that carries the enemy into our midst," and its treaties are nothing less than "a dagger pointed at our American Bill of Rights" (*Phyllis Schlafly Report* 1995f). The "New World Order," a term used by former President George Bush, is loathed as synonymous with totalitarianism, and both groups oppose international economic alliances such as the North American Free Trade Agreement (NAFTA), the General Agreement on Tariffs and Trade (GATT), and the World Trade Organization (WTO) as representing a dangerous drift toward the loss of national sovereignty (*Phyllis Schlafly Report* 1994b, 1994d, 1996b). Concerned Women for America charged that the U.N., "this forerunner of the anti-Christ's vehicle for world government," revealed its intentions to undermine "the basic precepts of our nation" in its fiftieth-anniversary celebration, at which children's choral groups celebrated "neopaganism" by performing songs to "The Great Mother Earth" (*Family Voice* 1995h, 1995i).

Not surprisingly, feminism functions as a bridge to mobilize women's opposition to the United Nations. Both groups articulate resentments against the international body derived from its capitulation to the "radical feminist agenda." This was Beverly LaHaye's argument against the second U.N. Conference on Human Settlements (Habitat II), which would "create 'gendered cities' where feminist groups would force communities to hire and plan based on gender," and probably on sexual orientation as well (CWA, LaHaye letter to membership, March 1996). Similarly, both groups denounced as a subterfuge the U.N. Convention on the Rights of the Child, supported by Hillary Clinton and her feminist friends. Under the guise of protecting abused children, the treaty would allegedly intrude on parental authority and allow children the freedom to join gangs and refuse to clean their rooms. It would also impede children's education, teaching them antitraditional values masquerading under the code words "diversity" and "multiculturalism" and inculcating feminist propaganda about equality of the sexes. To defeat the treaty, CWA launched a lobbying campaign, Operation Hands Off Our Kids (CWA, LaHaye letter to membership, March 1995; EF, Schlafly letter to membership, February 1995).

U.N. intervention in feminist issues has long been a source of contention among contemporary organized antifeminists, extending back to
their disapproval of the "extreme" document produced at the first World
Conference on Women in 1975 that allegedly "empowered the push for
the Equal Rights Amendment in America" (*Family Voice* 1995j). Although CWA objected to the 1995 conference location in a communist
country that practices infanticide, it fought without success to become a
part of the official U.S. delegation to Beijing, ostensibly to counteract
the "Marxist" influence of a U.S. delegate, Bella Abzug, the "notorious"
"grande dame of feminism" (*Family Voice* 1995f, 1995q). Beverly La-
Haye managed to invade the so-called "dragon's den" and reported
to her constituents that the Beijing meeting produced a controversial
"Platform for Action" supported by the Clinton Administration that
redefined gender and the family as diverse social constructions, opening
the door to "future protection of sexual orientation as a human right."
Warned CWA, "when true womanhood suffers a radical assault, true
concepts of manhood, family, and the place of children are not far
behind" (*Family Voice* 1995q).

Discussion

These findings challenge the "true womanhood" image promulgated by
contemporary antifeminist organizations. The maternalist vision of an
earlier era presumed women's unique capacities to solve social problems
within the traditional female domains of education, public health, and
social welfare (Skocpol 1992). Even the most conservative maternalist
organizations in the early twentieth century touted the power of motherhood while opposing federal oversight and reform legislation designed
to aid women workers (Michel and Rosen 1992). Contemporary antifeminist associations within the New Right coalition accept the idea of
"God-given" differences between the sexes and promote the ideals of
traditional motherhood, but their profamily politics differ from those of
their predecessors in two important ways: They reject the notion that
women constitute a unique political interest group, and they evidence
considerably more interest in protecting the authority and rights of
fathers or, at best, generic "parents."

The histories of Eagle Forum and Concerned Women for America,
each established to halt the ERA, demonstrate the effectiveness of using

grievances against feminism to further the political mobilization of conservative women. But the feminist movement also created political opportunities that Schlafly and LaHaye adeptly exploited. One such opportunity was the loosening of traditional norms against women's political participation, which made women more available for recruitment to activism. Another was the increased political salience of issues previously defined as private, such as sexuality and reproduction, which became the cornerstone of the "profamily" agenda. This essay argues that heightened attention to social issues by the New Right was in part an appeal to this newly mobilized constituency, and it worked, in large measure because women's organizations in the coalition performed bridge labor to move their constituencies from antifeminism to other conservative issues.

They accomplished this goal by using feminism as the basis for moral attacks on liberal policies. The feminist contention that gender inequality is socially based permitted assaults on "humanist" curricula that allegedly promotes disrespect for the beliefs of Christian parents. Its association with the 1960s sexual revolution facilitated allegations of excess and immorality; feminists were held responsible for injuries to children that included sexual victimization, homosexual recruitment, and juvenile delinquency. Welfare dependency was portrayed as the inevitable outcome of feminists' disparagement of fatherhood and traditional family life. The perceived radicalism of feminist ideology, which in their view deviated from holy Scripture and proposed a dangerous expansion of federal power to the detriment of individual liberty, combined with the dissolution of the Cold War to open the door to an opportunistic assault on feminism as part of a renewed fight against communism and pagan globalism. The success of their efforts to move beyond the "policy ghetto" of women's issues is illustrated in Phyllis Schlafly's promise to contributors that "Eagle Forum is a 'full-service' organization. That means we are effectively confronting America's enemies on every front . . . for our conservative cause" (EF, Schlafly letter to membership, December 1995).

The strategy of acquiring female recruits for the broader New Right agenda through assaults on feminism depends on a tolerant social climate. I have argued that continued cultural support for sexist attitudes, lower female social status and power, and women's relatively low group consciousness sustained aggressive assaults on feminism by right-wing women's organizations. These conditions also encouraged antifeminist groups to target prominent women, from the President's spouse to his cabinet appointments and members of the Supreme Court, as a way of ridiculing liberalism. Negative sexual stereotypes also encouraged right-wing paranoia about feminist political conspiracies, illustrated by repeated references to "hidden messages," "hidden agendas," and "secret plans" in everything from educational curricula to health care proposals and income taxes. Greater female vulnerability in U.S. society, along with the persistence of cultural approval for "gender-role traditionalism," helped normalize the radical accusations of right-wing rhetoric and legitimate the movement.

I further suggest that the division of labor among organizations within the New Right coalition was built on the existing gender stratification system so assiduously repudiated by antifeminist groups. While Ralph Reed of the Christian Coalition sought a more positive public image in a conference of reconciliation with African American ministers (DeParle 1996b), his female colleagues were engaged in the dirty work of mounting attacks on educational integration, affirmative action, and federal welfare policy that used gender as a proxy for race. The appearance of organized women speaking out against women's rights, moreover, only serves to reiterate restrictive gender stereotypes. Working out of the spotlight, these women may embody the "stealth" strategy that Reed credited with the Coalition's success, but at a cost of little public acknowledgment of their contributions to the cause.

REFERENCES

Barnett, Bernice McNair. 1993. "Invisible Southern Black Women Leaders in the Civil Rights Movement: The Triple Constraints of Gender, Race, and Class." *Gender & Society* 7, 2 (June): 162–82.

Barrett, Lawrence I. 1993. "Fighting for God and the Right Wing." *Time,* 13 September: 58–60.

Baxter, Sandra, and Marjorie Lansing. 1980. *Women and Politics: The Invisible Majority.* Ann Arbor: University of Michigan Press.

Blee, Kathleen M. 1991. *Women of the Klan; Racism and Gender in the 1920s.* Berkeley: University of California Press.

Blumenthal, Sidney. 1994. "Onward Christian Soldiers." *New Yorker,* 18 July: 31–37.

Boles, Janet K. 1979. *The Politics of the Equal Rights Amendment.* New York: Longman.

Bookman, Ann, and Sandra Morgen. 1988. *Women and the Politics of Empowerment*. Philadelphia: Temple University Press.

Conason, Joe. 1992. "The Religious Right's Quiet Revival." *Nation*, 27 April: 541–47.

Concerned Women for America (CWA). 1995–1996. Miscellaneous correspondence. In author's possession.

Conover, Pamela Johnston. 1988. "Feminists and the Gender Gap." *Journal of Politics* 50, 4 (Nov.): 985–1010.

Cook, Elizabeth Adell. 1989. "Measuring Feminist Consciousness." *Women & Politics* 9, 3: 71–88.

Cook, Elizabeth Adell, and Clyde Wilcox. 1991. "Feminism and the Gender Gap—A Second Look." *Journal of Politics* 53, 4 (Nov.): 1111–22.

Cott, Nancy F. 1977. *The Bonds of Womanhood*. New Haven: Yale University Press.

Crawford, Alan. 1980. *Thunder on the Right: The 'New Right' and the Politics of Resentment*. New York: Pantheon.

Crawford, Vicki, Jacqueline Rouse, and Barbara Woods, eds. 1990. *Women in the Civil Rights Movement*. Brooklyn, N.Y.: Carlson.

Deitch, Cynthia. 1988. "Sex Differences in Support for Government Spending." Pp. 192–216 in Carol M. Mueller, ed., *The Politics of the Gender Gap: The Social Construction of Political Influence*. Newbury Park, Calif.: Sage.

DeParle, Jason. 1996a. "The Christian Right Confesses Sins of Racism." *New York Times*, 4 August: 5E.

———. 1996b. "A Fundamental Problem." *New York Times Magazine*, 14 July: 18–44.

Doerr, Edd. 1995. "Pat's Patsy Political Program." *Humanist*, Nov.–Dec.: 39–40.

Eagle Forum (EF). 1995–1996. Miscellaneous correspondence. In author's possession.

Epstein, Barbara Leslie. 1981. *The Politics of Domesticity: Women, Evangelism, and Temperance in Nineteenth-Century America*. Middletown, Conn.: Wesleyan University Press.

Evans, Sara. 1979. *Personal Politics: The Roots of Women's Liberation in the Civil Rights Movement and the New Left*. New York: Knopf.

Family Voice. 1995a. "From the President's Desk: Family, Cornerstone of this Country." January: 3, 30.

———. 1995b. "The Failure of Feminism, Part 1." March: 24–27.

———. 1995c. "AIDS Training: Promoting a New Morality at Taxpayers' Expense." April: 4–12.

———. 1995d. "Time Out for Moms: Mom, I'm Home!" April: 13.

———. 1995e. "The Failure of Feminism, Part 2." April: 24–26.

———. 1995f. "A Look into the Feminist World: The 4th U.N. World Conference on Women." June: 3–6.

———. 1995g. "Making Room for Daddy." June: 7–14.

———. 1995h. "A Word for Dads: One-World Government." June: 17.

———. 1995i. "For the Pastor's Desk: The United Nations and Man's Wisdom." June: 28.

———. 1995j. "United Nations: Re-Designing Women." July: 4–15.

———. 1995k. "Boston Youth Parade A First in Homosexual Pride." July: 26–27.

———. 1995l. "Whatever Happened on the Way to the Clinic?" August: 4–11.

———. 1995m. "Moms: Harassment as Defined by the State." August: 24.

———. 1995n. "Making the Grade." September: 4–17.

———. 1995o. "A Word for Dads: The Grateful Dead." October: 15.

———. 1995p. "From the President's Desk." November/December: 3, 21–22.

———. 1995q. "Battling the Dragon in Beijing." November/December: 4–12.

———. 1994a. "Reform or Ruin? National Health Care." January: 4–9.

———. 1994b. "Free Speech Prevails!" January: 26.

———. 1994c. "From the President's Desk: An Exciting Opportunity." February: 3.

———. 1994d. "Clinton and the Family One Year Later." February: 4–10.

———. 1994e. "Pro-Life Movement Targeted by RICO." March: 17.

———. 1994f. "Time Out for Moms." March: 18.

———. 1994g. "For the Pastor's Desk: About My Father's Business." March: 20.

———. 1994h. "Crime: A Search for Justice." April: 4–14.

———. 1994i. "The Mainstreaming of Homosexuality." May: 4–15.

———. 1994j. "Navy Women Throw Effectiveness Overboard." May: 30.

———. 1994k. "From the President's Desk: Justice for All." June: 3, 22.

———. 1994l. "Welfare: Hidden Trap or Safety Net?" June: 4–11.

———. 1994m. "Time Out for Moms." July: 20.

———. 1994n. "From the President's Desk: CWA vs. Reno." August: 3, 28.

———. 1994o. "20% More in '94." August: 22.

———. 1994p. "For the Pastor's Desk: Responsible Christian Citizens." August: 25.

———. 1994q. "Educated Power and the NEA." September: 13.

———. 1994r. "For the Pastor's Desk: A Time to Wake Up!" September: 18.

———. 1994s. "Voting for Change." October: 4–11.

Felsenthal, Carol. 1981. *The Sweetheart of the Silent Majority.* Garden City, N.Y.: Doubleday.

Freeman, Jo. 1975. *The Politics of Women's Liberation.* New York: Longman.

Ginsburg, Faye D. 1989. *Contested Lives: The Abortion Debate in an American Community.* Berkeley: University of California Press.

Gurin, Patricia. 1985. "Women's Gender Consciousness." *Public Opinion Quarterly* 29, 2 (Summer): 143–63.

Gurin, Patricia, and Aloen Townsend. 1986. "Properties of Gender Identity and their Implications for Gender Consciousness." *British Journal of Social Psychology* 25, 2 (June): 139–48.

Hertel, Bradley R., and Michael Hughes. 1987. "Religious Affiliation, Attendance, and Support for 'Pro-Family' Issues in the United States." *Social Forces* 65, 3 (March): 858–82.

Himmelstein, Jerome L. 1990. *To the Right: The Transformation of American Conservatism.* Berkeley: University of California Press.

———. 1983. "The New Right." Pp. 13 30 in Robert C. Liebman and Robert Wuthnow, eds., *The New Christian Right: Mobilization and Legitimation.* New York: Aldine.

Jelen, Ted G. 1992. "Political Christianity: A Contextual Analysis." *American Journal of Political Science* 36, 3 (Aug.): 692–714.

Klatch, Rebecca E. 1987. *Women of the New Right.* Philadelphia: Temple University Press.

Kluegel, James R., and Eliot R. Smith. 1986. *Beliefs about Inequality: Americans' Views of What Is and What Ought to Be.* New York: Aldine.

Koonz, Claudia. 1987. *Mothers in the Fatherland: Women, the Family, and Nazi Politics.* New York: St. Martin's Press.

Liebman, Robert C., and Robert Wuthnow, eds. 1983. *The New Christian Right: Mobilization and Legitimation.* New York: Aldine.

Lofland, John. 1985. "Social Movement Culture." Pp. 219–39 in John Lofland, ed., *Protest: Studies of Collective Behavior and Social Movements.* New Brunswick, N.J.: Transaction Books.

Luker, Kristin. 1984. *Abortion and the Politics of Motherhood.* Berkeley: University of California Press.

Mansbridge, Jane J. 1986. *Why We Lost the ERA.* Chicago: University of Chicago Press.

Marshall, Susan E. 1997. *Splintered Sisterhood: Gender and Class in the Campaign against Woman Suffrage.* Madison: University of Wisconsin Press.

———. 1996. "Marilyn vs. Hillary: Women's Place in New Right Politics." *Women & Politics* 16, 1 (Spring): 55–75.

———. 1991. "Who Speaks for American Women? The Future of Antifeminism." *Annals of the American Academy of Political and Social Science* 515 (May): 50–62.

McAdam, Doug. 1992. "Gender as a Mediator of the Activist Experience: The Case of Freedom Summer." *American Journal of Sociology* 97, 5 (March): 1211–40.

McCourt, Kathleen. 1977. *Working-Class Women and Grassroots Politics.* Bloomington: Indiana University Press.

McNamara, Patrick H. 1988. "The New Christian Right's View of the Family and Its Social Science Critics: A Study in Differing Presuppositions." Pp. 285–

302 in Darwin L. Thomas, ed., *The Religion and Family Connection: Social Science Perspectives.* Provo, Utah: Brigham Young University Press.

Michel, Sonya, and Robyn Rosen. 1992. "The Paradox of Maternalism: Elizabeth Lowell Putnam and the American Welfare State." *Gender & History* 4, 3 (Autumn): 364–86.

Morris, Aldon D. 1984. *The Origins of the Civil Rights Movement: Black Communities Organizing for Change.* New York: Free Press.

Peek, Charles W., and Sharon Brown. 1980. "Sex Prejudice among White Protestants: Like or Unlike Ethnic Prejudice?" *Social Forces* 59, 1 (Sept.): 169–85.

Phyllis Schlafly Report. 1996a. "But Clinton Will Never End Big Government." February.

———. 1996b. "Free Trade, Protectionism, NAFTA, and GATT." March.

———. 1996c. "The Dumbing Down of America's Colleges." April.

———. 1995a. "Of Course, Congress Can Cut Federal Spending!" February.

———. 1995b. "Has the Navy Lost Its Manhood?" February.

———. 1995c. "How the Liberals Are Rewriting History." March.

———. 1995d. "The NEA Proves Itself Extremist Again." August.

———. 1995e. "Let's Abolish the Department of Education." September.

———. 1995f. "The United Nations—An Enemy in Our Midst." November.

———. 1995g. "English Should Be Our Official Language." December.

———. 1994a. "Colleges Should Display Warning Labels." April.

———. 1994b. "New World Order, Clinton-Style." June.

———. 1994c. "Stop Trying to Treat Christians Like Smokers." August.

———. 1994d. "What's So Wrong about GATT/WTO?" October.

———. 1994e. "The Feminists Have a Terrible Identity Crisis." December.

———. 1993a. "What's Wrong with Outcome-Based Education?" May.

———. 1993b. "Hillary, Health Care, and 'Remolding' Government." June.

———. 1993c. "Ruth Bader Ginsburg's Feminist World View." July.

———. 1993d. "NEA Steps Up Its Anti-Parent Policies." September.

———. 1993e. "Shenanigans of the Clinton Administration." October.

———. 1993f. "Men, Learn a Lesson About Feminists." October.

———. 1993g. "Clinton's Totalitarian Health Plan." November.

———. 1993h. "Eagle Forum Education Center Opens." December.

———. 1992a. "Feminist Goals vs. Fairness and Truth." April.

———. 1992b. "Women Don't Belong in Military Combat." July.

———. 1991a. "Feminist Falsehoods, Follies, and Funding." July.

———. 1991b. "Feminism Falls on Its Face." November.

———. 1990. "Time to Tell the Feminists Bye-Bye." December.

———. 1987. "The Discrimination of Parental Leave." March.

Piven, Frances Fox. 1985. "Women and the State: Ideology, Power, and the Welfare State." Pp. 265–87 in Alice Rossi, ed., *Gender and the Life Course.* New York: Aldine.

Reed, Ralph. 1995. "Ideas and Ideals: Let Us Begin the Important Work that Lies Ahead." *Vital Speeches,* 1 March: 309–12.

Robertson, Pat. 1991. *The New World Order.* Dallas: Word.

Robnett, Belinda. 1996. "African-American Women in the Civil Rights Movement, 1954–1965: Gender, Leadership, and Micromobilization." *American Journal of Sociology* 101, 6 (May): 1661–93.

Rossi, Alice S. 1983. "Beyond the Gender Gap: Women's Bid for Political Power." *Social Science Quarterly* 64, 4 (Dec.): 718–33.

Schlafly, Phyllis. 1981. *The Power of the Christian Woman.* Cincinnati, Ohio: Standard.

———. 1977. *The Power of the Positive Woman.* New Rochelle, N.Y.: Arlington House.

Schlafly, Phyllis, and Chester Charles Ward. 1976. *Ambush at Vladivostok.* Alton, Ill.: Pere Marquette Press.

Skocpol, Theda. 1992. *Protecting Soldiers and Mothers: The Politics of Social Provision in the United States, 1870s 1920s.* Cambridge: Harvard University Press.

Sears, David O., and Leonie Huddy. 1990. "On the Origins of Political Disunity among Women." Pp. 249–77 in Louise A. Tilly and Patricia Gurin, eds., *Women, Politics, and Change.* New York: Russell Sage.

Sigelman, Lee, Clyde Wilcox, and Emmett H. Buell Jr. 1987. "An Unchanging Minority: Popular Support for the Moral Majority, 1980 and 1984." *Social Science Quarterly* 68, 4 (Dec.): 876–84.

Smidt, Corwin. 1987. "Evangelicals and the 1984 Election: Continuity or Change?" *American Politics Quarterly* 15, 4 (Oct.): 419–44.

Snow, David A., E. Burke Rocheford Jr., Steven K. Worden, Robert D. Benford. 1986. "Frame Alignment Processes, Micromobilization, and Movement Participation." *American Sociological Review* 52, 4 (Aug.): 464–81.

Staggenborg, Suzanne. 1987. "Life-Style Preferences and Social Movement Recruitment: Illustrations from the Abortion Conflict." *Social Science Quarterly* 68, 4 (Dec.): 779–97.

Stearns, Cliff. 1996. "The Artificial GOP Gender Gap." *Washington Times,* 20 August.

Walker, Richard. 1989. "Falwell Claims Victory, Dissolves Moral Majority." *Christianity Today,* 14 July: 58–59.

Wall, James M. 1995. "Religiopolitical Operative." *Christian Century,* 24 May: 555–556.

Wirls, Daniel. 1986. "Reinterpreting the Gender Gap." *Public Opinion Quarterly* 50, 3 (Fall): 316–30.

Young, John Hardin, Sherry A. Swirsky, and Jay B. Myerson. 1995. "Going to the Grassroots: How the Christian Coalition Is Filling the Void." *Campaigns & Elections* 16, 7 (July): 34.

Chapter Nine

Reading Racism
Women in the Modern Hate Movement

Kathleen M. Blee

For a particularly striking example of the horrific logic of Holocaust denial you need look no further than the *True History of "The Holocaust,"* a book published by the Historical Review Press and distributed recently by one of the major Ku Klux Klan organizations. Created to explain what its adherents refer to as the "revisionist historical" position on the Jewish Holocaust, the book claims to proffer new evidence to refute standard estimates of the magnitude of killings of European Jews by the Nazis and their allies. Although what passes for evidence is a jumble of historical hyperbole, distortion, and omission, the book insists that its conclusions are solidly grounded in scientific fact and discovery. Like all works of Holocaust denial, the *True History* argues that the story of Jewish extermination was invented and perpetuated by Jews as the basis for receiving monetary and emotional reparations from the Aryan world. Thus, *True History* states its mission as refuting conventional interpretations of World War II by informing "British, Canadian and American churches and schools" of

> irrefutable evidence that the allegation that 6 million Jews died during the Second World War as a direct result of official German policy of extermination is utterly unfounded.... [I]n terms of political blackmail [the allegation] . . . has much more far-reaching implication for the people of Britain and Europe than simply the advantages it has gained for the Jewish nation. (Anonymous n.d.)

The ideological conviction of this published passage, however, is not echoed in the words of Jane, a California neo-Nazi, fervent adherent and practitioner of Holocaust denial, and leader in the white supremacist movement. When I interviewed Jane and asked her to explain how she understood the Holocaust, she replied:

> We kind of believe that, we don't kind of believe, we believe that the six million figure is greatly exaggerated and a lot of other things about the Holocaust that people accept as fact in fact were really war propaganda. . . . You know I'm not comfortable with doing it like, you know, I don't know what it has to do with it. If it has to do with history, it has to do with history, but I hate to see a political agenda in this particular issue because it doesn't really have a place in there. All these emotions, on both sides, you know, all this emotional crap issue. It should be an objective thing, like you know, a scholarly thing.[1]

The difference between these two passages is striking. Although her life has been dedicated to neo-Nazi activism, Jane waivers in her commitment to the core tenets of Holocaust denial: that far fewer than six million Jews perished during World War II and that Jewish deaths can be explained as a result of wartime hardship rather than deliberate policies of extermination. Moreover, Jane's comment that "if it has to do with history, it has to do with history" differentiates her from the historical revisionist argument that the memory of World War II was shaped by the subsequent political and monetary interests of powerful Jewish conspirators.

Jane's statements are typical of those of many women in white supremacist groups whose private racial beliefs often veer far from the official positions of their organizations (Blee 1996a). (There are no data on whether this pattern exists also for men.) These differences do not simply reflect diminished commitment to organized racist and anti-Semitic politics or groups, for discrepancies are found not only among rank-and-file members but also among the most active, visible leaders of the white power movement. At points the propaganda of white supremacist groups is mirrored in the beliefs of racist activists, but at others it is not. Such discrepancies suggest that in their continuing search for adherents, modern white supremacist organizations permit ideological latitude among their members. Understanding elements of commonality and disjuncture between the messages issued by modern racist organizations and the personal attitudes of active women members of these groups thus can provide insight into how the modern racist movement has begun to gain members, after decades of decline. It also provides important clues to the reasons that women join such groups and how they might be persuaded to leave.

Since the 1980s, organized racism has had a resurgence in the United States (Blee 1997; Ezekiel 1995; Ridgeway 1990; Ward 1996). At least part of the increase in membership and in the number and variety of racist groups can be attributed to a strategic decision by white supremacist leaders to focus on the recruitment of adult women and teenage girls and boys. As a result, women now constitute an estimated 25 percent of the membership (and nearly 50 percent of new recruits) in many segments of the racist movement. The secretive nature of organized racism makes it impossible to know precisely in which racist groups women are concentrated. However, women are quite visible in many rapidly growing neo-Nazi organizations, including violent gangs of racist skinheads. Women also are actively sought as members by the Ku Klux Klan, which is now splintered into at least two dozen competing Klans, many with strategic alliances to neo-Nazi groups.

To probe the comparability of personal belief and group propaganda among women activists in these groups, I use data from two sources. First, I analyze white supremacist propaganda from an extensive collection of contemporary white supremacist literature that I collected during a one-year period between October 1993 and October 1994. This includes the annual series of all newsletters, magazines, flyers, and recordings of music and speeches published by more than one hundred then-active self-proclaimed white power, white supremacist, white separatist, Ku Klux Klan, skinhead, Nazi/neo-Nazi, and similar groups operating in the United States.

Second, I draw upon in-depth (two- to six-hour) interviews that I conducted with thirty-four women racist activists in the United States between November 1994 and October 1995. These activists were identified and contacted using a variety of personal networks, including parole officers, correctional officials, newspaper reporters, other racist activists and former activists, federal and state gang task forces, attorneys, other researchers, and my own contacts. Respondents include four leaders who are known both within the movement and outside, ten leaders who are not known publicly, and twenty rank-and-file members of racist groups. They range in age from sixteen to ninety, with a median age of twenty-four. They are from fifteen different states, with the greatest concentrations in Georgia (six), Oklahoma (five), Oregon (four), and

Florida (four). Eleven live in the South, ten are from the West Coast, ten from the Midwest, and three from the East Coast.

The boundaries of many racist groups today are quite fluid, and respondents typically have moved in and out of a series of groups over time. Thus, few respondents can be definitely characterized by a single group membership, or even by a single philosophical position. If respondents are categorized according to their most significant involvement with an organized racist group, they include fourteen neo-Nazis (other than skinheads), six members of Ku Klux Klans, eight white-power skinheads, and six members of white supremacist Christian Identity or similar groups. To avoid creating publicity for the racist movement and to preserve the anonymity of my respondents, I use pseudonyms for both group and individual names, and I have changed identifying details.

It is commonly assumed that only poor or lower-working-class people join racist groups. However, the majority of my informants held middle-class jobs (as occupational therapists, nurses, teachers, and librarians), were attending college, or were not employed but were married to employed men. About one third of them were economically vulnerable; they held jobs as waitresses, lay ministers in tiny, nonaffiliated churches, or teachers in marginal private schools or were married to marginally employed men. In almost half of these cases, though, marginal employment was caused by involvement in racist politics.[2] Some had lost better jobs when they came to work dressed in racist regalia or Klan robes or sporting Nazi tattoos. Others were fired for giving racist literature to customers or fellow employees. Others decided to sacrifice wages for principle by working only for white supremacist organizations, for example as teachers in racist schools or as preachers in racist churches.

Organizational Ideology

Organized racism is unified by a set of common beliefs (Brustein 1993; Goldberg 1990; Weinberg 1993; Wetherell and Potter 1992). Most central to virtually all groups is anti-Semitic and conspiratorial thinking. Jews are almost uniformly identified as the principal conspirators, omnipotent yet anonymous. To most racists, Jewish control is absolute, and Jewish domination of the world—through the imposition of the so-called "new world order"—is just around the corner. Like all conspiratorial worldviews, it is the absence of confirming evidence that strengthens conviction. Thus, the failure of racist groups to identify specific conspirators or actions serves to underscore the power of the conspirators to remain hidden from public view (Blee 1996b).

Also common within organized racism is a belief that a "race war" is imminent, fueled by a conspiracy of hidden, evil powers. Most in the racist movement envision the future as an armed struggle between white Aryans and all other races. Whites, they insist, must prepare themselves for this inevitability by practicing techniques of survivalism and paramilitary training. Many racists thus maintain a substantial cache of foodstuffs, along with emergency medical supplies, water, guns, and ammunition in remote rural hideouts. The cities, they imagine, will be under the control of armed bands of African Americans, Hispanics, and other peoples of color, all operating under the careful watch of their Jewish overlords.

Moreover, belief in male domination and female subordination is common. White Christian women are rarely portrayed in the literature of organized racism except as ethereal Nordic goddesses, supporters of male racial warriors, or bearers of the next generation of Aryans. The procreative abilities of white Christian women are particularly heralded because of the emphasis in racist propaganda on securing numerical advantage for the next Aryan generation and safeguarding the purity of Aryan bloodlines. Women of color, Jewish women, and other non-Christian women are portrayed in racist literature either as irresponsible "baby breeders" or as sexual seductresses. Thus, racist propaganda tends to be strongly pro-natalist for whites but anti-natalist for people of color. Racist groups, for example, often support access to abortion for Jewish women and women of color while strongly opposing abortion for white, Aryan women.

Racist propaganda also warns the supposed unwary Aryan man that sexually aggressive Jewish women and women of color threaten his racial standing and his self-respect. Despite the increasing numbers of women racial activists, participation in organized racism is consistently depicted as the purview of Aryan men, with Aryan women in the background or missing altogether. Exaggerated stereotypic traits of masculinity, especially physical strength and aggression, are presented as both the prerequisite and the consequence of white racist activism. It is manly traits that are said to equip the Aryan racial warrior; battling the enemies of Aryan civilization is said to heighten masculinity. White women have little obvious place in the new racial order promoted in such propaganda.

Ideological unanimity across organized racist groups exists even in some aspects of racist ideology that have changed substantially over time. In the past, nationalism and xenophobia were staples of the propaganda of racist groups like the Ku Klux Klan, which argued for American superiority and warned that immigration from other nations posed a threat to the position of the United States in the world order. Such beliefs now are less common among racist groups, many of which have shifted their concerns from national loyalty to racial allegiance, largely in the attempt to foster links with their counterparts in Europe and southern Africa.

Comparison of Personal and Organizational Ideologies

The official positions of white and Aryan supremacist organizations are broadcast in newsletters, flyers, cartoons, and books and through computer bulletin boards and Internet sites. We know much less about the beliefs of individual racist activists. In this section, I compare the organizational propaganda of four groups that include substantial numbers of women members—neo-Nazis, white-power skinheads, Christian Identity sects, and the Ku Klux Klan—with the beliefs of women members of each of these groups as reflected in interview narratives.

Neo-Nazis

Women are highly visible as members and leaders in many of the most violent neo-Nazi groups. These groups, which celebrate Hitler's efforts to exterminate Jews, the disabled, and ethnic and sexual minorities, comprise an estimated one hundred groups and exist in thirty-one states. At least until a recent series of prosecutions and civil cases against the group, the most prominent of these has been the Movement for White Resistance (MWR), which espouses an anticapitalist, anticommunist, anti-elitist, and racist philosophy known as the "third position." MWR claims to take the side of white working people against both race mixing and capitalist exploitation, especially that by corporate elites. It began in the early 1980s with a declaration decrying the fate of the white working class in the era of deindustrialization and calling on Aryan "soldiers" to take up arms to resist. MWR leaders are extremely critical of others on the right, like David Duke and many Klan leaders (whom they see as not radical enough) and the new Christian right (whom they view as brainwashed by religion).

MWR has a female section, called the White Women's Council (WWC), which sees itself as having a definite mission in the white supremacist movement, distinct from that of men. It recruits from among young female skinheads and neo-Nazi sympathizers, and its newspaper, "Sister/Comrade," proclaims the centrality of "courageous young women warriors" to the struggle for white victory, searching for historical examples of female role models among Nazi leaders or mythical Viking warriors.

Although it is closely tied to MWR, the White Women's Council emphasizes the creation of an Aryan culture and a self-sufficient economic and social support and educational system as key to the future of the Aryan race. To that end, it publishes an Aryan parents' newsletter and Aryan coloring books, sponsors a personals column for Aryan singles and a pen pal exchange for Aryan children, and collects maternity and baby clothing and store coupons for an Aryan bartering exchange— all efforts to forge a white supremacist culture by building on women's traditional role in the family.

Consistent with its anticorporate stance and its concern for the future of the Aryan race, the WWC is also militantly pro-environmental, opposing the logging of old-growth forests and the use of disposable diapers. For the WWC, like many in the neo-Nazi movement, the Aryan future lies in the Pacific Northwest, where they see environmental spoilage as low and racial purity as high. They call for a "Great Northwestern Territorial Imperative," encouraging a paramilitary white supremacist network to colonize the Pacific Northwest as an all-white, all-Aryan homeland and then secede from the United States.

ALICE

Alice, a twenty-seven-year-old woman from Michigan, has been associated with MWR and the WWC for eight years. She initially heard of the group through her older brothers, who were longtime members and who convinced her to join the women's affiliate. While in MWR, Alice met and married Rex, a skinhead who later became peripherally involved in MWR. They have a five-year-old son. Since Rex is currently in prison, serving a sentence for armed assault, Alice has become more heavily involved with the racist movement, and she now sees MWR and WWC as her main source of emotional (and, at times, financial) support.

With her husband incarcerated, Alice is solely responsible for her son and has been unable to pursue her education beyond the G.E.D., but she hopes to begin college after his release. For now, Alice works odd jobs, most recently as a waitress at a local restaurant. Her ultimate occupational goals are uncertain. Since the birth of her child, she sees her life as mainly "getting through daily routines, dealing with society the way it is in my own way."

Alice's beliefs both mirror, and contrast sharply, with those of the Movement of White Resistance and the White Women's Council. Like those groups, Alice favors "separating ourselves from the nonwhites." Indeed, she insists that her interest in racial activism stemmed from her disgust with interracial couples. When asked what she sees as the biggest problems facing society today, Alice quickly lists "race mixing, [interracial] dating, marriage," and, like MWR and WWC, Alice attributes problems in the world to "Jews, NAACP, and the government," although she singles out Jews as the most powerful "because they get the votes." She concurs with the neo-Nazi movement that a race war is coming, although she is less certain about the timing: "I feel that [a race war] is due. I don't know if it's anytime soon. I feel it will be in the future."

Consistent with much racist propaganda, Alice insists that she does not hate other races, she "just chooses not to socialize with them," but when asked her vision for the United States in the future, she presents a scenario that is far less benign:

> I'd like separation ... if we have to live together I'd like punishment handed down to people of different races. I think the future will turn to violence. That's why I'm looking for a mostly white state if possible, a better place.

The most striking difference between Alice's rhetoric and MWR/ WWC propaganda lies in what is missing in Alice's commentary. Nothing in her three-hour interview ever suggested concern over issues of global economics, the decline of the middle class, or corporate ravaging of the environment—issues that are key to MWR/WWC's view of racial politics. More strikingly, Alice holds views on a number of issues that are at odds with some of the basic approaches to racial politics expressed in MWR and WWC propaganda. In contrast to MWR's (and, to a great extent, WWC's) insistence on armed resistance as the only way to avenge the interests of the average white and Aryan citizen, for example, Alice argues for a more cautious, electoral-based approach to racial politics. The best way to change the situation of "Jews, NAACP, and the government" running the world, she insists, is "just to get better people in office and in the political spotlight." Violent confrontation may be a major recruitment tactic of MWR/WWC, but to Alice it is just by "getting the word so people notice" that the racist movement will be built. Alice's emphasis on less violent forms of racial confrontation does not reflect a disagreement with the armed resistance talk of MWR/WWC propaganda. Rather, Alice's concerns are pragmatic, reflecting her situation as a single parent while her husband is in prison. Although she admits that she was initially attracted to MWR/WWC because of its reputation for violent rhetoric, she now insists that overt physical battles such as street fights with African Americans "need to stop, or all our people will be in prison." Taking a longer perspective on the goals of racial politics, Alice cautions that violence will not work because it leads to the incarceration of racial activists, thereby preventing them from influencing their children. However, such differences with MWR/WWC have not lessened her commitment to the organization or to the struggle for white supremacism.

Alice's views on issues of gender similarly reflect her particular life experiences. As such, they draw upon but do not mirror the gender ideology of MWR/WWC. Asked if she had any personal contacts with African Americans, for example, Alice relates a standard racist account of an African American coworker whom she describes as "a typical black male [because] he likes white girls." Contrary to the victimized position of white women relative to African American men in MWR literature, however, Alice argues that "I'm pretty much a bitch to him, I put him in his place." Such sentiments persist in Alice's opinions of the feminist movement, which she criticizes, not for intruding on men's prerogatives as the MWR literature proclaims, but for not being sufficiently assertive with men: "I don't really agree with some of the shit [feminists] say, you know. I think they're too wimpy. They're not strong enough to get along by themselves."

However, Alice by no means embraces a feminist ideology. Her gender identity, like that of many women in the racist movement, is torn between an aggressive assertion of white female privilege against white men and all peoples of color and an equally powerful conviction that the future of white supremacism rests on white women's procreative ability. Being in the WWC, Alice maintains, made her "think about my race more than I ever did and I just want to have babies, babies, babies, to help myself and my race."

Other aspects of Alice's dissension from MWR/WWC positions perhaps reflect a lack of understanding of organizational positions rather than ideological differences. For example, despite the virulent attacks on David Duke that pepper MWR and WWC literature, Alice immediately identifies Duke when asked to name her political heroes. Duke, she insists, "feels the same way I do. . . . He knows what he's talking about, about integration, schooling, the race mixing."

Skinheads

Another significant part of the neo-Nazi movement consists of teenage and young adult skinheads in loosely connected ganglike structures. These encompass an estimated 137 groups in twenty-nine states and number between two thousand and four thousand members. In the past, white-power skinheads were easily recognized by their shaven heads, black military combat boots, and Nazi insignia tattoos. Coached by older white supremacists about the dangers of being so easily recognizable by the police, however, many skinheads today forgo tattoos and skinned heads and essentially disguise themselves as ordinary-looking teenagers. Under such names as "romantic violence," "confederate hammer skins," and "reich skins," skinhead gangs have been responsible for a number of extremely violent assaults (and even murders) of African Americans, immigrants, and those they perceive to be gay men or lesbians.

Young women have been very active in the skinhead movement, particularly on the West Coast, and have been full participants in the movement's brutal practices of violence against racial, ethnic, and sexual minorities and against rival (and even allied) skinhead gangs. The loose confederation of most skinhead groups makes it difficult to assess any common ideological positions aside from their self-proclaimed racism, anti-Semitism, and homophobia, but it is clear that gender is a contested issue in many skinhead gangs. Certainly, virtually all skinhead propaganda projects images of hypermasculinity as central to racial activism. The *Code of the Skinhead,* for example, begins with a quotation from the philosopher Friedrich Nietzsche that "a more manly, warlike age is coming, which will bring valor again into honor!" and movement 'zines (magazines) commonly define skinheads as young men "that love to have fun, beer, and girls (not necessarily in that order)." A statement entitled "I Am the Wife of a Warrior" makes it clear that women's role in racial warfare should be distinctly in the background:

> My vows to my warrior-husband are as strong as fine tempered steel. . . .
> I am subject to long, lonely nights of worry and tears, while my warrior-husband fights our battles. I suffer his defeats, as I celebrate his victories.
> . . . Should he be wounded, I nurse him back to health, so that he can return to the forefront of the battle. I support my warrior-husband in all ways and through all circumstances [because] my warrior-husband fights for me. (Anonymous 1993)

In contrast to the submissive, background image of women in skinhead propaganda, the actual role of women in racist skinhead groups varies considerably. Although women exist as the compliant girlfriends of male skinheads in many groups, a number of women have been prominent as spokespersons for and even as leaders of skinhead groups, and some women have been prominent in the effort to link young skinheads to older, established fascist and racist organizations.

Not surprisingly, such conflicting portrayals of women's place in the movement have provoked considerable conflict. Gender friction among some skinhead gangs has become so intense that female-only "skingirl" gangs have been organized in states as different as California and Tennessee around the dual slogans of "white power" and "woman power."

JANICE

Janice, a twenty-two-year-old skinhead, lives in Seattle. Like many of her counterparts, she described her entry into the skinhead world as more a social than ideological process:

> I met people who were white supremacists, but it didn't faze me. I guess it didn't seem real at that point. It was just a social thing at first, and you met more people. The thing that, how I really started believing, thinking, in that white supremacist sense, it was really through the music. . . . It gives you an identity, it says you're special, you know, because you're white. . . . Once you start listening to the music, becoming familiar with the lyrics, you repeat them, you start to believe them.

Janice's introduction to the world of skinheads followed a predictable pattern of increasing involvement with more experienced skinheads and increasing detachment from outside relationships.

A man I'd had a crush on for a little over a year said to me 'You would look great with a shaved head,' and I said 'OK,' and I shaved my head. And that's when it got really hectic. That's when it all became very real. . . . People I worked with gave me a hard time. . . . My grades started to drop. My parents gave me the ultimate "No more of this." They started to really figure out what was going on [and told me], "You're getting out of here if this really keeps up." So I said to this guy, "Listen, I have nowhere to go" and he said, "Well, you can live with me." So I moved in with him, and we were together about two years.

In reality, the practices of skingirls in Janice's group varied considerably from the prototype displayed in skinhead propaganda. Far from lurking quietly behind skinhead boyfriends, many skingirls adopt both the aggressive stances and the symbolism of their male counterparts. As Janice commented, "You could tell a lot about the caliber of a girl by her tattoos. If she was like a tough fighting type, she had a whole bunch of homemade swastikas and Celtic crosses down her arm, but like the real feminine girls either didn't have any or they had only professional ones."

Janice did not have herself tattooed. Neither did she cultivate the tough street demeanor of other girls in her skinhead group. But it is not accurate to portray Janice's role in the skinhead movement as entirely subservient to male members. Even though she was living with and supported by her skinhead boyfriend, Janice was willing to challenge him, at least on occasion. This was especially true when Janice's relationships outside the skinhead world conflicted with the beliefs of her group. Commenting on her mother's sister, who was openly lesbian, Janice commented that she "didn't really mind . . . [to me] it wasn't really a big issue, [although] to some skins it was a huge issue." Specifically, she recalled that her boyfriend was "appalled" when he found out that she had been frequenting a local gay and lesbian dance club.

> I had gone in there a few times and when he found out he went nuts. But it wasn't that big of an issue at all for me. . . . Hey, to each their own. It's not something I'd be into.

Christian Identity

Christian Identity is a quasi-theological network of between two and three hundred churches across the nation linked by Christian Identity Family Bible Camps and radio shows that preach that Anglo-Saxons are the lost tribe of Israel and that Jews and African Americans and other people of color are inferiors sent to earth as a scourge from God. According to Christian Identity philosophy, when Eve fell from grace in the Garden of Eden she was impregnated with two seeds. From Adam's seed came Abel and the white race. From Satan's seed came Cain, Jews, and the nonwhite races, resulting in eternal racial conflict. Christian Identity targets both Jews and Catholics, peddling the viciously anti-Semitic tract the "Protocols of the Elders of Zion" through its newsletters and denouncing Catholicism as a "cult-religion." Christian Identity adherents also strongly oppose traditional Protestantism, even Christian fundamentalism, which they regard as eschewing direct action in favor of waiting for God's intervention. In contrast, Christian Identity insists that Aryans are the chosen people of God and that most government is illegal. They support home schooling to counteract the effects of "godless teachers" in public schools, regard abortion as promoted by Jewish doctors, and support a prohibition on racial intermarriage.

Although Christian Identity differs somewhat from other Aryan groups—seeing, for example, the Bible rather than Hitler's *Mein Kampf* as the source of its ideology—it is tied to other sectors of the white supremacist movement. These include a white supremacist prison network called the Aryan Brotherhood, the Aryan Nations (the infamous Idaho compound that sponsors the annual "Aryan World Congress"), and the Order, a violent underground terrorist network responsible for a string of bank robberies, bombings, and assassinations in the mid-1980s.

Christian Identity includes both men and women, but claims that Biblical tradition and moral righteousness prescribe a narrow role for women in the movement and a rigidly patriarchal gender ideology that opposes even women's suffrage. Christian Identity women—like the columnist Cheri Peters, wife of the Christian Identity leader Pete Peters—promote wifely submissiveness in the family and a role in Christian white supremacy that is supportive of political agendas defined by and directed by movement men. In her column "For Women Only" and in her Denver radio broadcasts, Cheri encourages women "to fulfill their ancient roles as wives and mothers," arguing that "a Christ-like woman wants a man who takes the lead and shows male dominance."

SHIRLEY

A twenty-four-year-old adherent of Christian Identity, Shirley lives with a group of other Christian Identity members in a remote rural area outside Wichita. Recently married, she has no children. Like many other young Christian Identity adherents, Shirley's commitment to Christian Identity started at an early age when her parents became involved with a Christian Identity group in rural Montana. From that point, Shirley's life was increasingly shaped by Christian Identity precepts. Her schooling, religious education, employment, and social life have been largely within Christian Identity–affiliated institutions, including schools, churches, and youth groups. Shirley has a high school diploma, but her plans for future education are complicated by what she fears would be the "indoctrination" she would receive in a secular university.

More so than Alice or Janice, Shirley's own beliefs and actions mirror the Christian Identity organizations to which she has pledged her life. In part this reflects Shirley's early socialization into Christian Identity ideologies. But it also reflects the all-encompassing nature of many Christian Identity groups, in which members are neither encouraged nor find it necessary to have significant contact with the non-Christian Identity world. Shirley avidly embraces both the white and the Christian supremacist beliefs of Christian Identity and its confrontational tactics. When asked what she liked about Christian Identity, for example, Shirley answered that she appreciated "its aggressive stance toward the need to have a movement for white people in America." Asked for her personal political hero, Shirley picked the Confederate Civil War general Robert E. Lee for what she regarded as his great military accomplishments against formidable odds.

Shirley's one dissension from the ideological propaganda of Christian Identity, surprisingly, centered around the idea of childbearing as an act of racial conviction for women. She stated that although she'd "like to have a few children," she was not interested in raising a large family of children for the movement. Moreover, Shirley's agreement with the doctrines of Christian Identity was based on a very shallow understanding of its philosophy. Asked to explain the beliefs or theology of Christian Identity, Shirley was unable to do more than parrot a few simple slogans. Like other Christian Identity adherents, Shirley evidenced a lack of dissent from the complex and convoluted principles of Christian Identity that stemmed more from a lack of knowledge than from considered agreement.

Ku Klux Klans

The Ku Klux Klan is not an organization per se but a name under which operate perhaps a dozen competing racist organizations organized in seventy-five factions in twenty-nine states. These groups have around ten thousand or so hard-core followers and five or ten times as many sympathizers. In recent years, Klan membership has declined, due both to bitter factional conflict between competing Klan leaders and to successful civil lawsuits against Klan chapters.

Today's Klans, like their predecessors, are deeply racist and anti-Semitic. They also target ethnic minorities, particularly Asians and Asian-Americans, and gay men and lesbians. Unlike earlier waves of Ku Klux Klan activity, however, modern Klans rarely promote anti-Catholicism, seeing Catholics as largely assimilated within white Aryan society.

In the Klan's effort to rebuild, it has targeted women and children as a main recruiting pool. Klan recruitment efforts now are likely to include social gatherings, family picnics, and volleyball tournaments, in addition to the traditional cross burnings and public marches. Many of the Klans also promise women the opportunity for leadership in the Klan, although the majority of Klan leaders continue to be men. Most contemporary Klan women leaders continue to be drawn from the families of male Klan leaders, but there is considerable pressure from women within the Klan to change this practice.

LUCY

A thirty-year-old Klanswoman from a small town in Tennessee, Lucy is a high school graduate. She has no concrete plans to attend college but expresses the vague desire to get a degree that would allow her to do child care work. She currently works as a cashier at a local video store. She is married but has no children.

Lucy's interest in the Ku Klux Klan began in high school when she was convinced to attend a Klan meeting by her cousin, a recent Klan recruit. At the meeting, Lucy says she was impressed by "people [who] could stand up for themselves and not be ashamed of it and really act on what they believe in." Through her cousin she was then introduced to the regional Klan leader, who convinced her to attend a meeting. Eventually, she decided to join and persuaded her husband to join at the same time.

> I was more for it, but he kind of wanted to join, but he just wouldn't, you know, put that last foot forward, and when I made my decision, he said, "What are you going to do?" And I said, "Well, I'm going to join." And he said, "Are you sure?" and I said, "Yeah, you can join with me." And

he was like, "Well, if you join, I'll join." But he wanted to, so I can't really say that I made the final decision, but with me joining, it let him take his last foot and step in the doorway.

Lucy's view of her Klan echoes the fraudulent message that some modern Klan leaders seek to project: that the Klan is a benign organization supporting the interests of white people. As Lucy maintains, "It's no different than being in Girl Scouts or anything else. It's just being involved in something you really want to do . . . just like a big family." Consistent with the Klan's recent efforts to deny its racist views, Lucy insists that her Klan membership does not mean that she is racially bigoted or even intolerant of other religions or sexual orientations:

In school my best friend was black . . . . I've got a family member that's bisexual, and the Klan's supposed to be against that. So you know it's just the person, not the race, not the religion. If I'm gonna like you, I like you for who you are, not what you are.

Lucy's departure from the Klan's ideology is largely around issues of gender. Like many Klanswomen, she expresses both privately and publicly a dissatisfaction with the limited role that women are allowed to play in Klan decision making and in Klan actions. But Lucy's gendered analysis goes beyond simple disagreement with organizational politics. Rather, Lucy argues that the very ways in which racial struggles are posed—by the Klan as well as by African Americans and other minorities—reflect a male pursuit of aggressive combat that overrides political and even racial considerations. In Lucy's view, racist violence is necessary but often misplaced. Violence lacks a strategic focus in many circumstances, she argues, because it is propelled by men's desires for physical superiority rather than by political concerns.

The biggest issue is probably the minorities and the whites. They've all gotta prove something, and that's the way they think they gotta prove it. "Oh, I'm a white guy and I beat up a black man yesterday. . . ." And you know, it's a power kick. They all want it and that's the way they think they gotta go about getting it.

Conclusion

This excursion into the biographies and beliefs of four women who are active in organized racist groups is instructive on several levels. First, it suggests that the ideologies of racist organizations are not fully encompassed within the texts of organizational documents. Women racist group members—even deeply committed and long-term activists—use the messages of organized racism in ways that do not necessarily parallel organizational positions. Such a discrepancy is not surprising. Indeed, it is this disjuncture between individual belief and organizational ideology that has allowed organized racism to broaden its organizational base beyond its traditional enclave of lower-middle-class, older, rural Southern male supporters and to build membership among women, the young, and the middle class without fundamentally changing its doctrines on gender, sexuality, and the nature of the racist agenda.

Second, at least among women racist activists, the points of disagreement with racist organizational doctrine fall within a relatively narrow range. Women are more likely to dissent on issues of gender, childbearing, and family life than on other issues. This largely reflects the constricted organizational role assigned to women in many parts of the white supremacist movement, which makes these concerns paramount to personal identity and activities within racist groups. On a broader level, however, this disparity suggests that adherence to racist groups may not require agreement with the groups' positions on issues of most immediate personal concern to members.

Finally, this comparison indicates the remarkable lack of understanding of organizational doctrine that exists among many members of organized racist groups. Indeed, it is impossible to fully assess the depth of ideological agreement among members because few of them command more than a shallow understanding of major organizational positions. Thus, the ideological engagement of members with white supremacist groups may be far less comprehensive—and reflect far lower levels of personal commitment—than is commonly understood. Differences between organizational propaganda and personal belief therefore provide a possible avenue for the recruitment of members *out* of the white supremacist movement.

NOTES

1. This and subsequent interview quotations are from interviews conducted by the author in 1994 and 1995.

2. The advantages of longitudinal studies of right-wing groups are discussed in Aho, *The Politics* (1990).

BIBLIOGRAPHY

Aho, James. 1990. *The Politics of Righteousness: Idaho Christian Patriotism.* Seattle: University of Washington Press.

Anonymous. N.d. *The True History of "The Holocaust"* (no place, no publisher), cover, 1, distributed by the Missouri Knights of Gladstone, Missouri.

Anonymous. 1993. *I Am the Wife of a Warrior* (no place, no publisher), 1.

Barkun, Michael. 1994. *Religion and the Racist Right: The Origins of the Christian Identity Movement.* Chapel Hill: University of North Carolina Press.

Blee, Kathleen M. 1997. "Mothers in Race-Hate Movements," in Alexis Jetter, Anneliese Orleck, and Diana Taylor (eds.), *The Politics of Motherhood: Activist Voices from Left to Right.* Hanover, N.H.: University Press of New England.

————. 1996a. "Becoming a Racist: Women in Contemporary Ku Klux Klan and Neo-Nazi Groups." *Gender & Society* 10 (December): 680–702.

————. 1996b. "Engendering Conspiracy: Women in Rightist Theories and Movements," in Ward (ed.), *Conspiracies,* 91–112.

————. 1993. "Evidence, Empathy and Ethics: Lessons from Oral Histories of the Klan," *Journal of American History* 80: 596–606.

Brustein, William. 1993. "The Rise of Xenophobic Movements in Contemporary Europe and the U.S." (Unpublished paper, University of Minnesota).

Christensen, Loren. 1994. *Skinhead Street Gang.* Boulder, Colo.: Paladin Press.

Ezekiel, Raphael. 1995. *The Racist Mind: Portraits of American Neo Nazis and Klansmen.* New York: Viking.

Goldberg, David T. 1990. "The Social Formation of Racist Discourse," in David T. Goldberg (ed.), *Anatomy of Racism.* Minneapolis: University of Minnesota Press.

Hamm, Mark S. 1993. *American Skinheads: The Criminology and Control of Hate Crime.* New York: Praeger.

Levin, Jack, and Jack McDevitt. 1993. *Hate Crimes: The Rising Tide of Bigotry and Bloodshed.* New York: Plenum.

Ridgeway, James. 1990. *Blood in the Face: The Ku Klux Klan, Aryan Nations, Nazi Skinheads, and the Rise of a New White Culture.* New York: Thunder's Mouth Press.

Ward, Eric (ed.). 1996. *Conspiracies: Real Grievances, Paranoia and Mass Movement.* Seattle: PPB.

Weinberg, Leonard. 1993. "The American Radical Right: Exit, Voice and Violence," in Peter H. Merkl and Leonard Weinberg (eds.), *Encounters with the Contemporary Radical Right*. Boulder: Westview.

Wetherell, Margaret, and Jonathan Potter. 1992. *Mapping the Language of Racism: Discourse and the Legitimation of Exploitation*. New York: Columbia University Press.

Chapter Ten

Report from Seneca
(1985)

Cynthia Costello and Amy Dru Stanley

> You can't kill the spirit
> She is like a mountain
> Old and strong
> She goes on and on

To this refrain, 2,000 women assembled at the Seneca Army Depot on August 1, 1983, to protest NATO deployment of first-strike nuclear weapons in Europe. Their verse testifies to the enduring character of feminist activism, the stubborn conviction that sustains women's resistance to militarism at Seneca, as throughout the world.

The Seneca Army Depot is located in Seneca County, New York, tucked away in the rolling farmland of the Finger Lakes region. The depot serves as a storage site for nuclear weapons and is also the departure point for U.S. nuclear missiles bound for Europe. Next to the depot, feminists have built a peace camp, the "Women's Encampment for a Future with Peace and Justice," following the example of British women who, in 1981, founded a peace camp beside the NATO base at Greenham Common, England. At Seneca, as at Greenham Common, the goal is not simply to expose and protest the threat of nuclear war and nuclear weapons. Women's peace camps seek to intervene directly—to block the deployment of 572 Cruise and Pershing II missiles in Great Britain, Italy, West Germany, Belgium, and the Netherlands which began in 1983 and is scheduled to continue through 1988.

The August 1 demonstration marked the culmination of a month-long protest during which some 150 women occupied the Seneca encampment on a daily basis, maintaining a constant vigil at the army depot, conducting outreach activities in the local area, and engaging in acts of civil disobedience on military property. The summer protests set the stage for a worldwide peace action—an International Day of Protest—on October 22, 1983. A month later, however, despite the rising tide of the international peace movement, the first missiles were installed in Europe on schedule. By the end of 1984, according to the Center for Defense Information, at least 118 nuclear missiles had been deployed in European NATO bases: fifty-four Pershing II's at the rate of one per week in West Germany; forty-eight Cruise missiles in Britain; and sixteen Cruise missiles in Italy. Yet even as the flow of weapons proceeds unchecked, women peace activists, at Seneca, at Greenham Common, and elsewhere, have refused to resign their posts beside military bases. Since the summer of 1983, women have occupied the Seneca encampment continuously.

This account of the origins of the Seneca encampment focuses on the mass demonstration of August 1, 1983, and offers a firsthand narrative of the events, written directly after the demonstration. Our purpose here is less to evaluate the record of Seneca from the long view of the international peace movement than to provide a more immediate, detailed portrait of feminist disarmament politics. August 1, 1983, has become a point of reference for female nonviolent resistance, a model for antinuclear protest. Yet the Seneca demonstration also revealed deep rifts among feminists, and between the women's peace camp and the local community. These rifts, involving differences over sexuality, patriotism, and feminist separatism, continue to divide the women's movement. They also shadow and threaten to dissolve the coherence of feminist peace initiatives.

The seeds of the Seneca encampment were first planted at a Global Feminist Disarmament Conference in June, 1982. The following spring, the Women's International League for Peace and Freedom announced that an encampment would begin in July, 1983, and run through that autumn. Together, American and Canadian feminists organized the peace camp—purchasing a fifty-one-acre site, raising funds, coordinating outreach activities, and educating themselves about the methods and legal implications of civil disobedience. Meetings were open, and the organizers were committed to collective decision making through consensus. Conceived in sisterhood with women's peace camps in Europe, the Seneca camp also drew on the experiences of the disarmament, antinuclear, and feminist peace efforts within the United States—in particular, the Women's Pentagon Actions; the Women's Strike for Peace; the Upstate (New York) Feminist Peace Alliance; and, in the Seneca vicinity, the Finger Lakes Peace Alliance.

For women, the symbolic significance of Seneca as a place of protest stemmed from more than the physical proximity of the army depot; the roots of the encampment reached into the past as well. In Seneca Falls in 1848, American feminists convened the first Women's Rights Convention and issued a Declaration of Sentiments that affirmed women's natural right to civil and political equality. "I could not see what to do or where to begin," wrote Elizabeth Cady Stanton, who presided at the meeting, "my only thought was a public meeting for protest and discussion."

Today a laundromat occupies the site of that historic convention; nonetheless, to an uncanny degree, the principles of the nineteenth-century women's movement infuse the peace encampment. Where Stanton propounded the need for an independent women's movement— "Woman alone," she said, "can understand her own degradation. Man cannot speak for her"—more than a century later feminists at Seneca defend the integrity of exclusively female peace actions and stress the value of women's perspective. As one woman put it, "An action of this length without men allows for creativity and a community unique within the American peace networks, a totally new direction emerging from the acknowledgment of women's experience." "To me," said another, "it is a vast statement . . . no longer will women sit back and allow men to make the decisions alone which affect the entire globe." The encampment challenges violence, feminists contend, "in a way that affirms our vision of a nonexploitive, nonauthoritarian, nonsexist, nonarmed future." Seneca prefigures such a future, free of psychological as well as physical forms of domination.

Precisely because it embodies the ideal of an alternative feminist experience, Seneca differs from previous women's disarmament actions in the United States. Seneca is a community of feminists, where women not only enact peaceful protest but also form close bonds and follow the daily routines of subsistence—eating, cleaning, cooking, mending—all against the backdrop of the adjacent military depot. The action is more than symbolic. By occupying land, by endowing the site with the peaceful force of their collective presence, feminists transform the conflict between nurturance and militarism from an abstraction into a lived reality.

Yet the values of the feminist community have been seen in a different light by residents of the small farming towns in Seneca County. For many townspeople, the sudden female influx is unwelcome, intrusive. At issue is not simply the legitimacy of nuclear arms or even entitlement to the land surrounding the depot but a more elementary question—the *propriety* of women's conduct. Unattached to family, seemingly unencumbered by jobs, the unfamiliar gathering of women does not conform to the social conventions of the rural farming district. The encampment's cultural aspects are most controversial: the exclusively female character; the communal practices; the close ties that flourish among women; and the freedom of lifestyle and sexual preference. If Seneca epitomizes a distinctive feminist vision, the content of that vision, particularly as regards sexuality, has proved confusing and alarming to local inhabitants. Unintentionally, the peace camp has disrupted townspeople's sense of authority over their community. Paradoxically, the values that underlie feminist antimilitarism—the commitment to creating nonhierarchical, life-sustaining, female communities—have enmeshed the encampment in conflict with the local population.

Saturday, July 30, 1983

Upon arriving at the main gate of the Seneca Army Depot, one was greeted with the sight of feminists and townspeople lined up uneasily under the watchful eyes of military police. Groups of local residents— indignant women, swaggering young men, parents with curious children—had turned out to jeer at the women protesters, punctuating their lurid threats with gestures of physical abuse. The main gate, which is the central focus of women's peace actions, lies directly on the route to the peace camp. For newcomers, it was a vivid introduction to the Seneca protest.

In contrast, two miles away, a flower and rock garden in the shape of a women's symbol marked the entrance to the women's peace camp. At the end of a rough dirt drive, an informal welcoming committee greeted new arrivals. By bus and by car, women arrived from across the United States and Canada, and from as far away as Germany, France, and

Australia. Most were white women; many were lesbians; several were elderly; some brought children. Very few were accompanied by men. Many belonged to disarmament church groups or feminist peace organizations.

In the main reception area of the women's camp, an old white farmhouse served as headquarters. Farther away, on uncultivated fields, women pitched tents and lean-tos for living quarters. A chain-link fence overhung with barbed wire formed a border along one side of the encampment—part of an unbroken barrier that circled the perimeter of the army depot, sealing off military property from the women's camp. In the reception area, men helped with support work but did not enter into the life of the camp itself. Inside the camp, signs of "women's work" were highly visible: a wooden pavilion to house meetings, ramps for disabled women, water lines, plastic outhouses, open-pit hearths, and a small vegetable garden. Each woman contributed $7 to meet the costs of the camp, including a nightly meal, and volunteered for work tasks: childcare, cooking, security, garbage pickup, and latrine maintenance. A series of daily workshops explored topics of concern to feminists, from health to racism to United States intervention in Central America. No uniform experience or single set of assumptions, beyond a broadly defined commitment to disarmament and feminism, united the women at Seneca. No particular political belief, religion, or lifestyle prevailed.

The encampment, like the depot, lies in the southern tip of Seneca County, adjacent to a handful of small farm towns—Romulus, Ovid, Varick, Waterloo, Seneca Falls, and Fayette. The total population of Seneca County is 34,000. The region is depressed economically, and the annual median income for a family is less than $16,500. In the southern part of the county the depot is a major source of employment. Most residents are conservative Republicans who consider themselves patriotic Americans.

More than any other single issue, the role of lesbianism at the encampment excited the fears as well as the prurient curiosities of Seneca County residents. Townspeople bearing American flags lingered at the camp to ogle the women, eager for a glimpse of the feminist way of life. "Nuke the dykes," they screamed, "Lesbian-communists go home." At the encampment lesbianism was neither expressly promoted nor in any way discouraged: it was viewed less as a formal concern of the camp than as a matter of personal choice. Yet at the same time, feminists at Seneca most emphatically recognized the defense of sexual freedom and the protection of gay rights as inseparable from the pursuit of noncoercive, peaceful coexistence. Accordingly, a vocal minority of townspeople reached the conclusion that lesbianism was the real meaning of Seneca—a belief that magnified local antagonism. Lesbianism became the focus of public outcry, a convenient target for allegations that the peace camp violated standards of heterosexuality, domesticity, civic pride, and moral decency.

A small, if highly visible, contingent of residents was overtly hostile. Among the majority, however, the most typical response appeared to be ambivalence. Others even returned women's outreach efforts: a local merchant donated pots and utensils; an Amish woman came regularly with food. But as the encampment expanded, encounters between feminists and townspeople grew increasingly strained.

Earlier in the day, in nearby Waterloo, a feminist peace march had exploded into a struggle among women protesters, townspeople, and police. Townspeople attempted to block the progress of the march, but the women refused to turn aside. Intervening, the police ordered the women to disperse. When fifty-three women resisted the order, they were arrested and jailed. Graphic reports of the skirmish, embellished with each telling, circulated throughout the encampment, underscoring a rising sense of anxiety. By evening, Waterloo was viewed as an ominous rehearsal for the mass protest on August 1. Suddenly persuaded that they had underestimated the depth of local resentment, feminists convened to suspend the vigil at the depot and to reconsider plans for August 1.

Sunday, July 31, 1983

It rained intermittently as women awoke to begin a day of meetings and training for the August 1 protest. An army helicopter circled above surveying the encampment. Below women ate and washed in open sinks behind the cooking area. Despite the rain, it was hot. The scene might have been an old-fashioned state fair—bustling activity, grassy fields, spreading trees, informal groupings, brightly colored clothing. But the serenity was broken by reporters looking for commentary on the arrests at Waterloo and the plans for the mass rally, and by the repeated intrusions of belligerent townspeople. One middle-aged man stationed himself at the entrance to the camp and propped up a large placard in front of his van: "Did The Russians Buy Your Land?" Behind the farmhouse, women gathered to paint a rejoining poster, "Bread Not Bombs," and to build model missiles.

The structure of authority within the encampment was democratic and unobtrusive. Along with a small paid staff, "affinity groups" served as the central unit of organization. Composed of five to fifteen women, the affinity group acted as both a support group and a decision-making body. Meetings of the whole considered policy affecting the entire encampment. A poster in what was known as the "nonregistration" tent announced the schedule for the day: meetings of affinity groups, training sessions for civil disobedience, a general meeting to complete the plans for the demonstration.

Three strategic issues preoccupied women throughout the day: use of the American flag, the forms of protest, and the question of lesbian visibility. Shaken by the example of Waterloo, feminists sought to discover, in each instance, a way to appease townspeople without betraying their own convictions. Many women stressed the urgency of highlighting shared values and characteristics, of cultivating a common perspective. According to this argument, the more controversial ideals of the encampment had to be muted in order to achieve a broader appeal. But if some women viewed the breach between townspeople and feminists as the governing consideration, others objected that such a position would, in practice, subvert both the specific ends and the animating ideals of the peace camp. Within this debate (which was less clearly drawn at the time), the controversies over strategy unfolded.

A month earlier, on July 4, a local man had offered the encampment an American flag. The gesture may have been meant either as an act of genuine courtesy or as a deliberate provocation. Whatever his motives, feminists rejected the flag. To townspeople, this refusal amounted not simply to a breach of etiquette but to an unwarranted act of hostility. During the following weeks, the incident was recounted widely and came to figure prominently in the local antipathy toward the camp. To make amends, some feminists proposed that on August 1 the entire encampment hold American flags aloft. But others found such an idea intolerable. It was not only that the last-minute patriotic gesture would prove ineffectual, they said; more importantly, as an emblem of imperialism, the flag was entirely inconsistent with the principles of feminist antimilitarism. Unable to achieve consensus on the use of the flag, the encampment instead resolved that the selection of a banner should be a personal one. In keeping with the camp's dedication to tolerance and pluralism among women, each was to obey the dictates of individual conscience where symbolic displays of national allegiance were concerned.

The dispute over the forms of protest summoned up an ostensibly different set of issues: feminist separatism; the characteristic "voice" of feminism; and the notion of an "innate" female sensibility. These issues, unlike concerns of patriotism, are considered central to the self-definition of the women's movement and have long been a focal point of disagreement among feminists. Yet in the context of the peace camp, the divisions internal to feminism closely reiterated the dilemma raised by the flag.

Several days earlier, the encampment had collectively adopted a five-stage scenario dramatizing women's horror at the prospect of nuclear destruction. Borrowing from the techniques of guerrilla theater, such ritual is a common feature of feminist peace protest. Through vivid gesture, creative props, and exaggerated expression, women were to enact the successive psycho-emotional states of denial, recognition, grief, rage, and empowerment. But on the eve of the mass demonstration, a group of women challenged the assumptions of the ritual. By enacting a drama predicated on nonrational, affective principles—what are often termed "female principles"—might not feminists inadvertently reinforce division based on gender stereotypes? That is, if the feminist perspective were narrowly defined as intuitive in essence and emotive in form, rational analysis, so they contended, could well become the exclusive province of men. Such an emphasis would simply lend credence to simplistic notions of women's innate capacities which in turn become justifications for restricting women's roles. The even more decisive argument against staging the scenario, however, turned on the effect of the drama on the local community—the likelihood that the ritual would appear incomprehensible and bizarre. Many women feared that in such a charged atmosphere the drama would confirm suspicions that the encampment housed a cult. They again struck a compromise by adopting a modified, toned-down version of the scenario.

Finally, the issue of lesbian visibility presented the Seneca encampment with the most perplexing dilemma. On this most volatile of questions—whether to stress or understate the lesbian presence at the peace camp—feminists were unable to achieve a compromise between the opposing values of the encampment and the community. The impasse

developed over the phrasing of a press statement to be issued on August
1. Several women had proposed a conciliatory statement.

> We are women who are old and young,
> black and white, mothers and wives. . . .
> We come to Seneca County not to
> threaten the people who live here but
> to peacefully protest the deadly nuclear
> weapons at the Seneca Army Depot.

But if the statement stressed marriage and motherhood, it failed to
mention, as one woman pointed out to a meeting of the whole, the
lesbian identification of many members of the encampment. Her observation evoked murmured commentary, hasty disclaimers, and explanations, but no sustained debate. The encampment never systematically
addressed the meaning of the omission the prejudices and denials
reflected in the press release; its evasion of the question of sexuality; its
equivocation over the status of lesbianism at the peace camp. Nor was
the statement revised. Rather, the Seneca feminists agreed to issue it as it
was, turning away from a series of provocative questions: was it really
the case that such efforts to establish common ground with the local
community actually convinced skeptics that feminists at Seneca were
typical Americans? Did the women seek to convey such an image?
Even if effective, did such self-definition not distort women's experience,
undermining the encampment's commitment to defending the rights of
all women, whether lesbian or heterosexual?

Feminists might easily have rewritten the release to acknowledge
lesbianism explicitly or, at the very least, to allude more obliquely to
diversity in lifestyles and relationships. Or, alternatively, if differences
over phrasing proved irreconcilable, they might have dropped the ques-
tionable passage altogether. But by failing to explore either alternative,
the encampment retreated from both the defense of sexual freedom and
the process of compromise. In this instance, the effort to court local
sympathy ended in the suppression of lesbian identity.

The strategic disputes implicitly required women at Seneca to evaluate
the convictions that united them as feminist peace activists. They found
that they differed—over allegiance to the state, over the rationalist/
intuitive split in feminist politics, and over sexuality. But for the most
part, they addressed these divisions in a preliminary and tentative way.

And where neither a pluralistic compromise nor a mediating alternative was readily discovered, feminists sidestepped divisive debate. The more pressing task was to organize a demonstration.

Monday, August 1, 1983

The demonstration was scheduled to begin at noon. But at 8:00 A.M., women began to gather in the parking area of a state park near the peace camp. The parking area was the starting point for the two-mile march to the depot gate where the rituals of protest were to be staged. A caravan of chartered buses arrived, dissipating fears that the rain, together with news reports of local harassment, might inhibit others from joining the protest. Women carrying every sort of flag, banner, puppet, and placard, burdened by raincoats and galoshes, with plastic garbage bags draped over their heads, milled about the parking area exchanging advice and encouragement, while "peace keepers" assigned to monitor the demonstration detailed final instructions. A flock of reporters questioned women about their expectations for the day. But no townspeople were present. To protesters, this seemed to suggest that conflict might be avoided. Across the expanse of the parking area, small circles of feminists began to sing, prompting a chorus of the whole.

In lines, five abreast, women marched on to state highway 96A. A gray-haired woman led the procession. Behind her, two Buddhist nuns with shaven heads, dressed in flowing robes, sounded a rhythmic drumbeat. Singing, praying, chanting, two thousand women followed in continuous rows that disappeared into the surrounding fields of corn and wheat. But within an hour police halted the march. Restive townspeople were massed at the depot gate, according to the police, and until they were quieted and order restored the march could not proceed. Women caucused in clusters and finally sat on the pavement. They shared canteens of water and sweated under the afternoon sun that had emerged from the cloud cover. An hour later, police told them to proceed. By midafternoon the police had interrupted the procession for the fourth time. Tired, hot, impatient with the repeated delays, women disputed whether to challenge the order and then, on impulse, surged forward. The police yielded. A hundred yards from the depot gate, members of the male support staff met the women with water, sandwiches, and fruit.

Over 250 townspeople waited at the depot gate. Police armed with guns and billy clubs lined up between advancing protesters and towns-people. Undaunted by the spectacle, some feminists grinned at the hel-meted officers and presented them with flowers. Others averted their eyes and refused to acknowledge the police presence.

Shielded by a chain of monitors, small groups of women edged closer to the chain-link fence of the depot. Behind it, at least two dozen soldiers stood impassively in full combat dress. Townspeople maintained a per-sistent chant: "Go home, damn queers, go home." The drone of an army helicopter overhead briefly muted the discordant screams, songs, and chants.

As if in slow motion, women began to enact the rituals of protest. With deliberate, exaggerated gestures, they advanced to the gate. Per-forming their assigned parts, they strung up banners, attached signs to the gate, and, laying a female claim to military property, wove fabric through the fence in intricate webs—a symbol of feminist unity and human interdependence. Seven women held hands in a circle. "The earth is our mother," they sang, "save the earth. The earth is our mother; she gave us birth." Near the gate another group with painted faces carried a net of black crepe while wailing in grief at the prospect of nuclear war. They chanted, tears streaming from the eyes of some, "We hate your weapons. We will not let you destroy us."

Civil disobedience began at a signal from the monitors. Individually, or in groups attached by strands of colored cloth, women scaled the seven-foot fence. Some paused on top, purposely inviting the media and military photographers to document their actions. "This one's for my mother," one woman cried. Others grimaced and gestured at the military police. Townspeople continued to howl imaginative variations on a single theme, "Queers. Nuke them till they glow." In the course of the day, 242 women committed civil disobedience.

By sundown, most women had returned to the encampment. Those who had come for the August 1 protest only collected their belongings and exchanged addresses. At the depot gate, a small group of feminists, townspeople, and police remained posted through the night.

Today, nearly two years after the August 1 demonstration, the Seneca encampment has become a landmark in the feminist peace movement. Sister actions include protests against Project ELF at Clam Lake, Wis-consin; against arms production at Honeywell Corporation in Minneap-olis; and against the presidential nuclear sanctuary at Mt. Weather, near

Washington, D.C. A web of women's peace camps extends from Seneca to Minneapolis, Tucson, and Puget Sound. At Seneca, women have installed water, sewage, and electric systems and have secured permanent legal status for the encampment. Although at times their numbers have dwindled to a handful, they continue to organize peaceful protests, to raise funds for the camp, and to sponsor workshops on feminism and disarmament. They focus on long-term projects of outreach that are designed both to connect the camp to the global peace movement and to implant it more firmly in the local community. Newsletters from the encampment report that "local support continues, while harassment has subsided"; that mailings reach 7,000 people; that classes visit from nearby schools and colleges; and that local newspapers run favorable editorials. "We have become a tourist attraction," a newsletter states, "along with the women's museums in Seneca Falls."

During the past two years women have made Seneca into a site of feminist political and cultural education. Yet, in the eyes of those outside the feminist and disarmament constituencies, has the peace camp simultaneously simply become a spectacle, a "tourist attraction," a curiosity to gape at, no different from those on display at women's museums? Museums present the past for contemplation; Seneca was meant to represent the future—through vital, creative, even shocking forms of protest.

In the summer of 1983, the feminist antinuclear protest was of consuming importance to the Seneca community, an object of bitter controversy, not benign contemplation. What has happened to the assembly of indignant townspeople? Why have the tensions that were so evident two years ago disappeared? The newsletters from Seneca do not say whether the truce has been modeled on the type of appeal devised for the August 1 demonstration. Nor do they indicate what, if anything, feminists have exchanged for the decrease in local hostility. Does the truce reflect the reversal of townspeople's original response or rather the muting of feminist ideals? Or is community acceptance perhaps the more mundane consequence of neighborly familiarity?

The terms of the truce will remain opaque until they are explored in relation to divisions among feminists at Seneca. The organization of the August 1 mass protest exposed such divisions. Through controversy—however uneasily stated—over patriotism, feminist separatism, and sexual preference, feminists began to elaborate a framework for addressing townspeople. And in so doing, they began, in practice if not expressly, to decipher the features common to the feminist and peace movements and to refine their understanding of the principles that distinguish and even divide these two movements. But although such concerns were addressed only tentatively in the summer of 1983, in the future feminists must submit them to more candid and searching consideration. The history of the mass demonstration on August 1 reveals at least three critical subjects for debate: the divisions among feminist peace activists; the methods of organizing an ambivalent public; and the relationship between feminist antimilitarism and the international peace movement.

Chapter Eleven

"It's Our Party—Love It or Leave It"

Jane Margolis

In 1997 I sat down with Kathleen Blee to explore my reasons for joining a radical left-wing party in the 1970s and my decision to leave the organization ten years later. What follows is a piece of the conversation that is emblematic of my thinking about this experience. For reasons of confidentiality, the party is not named, and pseudonyms are used. While a left-wing organization provides the context for my story, as a university teacher and researcher I am concerned with silencing and the struggle of individuals against the pressures of groupthink everywhere—in businesses, universities, classrooms, nonprofit organizations, church groups, and families.

What was your political background before joining the party?

Before I begin, I want to emphasize that I am mostly proud of my political past. During college I was an anti–Vietnam War activist. I went to University of California at Berkeley from 1965 to 1969, and I spent most of my time at demonstrations and thinking about social issues. My politics certainly were shaped by a historical time and place—as well by my parents, who were also vocally opposed to the war. During college, my own education seemed irrelevant and immaterial as long as the war was going on. Berkeley was one of the centers of the civil rights and antiwar movements. My mom has always said that I "majored in picketing and minored in leafleting." I, and so many other college students, saw our own lives in a context much larger than ourselves. What mattered to us was our efforts to stop the war, as well as our efforts to counter poverty and inequality. I will always have the image etched in my mind of screaming Vietnamese women, clutching their babies, running from their napalmed villages. I truly believed that business should not continue as usual as long as the war was being waged, and "business as usual" included my own education, as well as that of society.

In my junior year, I organized a course for ten students who received college credit for spending the summer helping to set up a Neighborhood Youth Corps in West Oakland, one of the poorest sections in the Bay Area. The teaching assistant for our course was Mel Newton, brother of the Black Panther leader Huey Newton. All of the students, including me, were white. We lived with African American families throughout the summer. I lived all summer with a family with ten kids. We were given seminars by Black Panther leaders, such as Eldridge Cleaver, Kathleen Cleaver, Bobbie Seale, and Huey Newton. In one seminar Bobbie Seale told us to go back and organize our own community, that we should get out of the black community. It was the first time that the Black Panthers had said this to white activists. That fall Huey Newton had a shootout with the police, and I became involved in his defense committee. I later became critical of the nationalist, black separatist turn taken by the Black Panthers—and of the sexist ways that they treated women.

How did you decide to join a Marxist-Leninist organization?

In 1969, as part of the movement against U.S. involvement in the war in Vietnam, I went to Fort Lewis, Washington, which is one of two army bases in the country from which soldiers were shipped to Vietnam. I was part of a group of antiwar activists who set up antiwar coffeehouses right outside or near the army bases. We showed films, had discussions with GIs about the war, provided antidraft counseling, and helped GIs write and put out an antiwar underground newspaper called Fed-Up. Through this work, I became friends with a GI named David, a Marxist who had been drafted. He said that all my activism was the equivalent of putting a band-aid on a problem. He convinced me that I needed to study the world as a system, that I needed to understand the root of all the injustices, and that I was mindlessly fighting from cause to cause. He offered to teach me Marxism. I will always remember the metaphor he used: Marxism is like a coat rack; once I understood Marxism I would be able to hang any event in the world—past, present, or future—on this coat rack, and it would all make sense. I felt the wonderful possibility of being able to understand history and all that was going on in the world.

David thought that I would really like his wife, Ellen. Both he and his wife were in the party—a Marxist/Leninist/Trotskyist organization. Ellen came up from the Bay Area to meet me, and we had endless conversations about Marxism, capitalism, and the world. We became close friends. We talked incessantly about the centrality of the organized working class for making systematic changes to capitalism, how it was the working class that had the power to bring the war and the system to a halt, and how it was through organized labor that people could see that their mutual interests were linked and that class transcended their different races and gender. To continue my friendship and political work with Ellen, I decided to move to the San Francisco Bay Area. I moved into the party's communal house in Berkeley and got a job at the phone company as a telephone operator. I then began to work with other party sympathizers in the phone company union, the Communication Workers of America [CWA]. I joined the party about a year and a half later.

I was ambivalent for quite a while about joining the party. I could sense the members' total commitment, and I wasn't sure that I wanted to surrender my personal freedom to this group. Most of the party members were much more doctrinaire and sectarian than I was. Some I even found to be eccentric, people whom I would not have befriended in any other circumstance. But I ultimately became convinced that the program and the principles that they adhered to were as right as could be, and I decided to make the commitment. I did believe in the need for a political organization—"vanguard party" was the term—to help link all the different struggles for justice, as opposed to having separate movements. I respected the program of this party. I believed the party stood up for what it felt was right, not what was trendy or politically correct at the time. Members were against black nationalism and black separatism; they were critical of Chairman Mao and Castro (feeling that China or Cuba did not have true socialism). They were against all forms of terrorism. They advocated an integrated international political working class movement. And, on paper and in the leaders' speeches, the party claimed to have a women's organization and a women's journal. As I had been active in women's liberation also, this was particularly important to me. I joined the party and remained a member for ten years.

What were your major activities in the party?

I was one of the trade union activists who were building radical caucuses in the labor unions. I worked for the phone company and was active in the Communications Workers of America. I spent the first two years as a telephone operator and was elected to the executive board of the Oakland branch of the union. Then I had an opportunity to become a telephone installer. The phone company, because of an early affirmative action decree, had to open the jobs to women. They went to their operators first and asked if anyone wanted to be a telephone installer, and I volunteered. So I got trained and spent the next seven years as a telephone installer, one of the first women in the job. I also remained very active in the union.

In the union our caucus was fighting for a more democratic and militant union. We felt that the current leadership was a "sellout." We had a caucus program that connected the little shop floor items to the larger political issue of a Labor Party; we argued that labor would continue to be in a weakened state if we continued to support either the Republicans or the Democrats. Labor, instead, needed to form its own working-class political party. Despite these controversial views, and a lot of anticommunist red baiting that came my way from the union leadership, I was elected by the membership to the executive board of the local union and as a national convention delegate.

How can you describe daily life as a party member?

Party life was all-encompassing and all-involving. We were engaged in constant conversation and thinking about history and current events. I loved this. It felt like our program was continually being confirmed—and even having an impact—even though we were a tiny sectarian organization chanting from the side. But then in the late seventies (maybe it happened earlier and I was not aware of it), being a member of the organization took on a distorted life of its own. We were always on a hunt for programmatic "deviations" in each other and in ourselves. Party members were rewarded for being uncritically loyal. Images of heroic communists, like the German Rosa Luxemburg, who weathered prison, struggled, and were singularly devoted to the party and the cause, were our ideals. We were contemptuous of ourselves and others who didn't live up to this commitment.

Being a member involved total surrender to the aims and needs of the organization. For instance, every week members would turn in copies of our work schedules to the party organizer. She or he would then write members into the party schedule that involved attending meetings during the week, selling the party newspaper early mornings or after work. Our lives were not our own—nor was our money. We turned in every pay stub, and our monthly party pledge was determined based on a sliding-scale formula. If we ever questioned the pledge, our commitment to the party was questioned. Money was equated with party consciousness.

My deep friendships were with party members. I had relationships with people outside the group—people in the union and my old college roommate, for example, whom I would see now and then—but my real friendships were inside the party. It wasn't that the party said I couldn't relate to other people; I didn't have the time. And, the real closeness was with people who shared the same level of commitment and world view. An "us versus them" mind-set—"them" being the world outside the party—pulled party members tightly together.

How did being in the party affect other people's reactions to you?

In 1979 I was elected as a national convention delegate from the San Francisco local to the CWA national convention. President Jimmy Carter had recently used the Taft-Hartley Act to break the miners' strike. His popularity was at an all-time low, but the national leadership of the union had invited him to address the convention. Our caucus held the position that no Democrat could legitimately be in the labor movement or speak at the convention. So I and other caucus members handed out a leaflet saying that Carter should not be at this convention and announcing that I was going to make a speech to this effect. All of the national media were covering the convention.

About forty-five minutes before Carter was scheduled to speak, I was approached by Secret Service agents on the convention floor. They flashed their badges at me and said, "Jane Margolis, come with us." I said, "Who are you?" They said, "Secret Service." I was a union officer, a shop steward, so my first reaction was, "Say what you want to say right here; I'm not going with you without representation." I walked over to one side of the convention floor to speak to some friends who were standing in the visitor's gallery, to tell them what was happening, and the Secret Service grabbed me. They literally dragged me off of the floor of the convention. They handcuffed me and took me up to a room upstairs. When I asked them what I was being held for, they answered: "For threatening the life of the president of the United States." Imagine being erroneously charged with threatening the life of the president! I was petrified. I kept demanding a lawyer. At one point a man walked into the room and I stood up and asked if he was a lawyer. He said "No, Channel 2 News." The Secret Service agent told him to get out of the room, and I told him: "I'm being held because I want to give a speech against Jimmy Carter." Apparently, he went to the head of the command post of the Secret Service and said, "Why are you holding that delegate back there?" They would give no response. He then made quite a ruckus, thank goodness, and after about twenty-five minutes I was suddenly released. They never frisked me. Instead, the Secret Service took away the notebook I was carrying in which I had written my speech criticizing Jimmy Carter's antilabor positions.

When I was released, I and other caucus members held a press conference to announce that I would be suing the Secret Service for violation of free speech. Their attempt had been to hold me away from the convention so I could not give my speech. For the rest of the convention, Secret Service agents followed me around. They waited outside of bathrooms. They said, "Drop the [law]suit." When I was hauled out of the convention, the San Francisco delegation had threatened a walkout until I got back in. But the national union leadership got on the stage and implied that there was something going on that the delegates shouldn't get involved in. The leadership spread rumors that I was going to do something. For the remaining four days, I was barraged with red-baiting and delegates shouting things at me like: "You caused embarrassment to our local. If you're so unhappy, why don't you go back to Russia?"

During the next year I and other caucus members spoke at numerous union meetings and gathered hundreds of signatures in support of my lawsuit. Exactly a year later, the Secret Service settled the case out of court. They wrote me a letter of apology, saying the incident had been a big mistake, and they paid me $3,500. I then signed the entire amount over to the union strike fund. At the next convention our caucus handed out a leaflet that showed a picture of the check signed over to the union strike fund. The same delegates who had red-baited me the year before now came up to me at this convention and said, "Honey, we knew you could do it. If anyone could do it, you could do it," "You showed them," "You should be president of the union." That whole incident was an amazing lesson for me—how quickly people will turn on you. The union leadership spread a rumor. People believed it. Mud sticks. Spines are weak.

What led to your decision to leave the party?

I guess that depends upon whom you talk to. The party leadership will say that I left because the Reagan years had discouraged me and I moved politically away from the belief in the centrality of a Marxist-Leninist party. The latter is true. They will say that I always had been a Menshevik, not a Bolshevik, and a "social worker"—someone who wanted to help people in the here and now more than believing in the need for a worldwide revolution. I believed that I was committed to the party for life. I remember standing on a bridge in Paris, when we had an international conference, with a woman comrade, saying we'd come back here when we're old comrades together.

Throughout the ten years, I had been critical of many of the party's positions, including its reliance on the writings of Lenin and Trotsky about Russia in 1917 as a guide for American political change, and, towards the end, I had more and more distaste for the way life was conducted inside the party. I had a reputation for voicing my opinion even when I disagreed with the leadership. But there was a cycle. I would disagree, I would get beaten down, I would self-criticize, repent, and denounce myself, and then I would get back up and continue to work hard. I worked hard to wrap my mind around the "party line" and to believe in it fully. I tried to reframe whatever party positions I disagreed with so that I wouldn't experience personal or political tension. Questions and reservations brought on intense political struggle inside the organization. We were essentially boxed in. The party leadership supposedly represented the interests of the working class. So, if we strongly disagreed with a party leader or his or her actions, we were attacking the interests of the working class.

In 1980 one of the party leaders became politically upset with a member and pointed a gun at his head. Even though the gun was not loaded, I was outraged when I heard about the incident. I kept talking about it with my close friends in the party. I compared this act to the type of behavior in Stalinist parties. While most of the leadership was also upset with this incident, I was told by the party leadership to cease and desist my campaign to condemn this leader's behavior, but I didn't. One day the national head of the party called. I brought up this issue to him, and he immediately screamed that I was "forming a faction" and slammed down the phone. Five minutes later, I got a call from the political chairman of the local branch accusing me of forming an anti-leadership clique. It was a nightmare from then on. Many lengthy party meetings were held in which party members had to take a position against me and other so-called "cliquists." A national convention was held in which party members rose and chanted, "It's our party—love it or leave it." I remember walking along the sidewalk and almost passing out at the thought of leaving the party. I felt as though the earth was ending. But I got myself together, denounced myself again, and announced my intention to rehabilitate myself. The party leadership said that my political consciousness had been eroded. They told me to resign my position from the union and move to Boston to focus on party work. So after nine years—within nine months of receiving a full pension from the phone company—I was told to leave the phone company, quit my position in the union, and move across the country. I did.

I was a good public speaker, so shortly after I arrived in Boston I was asked to give a talk for the party at Brandeis University about the Reagan years and about revolutionary will. I told the party leadership that I just couldn't speak about revolutionary will because I just didn't have it in me. They insisted. I ended up giving the talk without speaking about revolutionary will—and was again condemned by the party. The leadership told the membership that I was not to be trusted, and that I was still out to get the leadership. I was shunned by comrades. A bond then broke. Simultaneously something broke free within me. I found the courage to leave. I wrote a resignation statement saying that I had lost my revolutionary will and long live the vanguard party.

I felt so guilty, so awful for leaving, I spent the next year continuing to pay party dues and doing paper sales. During that year, I attended the funeral of Terri, a comrade in New York. Before the service I bumped into the party national chairman in the street, and he just screamed at me, "Terri hated quitters like you!" During the service, party leaders pronounced that the best way to honor Terri was to remain ever devoted to the party. I was sickened by the way her death was used to quell internal and external dissent. This was another breaking point.

While I was consumed with guilt, I also felt pride in my courage to quit. Even though I had written a self-denouncing resignation letter, I felt relief that I was finally acting on my beliefs. I began to take art classes. I will never forget the experience of drawing—with my freedom of expression not being inhibited. I had spent so many years trying to make my thoughts fit the party line. While doing art, I was making my own marks, speaking my own mind. I feared no retribution. For years thereafter drawing and painting helped piece me back together. I began to experience life on the outside. I started school in psychology at Harvard at night and eventually obtained my doctorate in education. There was a saying in the party: "Life on the outside is nothing but a biological existence." I found this saying not to be true.

How was your experience in the party gendered?

This is a very complicated question. I believe the party had a public and private face. Feminism was seen as bourgeois. "Women's issues" associated with the mass women's movement were suspect as middle class and discounted, while the party did publish a journal connecting issues of women's oppression to the class struggle. In terms of the private face, how was the party gendered? The top leadership was almost all male—the same men for the entire life of the party. At the same time, there were many women in local leadership positions. But women comrades who disagreed with a party position were called dumb, teased and taunted as they grew older for being "unmarketable." Personal relationships were manipulated to favor the sexual desires of the political chairman. Women's ways of behavior and concerns were considered deviant. Having children was discouraged and considered a distraction from one's revolutionary duty. While the party had a formal position for government-provided child care, there was minimal attention paid to the children of party members. I believe the party was gendered in the same way that a dysfunctional family is often gendered—with the patriarch at the head of the table, making everyone retreat into silence, denouncing everyone else as no good or dumb, and having special bile reserved for the women and the nonconforming males in the family who step out of line.

How do you now see your time in the party?

For a long time I felt I could never talk about the party, never say anything bad about it or the Left. I felt I was committing betrayal. Now, I feel differently. I feel that social change cannot occur until we understand how easily organizations can become ideological straitjackets and until we learn how to build healthy ones.

I stayed in the party for ten years because I felt that the world was unjust. I believed that there was a better way to structure society in which the needs of all people, such as education and health care, were taken care of for all. And I still do. I felt that capitalism was very exploitative. I really did believe that we had to do something to create a more equal world. And I believed that we needed an organization to do it, but once I joined the party it was hard to maintain my own critical perspective.

I have thought long and hard about why I was so vulnerable to the abuses of the party. I convinced myself that the political program was of primary importance and the internal deformations were secondary. I valued my political concern, activism, and commitment. But, why did I stay a party member so long when I was appalled by what has happening internally? Was my young age a factor? Was this a developmental issue? I think, for me, there was a complex matrix of factors. The most compelling reason was my outrage at the injustice in the world. There was also a very personal dimension. My younger brother had polio when he was one year old and I was four. His leg was paralyzed. As a kid, I used to take my brother around, and I saw how insensitive and cruel people could be to handicapped people. Having grown up and lived a little through the eyes of my brother, I think that my young psyche did not want to rest until I could make the world right. It was a drive in me. Nothing was more important to me than making a better world. In a way, I think I felt guilty for having two healthy legs, so when the party would say that I was a petit-bourgeois, privileged, middle-class woman who was not understanding this position from a working-class Leninist perspective, I bought it.

How does your experience in the party inform your thinking today?

I see things differently now than I did then, in the late sixties and seventies. Then I felt I would have been dead to the world's injustice had I not joined the party. I still feel good that I acted on my principles, but I no longer believe in the "coat rack." The forces in the world, and within human beings, are much too complicated to be explained through that one lens. The party went internally awry. I feel shame for the numerous times I did not stand up to the leadership when I disagreed. I am frightened by my and other people's weak spines. I am now compelled to understand and speak out about organizational abuse of power and groupthink. I don't have big regrets, though. I don't see those as ten wasted years. I learned so much, and I did it for good reasons.

The questions that remain for me are these: How do strong, courageous, independent-minded people like myself become sheeplike inside of organizations? And how can we build organizations that remain healthy and democratic? The irony here is that the party was made up of people who would go up against all of society and stand up against accusations of being communists. But within the party they became cowed and silenced. I believe that it is harder to disagree and stand apart in organizations brought together to pursue a common ideology, where all members are dedicated to a common cause. This is true especially if the organizational structure doesn't value and protect disagreement. And here is a very important point: While this phenomenon was extreme inside of the party, I believe that it occurs in everyday "normal" life as well—in corporations, in academic classrooms, in church groups. I am compelled to study and understand this social conformity and silencing within organizations, this groupthink, this individual lack of spine.

Part IV

Night and Day

Chapter Twelve

From the Fields to the Picket Line
Huelga Women and the Boycott, 1965–1975

Margaret Rose

One of the labor movement's most inspiring struggles during the post–World War II era was the unionization of farm workers in the National Farm Workers Association (NFWA), precursor to the United Farm Workers of America (UFW).[1] NFWA, founded in 1962 by César Chávez and Dolores Huerta, was an independent agricultural organization, composed primarily of Mexican and Chicano farm laborers.[2] It gained national headlines in 1965 when it joined Filipino workers in the AFL-CIO sponsored Agricultural Workers Organizing Committee (AWOC) in the now famous Delano grape strike. Defeated by the combined economic and political power of corporate agriculture and its allies, the union survived through a national appeal for consumer boycotts of agricultural producers. Since its inception, the UFW has targeted over two hundred different items in its campaigns against agribusiness. The public, however, is most familiar with its well-publicized boycotts of grapes, lettuce, and Gallo wines.

As part of its economic strategy, the union recruited male and female strikers from rural agricultural communities to live and organize boycotts in cities and towns across the U.S. Union leaders quickly recognized the key ingredient for a successful boycott formula. "Families are the most important part of the UFW," declared Dolores Huerta, "because a family can stick it out in a strange place, on $5 a week per person, the wages everyone in the union is paid (plus expenses)."[3] Echoing her sentiments Chávez emphasized, "We have not had one case of split families that has succeed [sic]. Ultimately the pressure gets too great and the husband returns to Delano."[4] The attitudes of the union leadership offer a contrast to the standard historical scholarship on the UFW. Displaying a male-centered perspective in their discussions and evaluations, writers have produced political analyses of the union and have not recognized the significance of the family in the farm worker struggle.[5] These perspectives have distorted the history of the union and the role of women in the movement.

While the family served as the core of the boycott strategy, this type of labor activism obscured women's centrality and contribution to the effort. The approach to community organizing respected a conventional division of labor along gender lines. Wives, mothers, and daughters experienced the boycott differently than their husbands, fathers, and sons—in rationale, content, and form. Women justified their participation as a defense of the domestic welfare of the family: their activism was to a considerable extent loosely tied to the organizational structure and was more cooperative.[6] Men justified their involvement in economic terms: their participation was explicitly incorporated into the union structure and was more individualistic. Furthermore, while men's militancy was more apparent and focused, women's activism was more complex as they juggled competing interests of family, work, and trade unionism.

Recent scholarship on women's labor history has uncovered the diversity and distinctiveness of women's working-class heritage. The protest of Chicanas and Mexicanas in UFW boycotts demonstrates a continuity with women in other labor struggles in the U.S. Female boycott volunteers share a rich tradition of militance with women unionists in the garment industry of the 1910s, in manufacturing and industrial concerns of the 1930s, and in the public service sector of the post–World War II era.[7] But the female boycott volunteers also display a special kinship with their ethnic forebears—striking Mexican laundresses in El Paso at the turn of the century, Mexican women in cannery organizing drives in California in the 1930s and 1940s, and wives of Mexican miners who formed women's auxiliaries in the copper strikes during the 1950s in Arizona.[8] Comparatively, little research has been done on the complex relationship between women's domestic roles and union activism. Most studies have analyzed women's experience in the labor force, their resistance to unjust working conditions, and their difficulties within the male-dominated labor movement. This work examines the protest of a selected group of Chicanas and Mexicanas in the UFW—married women with children, particularly in the Washington, D.C., boycott—who made the difficult transformation "from the fields to the picket lines" during the struggle for union recognition and collective bargaining rights.[9]

In the early years, Anglo volunteers dominated the boycott operations across the nation. Farm worker participation was minimal. Anglo boycott staff in the urban centers were isolated from the turmoil and pressing realities of the California struggle.[10] Originally, few Mexican or Mexican-American women and even fewer entire families went to boycott; the family pattern evolved gradually as the UFW experimented, through trial and error, with the most effective response to grower tactics and as union attitudes towards women began to change. Over the years, as the boycott strategy was refined, women were increasingly recognized as important players in the decision to relocate their families in urban locations.

When the union initially adopted the boycott strategy in 1965, it directed its first campaigns against highly visible major corporations, such as Schenley, DiGiorgio, and Perelli-Minetti, which depended on wine grapes for their products. In contrast to the later and much larger boycotts against the growers of table grapes and lettuce in the late 1960s and 1970s, the first boycotts were narrower in scope, concentrated primarily on the West Coast, and short in duration.[11] Reliance on Anglo boycott supporters in the cities with only the temporary assistance from farm workers, primarily young single men or husbands usually dispatched without their families, proved unsatisfactory in creating the sustained economic pressure campaign necessary in the later more protracted struggles.

For example, in 1966, Esther Uranday, a vineyard worker and early union member, stayed in California caring for her family and working in the Delano union headquarters while her husband, Manuel, staffed a boycott office in Oregon for several months. This practice created hardships for women who were often left with the primary responsibility for supporting families, raising children and running households with meager strike benefits. And for the married male workers separated from their families, once the novelty of their new job diminished, they became homesick in unfamiliar urban settings and quickly returned home. Esther described a typical pattern:

> He [her husband Manuel] was on the boycott for about two months and then he came back because I didn't go. I didn't go on the boycott so he came back. He was only gone for about two or three months.[12]

With lonely married men on the boycott for extended periods of time and women alone at home, there was the additional threat of family disruptions and divorce. This situation jeopardized farm worker cooperation with union boycott efforts.

Changes in farm worker organization began during the intensified boycott in 1968 against Giumarra, the largest producer of table grapes (and later extended against the entire industry). This long term effort which lasted two years required a greater financial commitment and a much larger staff in major cities all over North America. The union maintained operations in forty to fifty large urban centers. Usually one or two farm worker families, in addition to single men, were assigned to large cities to work with a UFW director and an Anglo support staff often recruited from the local community.[13]

In 1968, under pressure from her husband, Hijinio, and with urgent pleas from the union, María Luisa Rangel, a farm worker wife from Dinuba, a small agricultural town outside of Fresno, California, reluctantly agreed to transplant her family of eight children to Detroit to work on the Giumarra campaign. A writer who later interviewed her wrote:

> She had a hard time in Detroit; she didn't know much English, the climate was completely strange and she had two operations in the city.[14]

Nevertheless, María Luisa provided essential stability for family life and the boycott as she worked alongside her husband and children until the historic grape contracts were secured in 1970. Soon after the announcement of the agreements, the Rangels returned to California. From her Detroit experience, María Luisa emerged a strong advocate of the union's cause as evidenced by her comments about a subsequent boycott.

> It's just like it was then. The struggle is for the people to win, not the growers but the people. I know it, and they—the growers—know it.[15]

However, convincing farm worker women to leave their homes and communities during these early years proved difficult for union officials.

With the strike and boycott against lettuce growers in 1970, new personnel were needed. This time recruitment of farm worker families was facilitated by changing attitudes towards and more recognition of Chicanas and Mexicanas in the UFW. In part a response to urgent staffing requirements and in part an outgrowth of the emergence of the women's movement, these new views regarding the importance of women in the union effort were expressed in an increase of articles about women in union publications. For example, news stories like "A Woman's Place Is . . . on the Picket Line!," which featured the contributions of four women field workers to *la causa,* appeared in *El Malcriado.* [16] And also by the early 1970s, the union leadership and the permanent boycott staff had more experience in preparing for, accommodating, and utilizing farm worker families to maximum effect in the boycott.

During this period, the Juanita and Merced Valdez family and their seven children left the lettuce and strawberry fields in the Salinas Valley in northern California and moved to Cincinnati to help with the lettuce campaign. The parents tended to the day-to-day chores of the boycott. Their children—Sergio (eighteen), Mary (seventeen), Rego (fifteen), Olga (fourteen), Milly (ten), Lucy (nine), and Enedella (eight)—devoted their summers, weekends, and afterschool hours to picket lines. One leaflet the family distributed at bus stops and shopping centers, to church groups, and at Kroger stores (a large midwestern chain that refused to honor the lettuce boycott) implored consumers, "Please Do Not Shop at Kroger Until the Valdez Family and 3 Million Farm Worker Families Secure Justice." [17] During the week the parents and older children appeared before community meetings to talk about their work in the fields, their strike experiences, and to appeal for help for their union. Their activities generated publicity for the boycott in the local press and on television news and public affairs programs. In this effort, the family worked with an Anglo staff, volunteers, and a local community support group [18]

By 1973, when the UFW had intensified its lettuce campaign, renewed its boycott against table grapes, and initiated its drive against Gallo wines, the family pattern of boycott participation was firmly entrenched. Some single Chicano and Mexican men and women participated in boycotts, but married men were discouraged from doing so unless accompanied by their wives and children. "This time," observed Dolores Huerta in 1973, "no married man went out on the boycott unless he took his wife." [19] The family pattern exposed farm workers—husbands, wives, and children—to a new world of social activism and political protest. The Washington, D.C., union operation provides a good example of the family pattern of boycott participation. In the family, in the fields, and in the boycott, responsibilities for men and women were divided along gender lines. A patriarchal order characterized the organizational structure and personal relations from the leadership down to the rank-and-file level.

Gilbert Padilla coordinated the union's effort in the nation's capital from 1973 to 1975. California-born Padilla, one of nine children, migrated with his family throughout the agricultural valleys in the state, quitting school after the seventh grade to work full time in the fields. As a young adult, however, he obtained nonagricultural employment and other experiences that gave him greater exposure to Anglo culture and customs. He served in the U.S. Army during World War II and after his discharge had operated a dry cleaning business with his brothers. In 1955 he returned to field work, securing a position as a foreman for a labor contractor in cotton production. Meeting César Chávez in 1957, Gilbert was impressed with his determination to stop abuses by labor contractors and to obtain minimum wage and unemployment legislation for farm workers. He joined the local chapter of the Community Service Organization (CSO) being established by Chávez and later helped Chávez and Dolores Huerta found the Farm Workers Association in 1962. Subsequently, he led union membership drives in California and South Texas; headed the union's Selma field office near Fresno; participated in boycotts in Philadelphia and Wisconsin, and served as secretary-treasurer of the UFW.[20]

Thus, by the time the forty-six-year-old Gilbert became the director of the Washington, D.C., office in 1973, he already had extensive labor organizing and administrative experience. With a minimal staff, he went to Washington, D.C., to rebuild the lettuce boycott, which had been suspended while the union tried to reach an agreement with lettuce producers, and to campaign against Safeway stores, which had steadfastly resisted UFW pressure to remove nonunion produce from its shelves.[21]

As director of the Washington, D.C., boycott, Gilbert was the chief spokesman and strategist for the union in the federal district and the surrounding area. He coordinated picketing and sought the support of labor groups and politicians as well as clergy, students, and the general public. He concentrated on the male-dominated labor community. Unlike New York or Detroit, Washington, D.C., was not a strong union town. The fairly small local labor leadership, however, did respond to appeals from Gilbert and his staff. The Washington, D.C., Central Labor Council endorsed the boycott, sponsored luncheons, and recruited union members to participate in UFW picket lines. Gilbert cultivated ties with national labor officials, such as Tom Donahue, executive assistant to George Meany, at the Washington, D.C., office of the AFL-CIO. He also sought to develop regional labor support. Gilbert addressed AFL-CIO state conventions in Maryland, Virginia, and the Carolinas seeking cooperation and soliciting donations from delegates to sustain the boycott. Different segments of the labor movement responded more favorably than others. The steel workers' union, for example, contributed important moral and financial support.[22]

Gilbert was joined by his second wife, Esther, whom he married in 1971, and their baby daughter, Adelita. The twenty-nine-year-old Esther Negrete de Padilla, a California-born Chicana, brought sensitivity, educational training, and administrative experience to the Washington, D.C., enterprise. The youngest of fourteen children born to an immigrant farm worker family, Esther labored briefly in the fall cotton harvests in the Fresno area after school. Heeding the advice of her parents to "get a good education and do something positive," she finished high school and earned a bachelor's degree from the local college in 1966. Her academic training offered the opportunity for white-collar employment; she became a social worker in the Fresno Department of Social Services and later was a supervisor with the Head Start program. After several years of volunteer activity with the union, she officially joined the UFW in 1971.[23]

While Gilbert oversaw the entire boycott operation, he received valuable help from Esther in gender-specific areas. This service, while critically important, did not attract wide notice because of its traditional nature and because it often occurred behind the scenes. A conventional female concern in the home was the care and management of the family. Esther not only met these responsibilities but also managed the domestic side of the boycott. The two-story frame house in Takoma Park, a suburb of Washington, D.C., that served as headquarters for the boycott sheltered up to fourteen people. Its four bedrooms, with a makeshift dormitory in the basement, was home to the Padillas and to the families and individual organizers who came and went in the course of the two-year campaign.[24]

Esther dealt with the problems that inevitably arose from the interaction of many people. Using her knowledge of the welfare system, she obtained food stamps and medical benefits for the transplanted farm workers. When one farm worker woman required emergency care upon arrival in the city, Esther arranged for her hospitalization. Children required visits to the doctor and glasses.

The winter months brought additional health problems. "Prolonged illnesses among over 50 percent of the farm workers' families in Washington, including hospitalization for pneumonia, have resulted from our lack of money for warm clothing, nutritional foods, vitamins, medications, and heating fuel . . . ," noted an appeal for donations in *¡Acción!*, the local boycott newsletter. "At the present writing," it continued, "two adults are recovering from pleurisy and pneumonia, another is housebound with pneumonia, one is recovering from surgery and another is due for surgery. Adults and children are suffering from flu, lung infections, tonsillitis, head colds, and muscular pain."[25] For the new boycott recruits from the fields, Esther sought medical attention and acted as a counselor and morale booster. As such she served as a liaison between the boycott leadership and the farm worker families scattered around the metropolitan area.

Esther's contribution was not limited to personal and domestic details. Because of her educational and work experience, she was a valuable asset in the formal administration of the boycott. Her public duties ranged from dealing with produce managers and political representatives to office work. Esther's day began with early morning visits to the central produce market. Along with staff members Mike Angelo and David Urioste, she harangued uncooperative fruit and vegetable dealers who continued to purchase boycotted grapes and lettuce. Describing these clashes as "rough times," she and her coworkers depended on Gilbert, who waited at the boycott office, to authorize bail if necessary.

After these 5:30–7:30 A.M. daily encounters, she devoted the bulk of her time to political lobbying on Capitol Hill. After Gilbert arranged formal introductions to elected officials, Esther directed this effort. She intervened with influential Senators Walter Mondale and Alan Cranston on labor legislation of interest to the union. She prevailed on long-time supporters Representatives Philip Burton and Edward Roybal, to help; both supplied staff assistance and, in some instances, access to their telephone lines. Through her lobbying, other members of the California congressional delegation lent their important backing: Representative Don Edwards returned to California to attend the funeral of a slain UFW member, and Representative Jerome Waldie flew to a UFW rally in Fresno to offer his endorsement of the union. Public officials who were not sufficiently supportive of the union became the target of UFW campaigns. Esther organized a sit-in at the Washington, D.C., office of California Senator John Tunney in response to his failure to support UFW boycotts and his advocacy of labor legislation opposed by the union.[26]

In addition to personal contacts with legislators and their staffs, Esther testified before congressional committees. One appearance arose out of the UFW recall campaign against Arizona Republican governor Jack Williams, who had signed into law a restrictive bill intended to thwart agricultural unionizing in the state. She alleged that local officials impeded the UFW voter registration drives in this recall effort through a series of arbitrary rulings, particularly the action of the Maricopa county recorder who refused to recognize the authority of approximately three thousand new deputy registrars and issued revised testing procedures for certification of these officials. Presenting a copy of the new, cumbersome exam to the committee, she implored, "We, of the farmworkers, urge you to enact legislation that would put Federal machinery to work on behalf of citizens all over the country, so that we will not have to depend on the goodwill or absence of it on the part of county recorders, whether they be in Arizona or elsewhere in our great country." She also made a plea to the committee to hold a hearing in Arizona to investigate the practices of local officials.[27]

When she was not on Capitol Hill, Esther helped in the day-to-day operations of the enterprise. Working out of the boycott house in Takoma Park, she handled correspondence, issued press releases, supervised Anglo supporters who volunteered to help in the office, attended staff meetings, and kept minutes for important regional boycott conferences.[28] With her expertise on congressional matters, her knowledge of the Washington, D.C., office, and her dealings with farm worker personnel, she also served as a confidante and advisor to her husband. Thus besides being a family unit, the Padillas were a political team—Gilbert the official head of the boycott and Esther his trusted assistant. But within this formal patriarchal arrangement, there was a great degree of mutuality, cooperation, and female autonomy.

This family model of union activism also characterized the Washington, D.C., boycott venture at the rank-and-file level. Initially, the Padillas supervised a staff of only four recruits from the local community, but with the announcements of the grape and Gallo boycotts the number of personnel increased rapidly. By 1974 there was a staff of twenty-three, supplemented from time to time by temporary non-Hispanic and non-paid volunteers. This figure did not take into account the younger children who often participated in the boycott. The majority of the staff consisted of five farm worker families—the Castillos, the Herreras, the Baldwins, the Salinases, and the Rodríguezes and three single males, José Salzar, Daniel Terrones, and David Urioste.[29]

The family of Herminia and Conrado Rodríguez resided in the Arvin-Lamont area, south of Bakersfield, before their move to Washington, D.C. Their background and experiences were typical of the families who left their homes to work in the boycott during the 1973–1975 campaign. Born in Brownsville, Texas, in 1935, Conrado Rodríguez married eighteen-year-old Herminia Vargas, a native of Matamoros, Mexico, in 1957. Conrado (also called Lalo) supported his family as a farm laborer, supplementing his income with carpentry jobs during the winter months. Herminia, following a traditional female pattern of part-time, seasonal work, contributed to the household economy as a field worker during harvest time. The young family migrated annually between Texas and California. In the Arvin-Lamont area, where they eventually settled, the Rodríguezes worked primarily in table and wine grape production and occasionally in the harvest of other local crops, such as carrots and cotton.[30]

Like many other families, the Rodríguezes' politicization became a family affair. During the summer of 1973, the family participated in the widespread protests against local grape growers who balked at renewing the UFW contracts negotiated three years before. As a local leader at his company, Conrado hosted strategy meetings in his home attended by his coworkers and his family. As talks between grape producers and the union stalled, demonstrations intensified. When local grape industry representatives hastily concluded contracts with the Teamsters Union, protests heightened.[31] While picketing against local growers, Conrado and his eldest teenage daughter, Lupe, were arrested along with other union supporters and transported to the county jail in Bakersfield. Herminia and the remaining children, together with other detainees' families, went into the city and denounced the incarcerations. Lupe Rodríguez stayed in jail for three or four days; her father was held a few days longer and then released.[32]

The calamitous confrontations between agribusiness and the union in the summer of 1973 that resulted in the mass arrests of farm workers (men, women, and children) and their supporters politicized many families. When the UFW suspended picketing after the deaths of two union supporters in August, the activism of the Rodríguez family did not diminish. Packing up their personal belongings, they joined the caravans of farm worker families who left in the late summer and early fall 1973 to launch a renewed boycott campaign against corporate agriculture on a distant urban front, far away from the recent turmoil in the fields.[33]

As with the Padillas, the Rodríguezes followed the family model of boycott participation with activities divided along gender lines. Herminia Rodríguez oversaw the domestic needs of her family and participated in traditionally female-defined boycott work. Like Esther Padilla, Herminia received much less attention than her husband and refrained from public speaking with the result that her actions, like those of most other Chicanas and Mexicanas, seemed "invisible." Since they appeared infrequently in news accounts and official union records, it is difficult to quote directly their personal reactions and experiences.[34]

The traditional responsibility of making her family comfortable was not an easy task for Herminia Rodríguez given the disruptions in family life caused by the boycott. The Rodríguez family, like others, had to adjust to a strange environment, new people, different climate, an unfamiliar culture, and difficult living conditions. An entirely new system of survival and domestic decisions had to be adopted. For food, clothing, and housing, the family relied on the local community and fundraising drives. Financial support from the union was kept to a minimum in order to remit the maximum of surplus funds to California.[35]

As boycott wives and mothers learned quickly, domestic stability became secondary to the demands of the boycott. When organizing needs shifted, the family relocated. Herminia moved her family four times during their two-year stay in Washington, D.C. First, they lived in the Takoma Park boycott house with the Padillas and other boycotters. Later, they shared another house, a block away, with the Salinas family. Another move took them to an apartment downtown near the White House. Finally, the family stayed in the basement of a house in the same area. Frequent residential changes necessitated different arrangements for the entire family.[36] Herminia's patient acceptance of this instability contributed to the smooth functioning of the boycott. Furthermore, her sacrifices of domestic tranquility were directed towards political ends. Herminia and other wives endured these dislocations to advance the goals of better wages, decent living conditions, and the opportunity for a better future in California. "The union has to win," declared Rosa

Martínez, a farm worker and mother of twelve, "we're making this sacrifice so they [growers] will pay us so we can educate our children."[37] In the boycott the thin line between personal family concerns and political action blurred in the lives of Chicanas and Mexicanas. Personal discomforts and domestic duties translated into a strong female political statement.

In addition to managing difficult living conditions and family affairs, Chicanas and Mexicanas also participated in public boycott activities, short of public speaking which was left to the men. Here a more direct connection between personal activism and political goals appeared. The most tedious, but most essential, task was picketing. Chicanas and Mexicanas spent hours on picket duty, particularly during the summers when the objective was to maintain daily picket lines. At grocery stores, like Giant and Safeway, and at local liquor stores, such as Woodley Discount Liquor, Esther Padilla carried her two-year-old daughter, Adelita, and Herminia Rodríguez took her five children—Lupe, Oralia, Eduardo, Daniel, and Dalia. At times picket lines were composed of women and children. Promoting a spirit of female solidarity with farm worker women, the local chapter of the Coalition of Labor Union Women (CLUW) sponsored a picket line at the Newark Street Giant Food Store in Fall 1974.[38] Philippine-born Luming Imutan related the typical difficulties picketers encountered from unsympathetic members of the public:

> One of the hardest parts about being on strike and being on picket lines is taking the insults that people give you. When I was in Los Angeles for the factory gate collections and the boycott lines for S & W [DiGiorgio product brand], people would ask, "Why should you tell us what to buy?" "Why do you have to beg?" "Why don't you go to work?" There were many people who called us a disgrace to the public.[39]

Becoming active participants in the boycott propelled Mexicanas and Chicanas out of the private sphere and into the public domain in ways they were unaccustomed to in rural California. While picketing was a temporary activity in California, in the boycott it became a regular part of the work week. But while these pursuits expanded the public role of Mexican and Mexican-American women, it did not fundamentally alter gender roles. To the contrary, boycott women relied on a shared domestic culture and female reciprocity to relieve the hardships of their new urban lifestyle.

Farm worker women engaged in supportive jobs in the office, depending on their skill level, but did not participate in the formal decision-making process which was reserved for men. Because of her education (and her position as wife of the director), Esther Padilla assumed a more visible role than did Hermenia Rodríguez, who had received no formal education while growing up in Mexico. Herminia and other Mexicanas answered phones, stuffed envelopes, or ran office equipment. María Castillo, Herminia's friend, assumed the task of selling union bumper stickers, buttons, key chains, and other items at union-sponsored events. Noting that María was "real good" in this capacity, Esther Padilla explained that she helped raise needed funds as well as awareness of the union's cause. Possessing a fine singing voice, María also provided entertainment performing Mexican folk songs and *corridos* (ballads), such as "De Colores," a union favorite, accompanied by guitar-playing Conrado Rodríguez.[40]

The domestic skills of Herminia, María, and other boycott wives also served the boycott. Herminia shopped, cooked, and cleaned so that other women could perform office duties. While Esther lobbied on Capitol Hill, Herminia babysat her daughter, Adelita.[41] Farm worker women contributed their domestic talents in other ways at the UFW-sponsored fundraising dinners attended by the Democratic political establishment. Eunice and Sargent Shriver lent their Maryland estate for several of these affairs. Liberal senators, such as Edward Kennedy and George McGovern, and sympathetic House members, such as Bella Abzug and Patricia Schroeder, along with other influential union and community leaders, appeared at these functions, which generated important support for the boycott. At these events, some attended by as many as 2,000 guests, and at smaller gatherings, Herminia, María, and other farm worker women collected tickets at the door or assisted in the preparation and serving of food, similar to the vital work of the women who ran the strike kitchens in California.[42] In this context, the economically essential work of cooking was converted into a political act.

In contrast to Chicanas and Mexicanas at the rank-and-file level, their husbands exerted a more public and readily recognized presence in the boycott. The family model of social activism gave the male head of household more prominence, authority, and responsibility. Media coverage reinforced this division. When a news story appeared in the *Washington Post* that mentioned boycott families, Conrado Rodríguez, as "head" of the family, was the natural choice to respond to the interview-

er's questions. He commented on his boycott experience and of his need
to learn English.

> When I came to boycott I speak only about 10 percent. Now I speak about
> 50 percent. . . . It's difficult to understand when people ask questions. I
> never had an education. I had to work in the fields . . . in the fields it is
> not necessary to speak English.

> In this kind of cause, sometimes people don't understand what you want.
> . . . I have to learn the words. Boycott grapes. Boycott lettuce.[43]

Though speaking for himself, Conrado provided an insight into the
challenge the boycott provided for his wife, who struggled with her
limited English, and other farm worker participants.

While both men and women walked picket lines, the men were photographed more frequently for union publications and were often jailed—
a very public event—for their activities.[44] Whereas in rural California
mass arrests of both men and women occurred, especially during the
summer of 1973, in the cities men were more frequently arrested than
women. If both husband and wife underwent arrest, there was no extended family to care for the children; thus, the less public responsibility
to stay out of jail usually fell to the wife.

By virtue of gender and patriarchal standing in the family, male farm
workers in the boycott assumed more administrative duties. For his
special project, Conrado Rodríguez teamed with an Anglo staff member,
Kay Pollock, to develop support for the boycott among religious groups.
Together with his female mentor, he wrote letters to churches and syna-
gogues, asking for the opportunity to address their memberships. Along
with Pollock, he attended church-sponsored gatherings, spoke briefly
about his experience in California agriculture, showed farm worker
slides or films, and appealed for help to walk picket lines, write letters,
donate food and clothing, and provide financial assistance.[45]

Despite his third-grade education and difficulty with the English language, Conrado and Kay won the strong support of the religious community. The Catholic archdiocese early pledged its backing, provided
financial aid, in some areas on a monthly basis, and furnished food and
housing for farm workers and Anglo staff alike. Protestant denomina-
tions, especially Episcopalian, Unitarian, and Congregational, sponsored
"fiestas" and donated the proceeds to the union. A coalition of rabbis
and Jewish groups organized community fund-raisers and sent letters to
Jewish caterers asking them to honor the boycott in their purchases.[46]

The backing of the religious community proved an essential mainstay of the boycott effort. The overall effectiveness of Rodríguez' appeal relied on domestic cooperation and support from his wife, Herminia, and the able assistance of his Anglo female coworker.

Farmer worker children were also an important element in the family boycott model. Children's contribution to the boycott extended from their economic role in the farm worker family; as they had helped their parents in the fields, they also participated in boycott work in the cities. During the summers, on weekends, and after school, they joined their parents on picket lines. Besides providing more personnel to maintain between nine and twenty-five picket lines (depending on the time of year), children had a special persuasive effect on consumers. On Saturdays and Sundays, families also leafleted neighborhoods, shopping centers, busy bus stops, and other heavily traveled areas. Energetic youngsters added a festive spirit to the job. Occasionally, entire families attended the more social evening gatherings, and the parents, usually the father, made brief presentations to civic, community, or church groups.

Children born to parents participating in the boycott received special recognition. When asked by a reporter how many individuals lived in the union house, Esther Padilla enthusiastically replied, "The fourteenth is newborn Ernesto . . . , the 'boycott baby' " (son of María and Leo Castillo). *El Malcriado* announced the birth of Celestina, daughter of Juanita and Alfredo Herrera, in Washington, D.C., with "Congratulations y Vivan las Boicoteritas y Boicoteritos."[47] Baptismal rites were an occasion of community celebration. Esther and Gilbert Padilla served as *compadres* [godparents] for babies born in Washington, D.C. At UFW gatherings, union leaders often asked that all boycott babies come forward to be honored. Often caught up in the movement culture, older children made unique individual contributions. The 12-year-old daughter of Herminia and Conrado Rodríguez presented an essay on the UFW to her classmates and enlisted the support of a sympathetic teacher. During Halloween farm worker children in the nation's capital passed out cards listing boycott targets as they made their rounds for treats.[48]

For children, the boycott became a novel and exciting experience, offering a dramatic exposure to a different style of life. Toddler Adelita Padilla was the subject of much attention from boycott supporters as she appealed to them not to shop at the "caca" (poopy) stores.[49] But gender divisions prevailed here also. In the Cincinnati boycott, for example, sons Sergio (eighteen) and Rego (fifteen) Valdez often took charge of speaking duties and other responsibilities from their father, while their sister Mary (seventeen) performed a more auxiliary and less public, though no less vital, role in the office. Thus, while teenage boys often served as spokespersons for their families, their sisters were expected to assume a supportive and behind-the-scenes presence, like their mothers.[50]

The progress of the Washington, D.C., boycott accelerated after the arrival of farm worker families in the city. The immediate attention of the boycott focused on pressuring supermarkets to remove nonunion products and to create strong grass-roots support for UFW collective bargaining demands. Farm worker families, like the Rodríguezes, the Castillos, the Herreras, the Baldwins, and the Salinases, were essential in the picketing strategy. Within the first three months of their arrival in the nation's capital, they had succeeded in gaining the cooperation of 137 independent and "Mom and Pop" stores. Local co-ops, such as the Beltsville Consumes, a group of ten stores, joined the boycott. After the arrests of three farm workers, another small independent, Snider's market, agreed to remove grapes from its shelves. The California boycotters also achieved success in their campaign to pressure 275 liquor stores to stop selling Gallo wine products. Cooperation from black groups was notable in this effort; 110 stores in the black community quickly responded to the boycott. But as the local boycott leadership and farm worker families soon realized, the most difficult targets were the large supermarkets. After their initial accomplishments with small stores, farm workers and their supporters began picketing Giant Foods, a chain of one hundred stores in the Washington area. The largest and most intransigent chain was Safeway with 234 stores in the vicinity. Despite almost constant picketing at their stores and warehouses, and despite financial losses, both chains resisted demands of farm worker families to honor the boycott.[51]

To create the necessary pressure to make the UFW campaign effective, the boycott leadership turned to the development of long-term community and regional support. Through the sustained cooperation of farm worker families, local organizers, and with the backing of labor, religious, political, consumer, and student groups, the Washington, D.C., UFW office mounted a viable boycott effort.[52] After organizing the nation's capital, the boycott spread to other areas. Using the experience they had gained in Washington, D.C., farm worker families moved to other cities. Juanita and Alfredo Herrera and their five children went to

Baltimore to build a campaign against the A & P grocery chain. Still other families accepted assignments in Norfolk and Alexandria, Virginia.[53]

In this region, the most successful campaign was directed against Gallo wine because of its highly recognizable labels and the availability of other easily substituted brands. Although significant, the boycotts against grapes and lettuce yielded less impressive results.[54] Overall, the nationally coordinated campaign finally convinced agribusiness in California to endorse legislation, the Agricultural Labor Relations Act (ALRA), which guaranteed secret-ballot elections—an historic step in the state.[55]

With the passage of the ALRA in summer 1975, a major shift occurred in the boycott structure. As a member of the UFW Executive Board, director Gilbert Padilla and his family returned to California. Announcement of their departure appeared in the local boycott newsletter.

> Gilbert and Esther Padilla have been called back to California to organize farm workers for the coming elections. They say good-bye and thank you to all of you who have supported them, also that they know you will support their replacements. . . .[56]

A challenging and difficult job awaited the two in California—confronting growers who continued to resist attempts at unionization.[57] Farm worker families also returned to California in anticipation of participating in field election campaigns. Herminia and Conrado Rodríguez moved their family back to the Arvin-Lamont area to cast votes for UFW representation at their struck ranches. In Washington, D.C., boycott operations were transferred to the local Anglo staff, who sponsored vigils and picket lines to publicize and protest grower infractions of the new California law, the mistreatment of union organizers, and the intimidation of workers.[58]

The ultimate success of the two-year struggle, from 1973 to 1975, against the agricultural industry depended on a remarkable cooperation between Mexican and Chicano activists and field workers, Anglo organizers, and middle-class supporters in cities across the U.S. and Canada. Farm worker commitment to the boycott was intricately tied to the family approach to organization that preserved gender designated forms of labor activism.

The variety of Chicanas' and Mexicanas' participation in the Washington, D.C., boycott reflected the diversity of experience of women of Mexican heritage in the U.S. during the second half of the 20th century. Class and generational distance from Mexico, in particular, shaped female activism. More acculturated and educated, U.S.-born Chicanas, like Esther Padilla, often exerted a prominent and visible position in the boycott and experienced more flexibility regarding their social activism. Recently immigrated, poorer farm worker women from Mexico, such as Herminia Rodríguez, influenced by a more conservative definition of female activism and limited by inadequate educational and language skills, received little recognition of their quiet, but vital, contributions to the boycott.

Regardless of ethnicity or class, gender remained the preeminent force shaping women's activism on the boycott. The family model of boycott organization reinforced the general expectation that Chicanas and Mexicanas would exert a crucial, but less visible, role in the boycott. Female cooperation and community prevailed over individual ambition. A familiar domestic culture eased the transition from the fields to the cities.

But because of its unconventional nature and its unorthodox and radical challenge to the established economic order, the boycott had perhaps the unintended consequence of undermining traditional social and gender relationships for this generation of women. New Mexican-born Carolina Vásquez, a grape striker from the Schenley company who worked in the boycott as a single woman in Philadelphia and later as a wife, after her marriage in 1969 to a farm worker boycotter in Connecticut, hinted at the potential of the boycott for relaxing conventional relationships between spouses.

> Now my husband and I work together, and sometimes we have different points of view, but we help each other as much as we can. We are up to our nerves in this strike most of the time from responsibilities we've confronted on the boycott.[59]

Vásquez also demonstrated the impact of the boycott on raising the self-image and outlook of Chicanas and Mexicanas. An interview with her in the union's publication, *El Malcriado,* revealed this change.

> Carolina feels the boycott has personally educated her by improving her English (speaking before the public and media), and knowing how people live in the large cities. Also, she now realizes that "education is important, and I have a lot to learn," she concludes.[60]

A few women, like Esther Padilla, developed feminist leanings. When she first participated in the boycott she became defensive when middle-class female supporters challenged the UFW's traditional attitudes towards women. As she observed that other unions in Washington, D.C., had established bureaus and committees to address the concerns of women, she became more sensitive to the issue. By the late 1970s her raised consciousness moved her to write to César Chávez to advocate the formation of a women's department in the UFW.[61] The unusual circumstances of the boycott created a climate for altering traditional male-female relationships within marriage and in the union and for providing Mexicanas and Chicanas with new opportunities for personal growth.[62] But the feminism of Esther Padilla remained an exception.

While the UFW provided an outlet for class solidarity and a means for expressing ethnic pride for an exploited minority, it reinforced traditional gender relations by confining women to traditionally female-defined work and social activism. However, by raising the ethnic and class consciousness of its female membership and by exposing them to novel situations, new ideas, and different cultural expectations, the UFW may have inadvertently laid the foundation for the emergence of a greater awareness of gender issues among Mexicanas and Chicanas.

NOTES

1. The union has had several different names. Originally what was the Farm Workers Association (FWA) in 1962 soon expanded to National Farm Workers Association (NFWA). In 1966 when the NFWA merged with the Agricultural Workers Organizing Committee (AWOC), it became the United Farm Workers Organizing Committee (UFWOC). UFWOC became a chartered affiliate of the AFL-CIO and adopted its current name, United Farm Workers of America (UFW), in 1972. For simplicity's sake, I refer to the union as the UFW in this chapter.

2. The terms Chicano and Mexican-American refer to persons of Mexican descent born in the U.S. and are used interchangeably. Chicanos can refer to males only or to both males and females, but Chicanas are Mexican-American women. Mexican or Mexicano/a signifies persons born in Mexico.

3. Quoted in Barbara L. Baer and Glenna Matthews, " 'You Find a Way': The Women of the Boycott," *The Nation*, Feb. 23, 1974, 233.

4. Quoted in boycott newsletter [undated] [c. Jan. 1969] Dear Boycotters from Cesar, UFW Philadelphia Boycott Office (acc 376), Box 4, Folder 3,

Archives of Labor and Urban Affairs, Walter P. Reuther Library, Wayne State University (hereafter ALUA).

5. The literature on the UFW is varied. Activists and writers penned the earliest treatments. These include Eugene Nelson, *Huelga: The First Hundred Days of the Delano Grape Strike* (Delano, 1966); John Gregory Dunne, *Delano: the Story of the California Grape Strike* (New York, 1967); Peter Matthiessen, *Sal Si Puedes: Cesar Chavez and the New American Revolution* (New York, 1969); Mark Day, *Forty Acres: Cesar Chavez and the Farm Workers* (New York, 1971); Joan London and Henry Anderson, *So Shall Ye Reap* (New York, 1970). In the mid-1970s, several journalists who had covered the farm worker movement for a decade prepared accounts: Ronald B. Taylor, *Chavez and the Farm Workers* (Boston, 1975); Sam Kushner, *Long Road to Delano* (New York, 1975); Jacques E. Levy, *Cesar Chavez: Autobiography of La Causa* (New York, 1975); Dick Meister and Anne Loftis, *A Long Time Coming, The Struggle to Unionize America's Farm Workers* (New York, 1977). Only two scholarly monographs have been published: Linda C. Majka and Theo J. Majka, *Farm Workers, Agribusiness, and The State* (Philadelphia, 1982) and J. Craig Jenkins, *The Politics of Insurgency: The Farm Worker Movement in the 1960s* (New York, 1985). There are no published texts on women in the UFW. For an article on one woman in the UFW, see Ellen Cantarow, "Jessie Lopez De La Cruz: The Battle for Farmworkers' Rights," in Ellen Cantarow et al., *Moving the Mountain: Women Working For Social Change* (Old Westbury, N.Y., 1980), 94–151.

6. Maxine Baca Zinn, "Political Familism: Toward Sex Role Equality in Chicano Families," *Aztlan* 6:1 (1975), 13–27, notes the significance of family participation in the Chicano movement. Although their works deal with different eras, locations, and industries, the following authors' observations on women's collective action and female consciousness have influenced my discussion: see Louise A. Tilly, "Paths of Proletarianization: Organization of Production, Sexual Division of Labor, and Women's Collective Action," *Signs,* 7 (Winter 1981), 400–417; Temma Kaplan, "Female Consciousness and Collective Action: The Case of Barcelona, 1910–1918," *Signs* 7 (Spring 1982), 545–566; Jacquelyn Dowd Hall et al., *Like a Family: The Making of a Southern Cotton Mill World* (Chapel Hill, 1987), 226–231, esp. 227.

7. Alice Kessler-Harris, *Out to Work: A History of Wage-Earning Women in the United States* (New York, 1982); Ruth Milkman, *Gender at Work: The Dynamics of Job Segregation by Sex During World War II* (Urbana, 1987); Nancy Gabin, " 'They Have Placed a Penalty on Womanhood': The Protest Actions of Women Auto Workers in Detroit-Area UAW Locals, 1945–1947," *Feminist Studies,* 8 (1982), 373–398; Marjorie Penn Lasky, " 'Where I Was a Person': The Ladies' Auxiliary in the 1934 Minneapolis Teamsters' Strikes," in Ruth Milkman, ed., *Women, Work, and Protest: A Century of U.S. Women's Labor History* (Boston, 1985), 181–205.

8. Mario T. Garcia, "The Chicana in American History: The Mexican Women of El Paso, 1880–1920—A Case Study," *Pacific Historical Review,* 49 (1980), 315–337; Vicki L. Ruiz, *Cannery Women, Cannery Lives: Mexican Women, Unionization, and the California Food Processing Industry, 1930–1950* (Albuquerque, N.M., 1987); Patricia Zavella, *Women's Work and Chicano Families: Cannery Workers of The Santa Clara Valley* (Ithaca, 1987); Sarah Deutsch, *No Separate Refuge: Culture, Class, and Gender on An Anglo-Hispanic Frontier in the American Southwest, 1880–1940* (New York, 1987); Michael Wilson, *Salt of the Earth,* Commentary by Deborah Silverton Rosenfelt (Old Westbury, N.Y., 1978).

9. There are exceptions to the family pattern of union activism: see Margaret Eleanor Rose, "Women in the United Farm Workers: A Study of Chicana and Mexicana Participation in a Labor Union, 1950 to 1980" (unpublished Ph.D. of diss., University of California, Los Angeles, 1988), chapters a, 5, 7.

10. Taylor, *Chavez,* 233. Taylor commented that when farm workers appeared on picket lines in the cities the morale of Anglo volunteers soared and that workers' presence also created a noticeable effect on supermarket customers.

11. Jerald Barry Brown, "The United Farm Workers Grape Strike and Boycott, 1965–1970: An Evaluation of the Culture of Poverty Theory" (unpublished Ph.D. diss., Latin American Studies Program, Cornell University, 1972), 191. The largest of the three early boycotts was the DiGiorgio campaign. According to Brown it "involved a staff of 53 people—31 of whom were based in California—in 12 major cities."

12. Interview with Esther Uranday, Delano, California, July 12, 1983, 29. Hereafter Uranday Interview. Uranday had three children. Interview with Dolores Huerta, 3, Kenne (La Paz), Calif., Feb. 8, 1985, 118–119 and 121–122. Hereafter Huerta Interview, 3. Huerta talks about the young Filipino and Mexican men she recruited to work on the boycott in Los Angeles.

13. Taylor, *Chavez,* 229–230.

14. Quoted in Baer and Matthews, " 'You Find a Way,' " 236. For brief comments on other Chicana boycotters in Toronto and New York, see Taylor, 233–234.

15. Quoted in Baer and Matthews, " 'You Find a Way,' " 236. Another article written on the Rangels appeared in the union newspaper. It referred to Hijinio and the children but did not mention María Luisa. See *El Malcriado* (Nov. 1, 1970).

16. *El Malcriado* (July 1, 1970), 4. Up to this time features directed toward women consisted of a recipe and poetry page and an advice column, "Dear Alma."

17. Quoted in *El Malcriado* (Dec. 15, 1970), 4:11.

18. Ibid.

19. Quoted in Baer and Matthews, "You Find a Way,' " 234. Young unmarried Chicanas went to the boycott, though they were usually attached to family units. Despite the objections of her father, Linda Chávez Rodríguez, daughter of César and Helen Chávez, went to the Detroit boycott with her older, married sister and her husband, Sylvia and George Delgado. See interview with Linda Chávez Rodríguez, Kenne (La Paz), Calif., Mar. 28, 1983, 3–4 and 16–20. Susan Chávaz Valle and Rebecca Chávez, daughters of Richard and Sally Chávez, participated in the San Diego boycott. See interview with Susan Chávez Valle, Kenne (La Paz), Calif., June 23, 1983, 43–45.

20. Taylor, 88–90. Meister and Loftis, 118–119. Levy, 181. See also "Biography," Gilbert Padilla, UFW, Washington, D.C., Boycott (7–77) Box 5, Folder: Padilla—Biography, ALUA. (Hereafter D.C.B. [7–77]). This brief biographical summary states that Padilla was born Dec. 21, 1927, in Los Banos, Calif., in a labor camp. Padilla had seven children from his first marriage, some of whom worked in the boycott.

21. For another, shorter biographical sketch on Gilbert Padilla, see *El Malcriado,* Oct. 19, 1973. His arrival in Washington, D.C., was noted in *Washington Post,* Feb. 19, 1973.

22. Report of the Washington, D.C., Boycott Director, Gilbert Padilla, Oct. 9, 1974, UFW Boycott Central (acc. May 1977), Box 3, Folder: Washington, D.C., Boycott, 1974, ALUA. (Hereafter Boy Cen [5–77]).

23. Interview with Esther Padilla, Fresno, Calif., Nov. 30, 1988. (Hereafter Padilla Interview). *Washington Post,* Aug. 15, 1974. For quoted material see *Fresno Bee,* Aug. 9, 1987.

24. *Washington Post,* Aug. 15, 1974.

25. Padilla Interview. Quoted material in *!Acción!,* Dec. 1973 and Jan. 1974, D.C.B. (7-77), Box 13, Folder: Layout and Materials for Leaflets and Newsletters, 1973–1977. ALUA.

26. Padilla Interview. For relations with Cranston, see Levy, 112, 133, 302, and Majka and Majka, 193. For the union's discordant relationship with Tunney see ibid., 239, 246, and 296.

27. Quoted in U.S. Congress, Senate, Post Office and Civil Service Committee, "Voter Registration: Hearing on S. 352 and S. 472," 93rd Cong., 1st sess., 16 March 1973, 250. Father James L. Vizzard also lobbied for the UFW from 1972 and 1977. Vizzard concentrated on such legislation as the Farm Labor Contractor Registration Act Amendments of 1974. For his legislative files, see James L. Vizzard Papers, Box 18, Folders 5, 7, 8, 10, Dept. of Special Collections, Stanford University Libraries, Stanford University. His activities remained separate from Esther's.

28. For an example of Esther Padilla's office work, see Minutes—Boycott Coordinators' Meeting, East Coast, Northeast, Southeast, and Eastern Canada, Feb. 9–12, 1974, Washington, D.C., UFW Boycott Central Files, 1973–1977,

Box 6, Folder: Barbara—Personal, ALUA. These minutes were prepared by Esther Padilla and Kay Pollock. Press Release, 9 Sept. 1974, D.C.B. (7–77), Box 10, unlabeled folder, ALUA.

29. Active Union Personnel According to January 1974 Budgets, III Boycott Cities, Boy Cen (5–77), Box 1, Folder: Keene (La Paz) Boycott Office, ALUA. See also letter from Kay Pollock to Rt. Rev. John T. Walker, Sept. 19, 1973, D.C.B. (7–77), ALUA. Pollock noted that there were twenty-one children ranging from 5 weeks to 16 years. For mention of additional nonpaid volunteers on the staff, see *Washington Post,* Aug. 15, 1974.

30. Interview with Oralia Rodríguez Mata, Martin Luther King Farm Workers Service Center, Lamont, CA, May 21, 1984. (Hereafter Mata Interview). Oralia Mata is the daughter of Herminia and Conrado Rodríguez. She worked in the UFW's service center at the time of this interview. Mata gives a birth date of 1934 for her father. His birth date is listed as 1935 in union records. See, D.C.B. (7–77), Box 10, Folder: Car—titles, repair estimates, 1974–1975, ALUA.

31. Levy, 475–510. Levy discusses the Teamster incursion and the resultant turmoil and arrests during the summer 1973 in the agricultural valleys throughout California.

32. For samples of the unrest and protests in this area see *Lamont Reporter,* April 11, 1973 and *Bakersfield Californian,* April 18, 19, 1973. See also Mata Interview.

33. For reports of boycott car caravans leaving California, see *Bakersfield Californian,* Aug. 31, 1973, and *The McFarland Press,* Sept. 7, 1973. See also Meister and Loftis, 181–194.

34. Conrado "Lalo" Rodríguez was written about and was pictured in several *Washington Post* news stories. For example, he appeared in a captioned photograph playing the guitar on a picket line: see *Washington Post,* July 27, 1975. Another photo of Rodríguez and other male picketers was included in a story: on the Washington, D.C., boycott in the union newspaper: see *El Malcriado,* Dec. 28, 1973. I could locate no captioned photos of his wife. It is interesting to note that the Washington, D.C. boycott records reveal most information on Gilbert Padilla and the Anglo staff; relatively little data is provided on farm worker families who are often referred to as a group and not as individuals. When referred to singly, however, Conrado Rodríguez and other male farm workers appear more than their wives.

35. In 1974 the Washington, D.C. boycott raised 79% of its expenses: see Boycott City Income and Expense Summary, February 1974, Boy Cen (5–77) Box 1, Folder: Keene (La Paz) Boycott Office, ALUA.

36. Mata Interview. See also *Washington Post,* Aug. 15, 1974.

37. Quoted in *El Malcriado,* July 1, 1970.

38. For a story on and photo of Esther Padilla and her daughter, see *Wash-*

ington Post, Aug. 15, 1974. For a photo of female picketer Margo Lopez, see *Washington Post,* Aug. 11, 1974. Oralia Mata provides an account of her mother's (Herminia Rodríguez's) and siblings' picketing in her interview; see Mata Interview. For mention of the Coalition of Labor Union Women's (CLUW) picket line, see Report of Washington, D.C. Boycott Director, Gilbert Padilla, Oct. 9, 1974, UFW Boy Cen (5–77), Box 3, Folder; Washington, D.C. Boycott, 1974, ALUA. See also (The Metropolitan D.C. Area) *CLUW News,* December 1974.

39. Quoted in *El Malcriado,* June 10, 1967.

40. Mata Interview, Padilla Interview.

41. Padilla Interview.

42. For accounts of several of these fundraising events at the Shrivers' estate, see *Washington Post,* July 20, 1973 and Sept. 9, 1974. At the former event $6000 was raised, at the latter another $11,000 was collected for the union.

43. Quoted in *Washington Post,* Aug. 15, 1974.

44. For Conrado Rodríguez's picket line activity, see *El Malcriado,* Dec. 28, 1973.

45. For Conrado Rodríguez's attendance at important union meetings, see Minutes—Boycott Coordinators' Meeting, East Coast, Northeast, Southeast, and Eastern Canada, Feb. 9–12, 1974, Washington, D.C., UFW Boycott Central Files, 1973–1977, Box 6, Folder: Barbara—Personal, ALUA. For an example of his correspondence, see Letter to the Urban Affairs and Social Action Committee of the Jewish Community Council of Greater Washington from Kay Pollock and Conrado Rodríguez, Feb. 15, 1974, Boy Cen (5–77), Box 3, Folder: Washington, D.C., 1974, ALUA.

46. For public support from the religious community, see, for example, *Washington Post,* July 6, 1973, and *El Malcriado,* Oct. 18, 1974. For internal union records commenting on help from religious groups, see Report of Washington, D.C., Boycott Director, Gilbert Padilla, Oct. 9, 1974, Boy Cen (5–77), Box 3, Folder: Washington, D.C., Boycott, 1974, ALUA.

47. For Esther Padilla quote: see *Washington Post,* Aug. 15, 1974. For Herrera family, see *El Malcriado,* Nov. 2, 1973.

48. Mata Interview, Padilla Interview. For a photo of a christening in which the Padillas are godparents, see UFW Photographic Archives, Padilla File, ALUA.

49. Padilla Interview.

50. *El Malcriado,* Dec. 15, 1970. This article on the Valdez family in Cincinnati indicates how Sergio, 18, the eldest son, often spoke for the entire family. The father and sons are more dramatically featured in this story. The Rodríguez daughters Lupe and Oralia, had more prominence in the D.C. boycott because they were the eldest children, and the sons in the family were very young at this time.

51. *El Malcriado,* Dec. 28, 1973.

52. For an analysis of the contribution of various sectors of the Washington, D.C., community, see Report of Washington Boycott Director, Oct. 9, 1974, Boy Cen (5–77), Box 3, Folder: Washington, D.C., Boycott, 1974, ALUA. The above report also indicates that the union and farm worker families also interacted with students organizations, particularly the National Student Association (NSA). The NSA, whose national office was located in Washington, DC, played a significant role in revitalizing the boycott on college campuses. Two student members of the NSA lived for a time at the boycott house and worked with farm worker families. This close relationship helped create the pressure nationwide for the removal of grapes and lettuce from universities across the nation and from three campuses in the immediate Washington, D.C., area. See also *Washington Post,* April 21, 1975, for an example of the cooperation between student groups and the farm workers.

53. *El Malcriado* (November 2, 1973) reported on the Herrera's move. The Baldwin family went to Alexandria. The Rodríguez family stayed in Washington, D.C. Padilla Interview.

54. Opponents of the union boycott also rated the Gallo effort as the most effective campaign. See, for example, a pamphlet produced by one of their professional organizations, "Boycott: A Background Perspective," prepared by the Food Distribution Information Council, Supermarket Institute, Chicago, 1975, 51, Vizzard Papers, Box 16, Folder 6, Stanford.

55. For the most thorough discussion of the Agricultural Labor Relations Act and the conflicts between growers and the UFW after its enactment, see Majka and Majka, 233–247. See also, Meister and Loftis, 215–228 and J. Craig Jenkins, 196–200.

56. Quoted in (Washington, DC, boycott newsletter) *!Acción!* (summer 1975), D.C.B. (7–77) Box 13, Folder: Layouts and Materials for Leaflets and Newsletters, etc., 1973–1977, ALUA.

57. The Padillas returned to Washington, DC in 1979 for the Chiquita banana and Red Coach lettuce boycotts. They resigned from the union in 1980. Gilbert is now a consultant to California Rural Legal Assistance and Esther is a community advocate and social worker at Centro La Familia in Fresno, CA. She served as president of the local chapter of the Mexican American Political Association (MAPA) for 1986–1987. Padilla Interview. *Fresno Bee,* Aug. 9, 1987.

58. For the departure of the Rodríguez family, see Mata Interview. See also *Washington Post,* Aug. 4, 1975, and Sept. 10, 1975. The *Washington Post* coverage of events in California was fairly comprehensive; however, publicity on the local boycott was not regular. Reporters in the above two stories made a point of noting the preponderance of Anglo organizers and the lack of farm

worker participants after the Padillas and farm worker families returned to California. The boycott officially continued for three more years when it was suspended in 1978 because the UFW diverted its boycott staff to California to administer the contracts it already held: see Delano Record, Feb. 2, 1978. For the UFW's shift in emphasis to contract administration: see, California, *Second Annual Report of the Agricultural Labor Relations Board,* July 1, 1977 to June 30, 1978, Sacramento, California, 1. The diversion of the union's resources did not last long; the boycott apparatus was reactivated a year later for the Red Coach lettuce boycott.

59. Quoted in "From the Fields to the Picket Line: Huelga Women and the Boycott,"*El Malcriado,* Aug. 15, 1970.

60. Quoted in *El Malcriado,* Aug. 15, 1970.

61. Padilla Interview. According to Esther, her letter drew no response. I have not been able to locate this correspondence in the union's archives. For an example of advocacy for women's issues within the labor movement, see Nancy Gabin, "Wins and Losses: The UAW Women's Bureau After World War II, 1945–1950," in Carol Groneman and Mary Beth Norton, eds., *"To Toil the Livelong Day": America's Women at Work, 1780–1980* (Ithaca: Cornell University Press, 1987), 233–249.

62. Other scholars have noted a similar phenomenon of increasing confidence and self-esteem as a result of labor union participation. See Laurie Coyle, Gayle Hershatter, and Emily Honig, "Women at Farah: An Unfinished Story," in Magdalena Mora and Adelaida R. Del Castillo, eds., *Mexican Women in the United States: Struggles Past and Present* (Los Angeles: UCLA Chicano Studies Research Center, 1980), 117–143. See also Vicki L. Ruiz, "Obreras y Madres: Labor Activism among Mexican Women and Its Impact on the Family," in *La Mexicana/Chicana,* The Renato Rosaldo Lecture Series Monograph, 1, Ignacio García and Raquel Rubio Goldsmith, eds. (Tucson: University of Arizona Press, Mexican American Studies Research Center, 1985), 19–38.

Chapter Thirteen

From Housewives to Activists
Women and the Division of Political Labor in the Boston Antibusing Movement

Julia Wrigley

In September 1974, national news programs showed scenes of white protesters, mainly women, screaming at black schoolchildren. The protesters denounced suburban parents as hypocrites for calling them racists while sending their own children to protected schools. These scenes took place, not in the South, but in Boston, where antibusing protesters plunged the city into turmoil and radically changed its image from a city of liberal tolerance to one of racial antagonism. The drive for desegregation had come down to a battle between poor whites and even poorer blacks, fighting over schools that the middle class had long since fled.

The 1974 Boston busing protest signaled the gathering force of white backlash (Hochschild 1984). Racial change in the North would come no more easily than it had in the South. While Northern ghetto blacks waged their own rebellion in the streets, judges began interpreting a body of federal law as requiring school desegregation in the North. Whites reacted with outrage, and the Democratic party coalition of blacks and whites began to fissure (McAdam 1988, 192–97). The Boston antibusing protest was perhaps the most traumatic event in the unraveling of the civil rights coalition.

While the Boston protest's larger significance lay in what it meant for the Northern civil rights drive, this conflict stood out because it was a movement largely organized by white working-class women. Such women are usually not very visible in politics (Chafetz and Dworkin 1986, 161–62). In the antibusing struggle, however, they organized the school protests, distributed flyers, staffed offices, and made public statements. Men helped, and some were leaders, but women did most of the organizing work. They also filled most of the slots on the executive board of ROAR (Restore Our Alienated Rights), the main antibusing organization.

By looking at the paths Boston's antibusing women took into political life, we can learn how strongly sex-segregated cultures can still support certain types of women's activism. More broadly, the history of the Boston antibusing movement can clarify what it means to have a division of political labor within a community. The protest engaged whole neighborhoods within the city, with young and old, men and women, parents and nonparents finding their own tasks. The busing protest was a right-wing movement in support of long-standing racial patterns within the city; as such, it evoked little conflict *within* Boston's neighborhoods, segregated along lines of class and race as they were. It also evoked little conflict within families. This was not a movement that challenged tradition, but one that sought to reinforce it. Boston's white working-class women, the movement's primary organizers, did not have to fight their own husbands or fathers when they joined the movement. They received instant community legitimation, since they were fighting on behalf of what was perceived as a collective goal, the maintenance of politically guaranteed segregation in the city, a segregation that had long operated in the realms of housing, city jobs, and the schools.

There is a growing literature on women and politics, one that emphasizes that women are indeed politically active, but sometimes in different ways from men (Chafetz and Dworkin 1986; Laslett, Brenner, and Arat 1995; Ridd and Callaway 1987; Reynolds 1987; Tilly and Gurin 1990; West and Blumberg 1990). They are more likely to engage in "protopolitics," that is, political activity divorced from recognized political institutions, although this tendency is diminishing (Tilly and Gurin 1990a). In this chapter, I argue that these discussions of "protopolitics" identify a characteristic form of women's political activity but have failed to address the division of political labor along lines of sex and age. To understand women's activism, researchers must clearly distinguish between activism in support of goals held by communities, or major parts of communities, and those endorsed by politically active women even over the opposition of men. In the first case, women's activism may seem divorced from that of men and spontaneous or highly combustible, but in reality it may be part of a much more complex and ordered arrangement that involves a gender-specific assignment of political tasks. To demonstrate in practice how such an assignment of political tasks can occur, I analyze the Boston antibusing movement, a protest that mobilized large sectors of Boston's white working-class communities in 1974 and for several years thereafter before waning.

The Boston protest involved not just women's activism but a specific type of activism, a right-wing political protest directed against changes in the racial status quo. As a struggle in support of racial tradition in Boston, many different people in the protesting communities had roles to play, including men, women, youths, and even the aged. This facilitated a gender-based division of labor. It is striking, however, that working-class women took the lead in the protest, which raises the question of why they did not play supporting or auxiliary roles, as women often have in other political struggles. Suffering the double disadvantage of class and sex, working-class women rarely emerge as political leaders. As a rule, they have limited access to political institutions such as unions and political parties. Studies of political participation show that education and social position are positively correlated with involvement (McCarthy and Zald 1987, 342). Working-class women have lower rates of organizational participation than do men or middle-class women, and they tend to join locally based organizations, such as volunteer groups or churches, rather than citywide, regional, or national organizations. Their localized involvement means that they seldom receive the training in public speaking or in running meetings that comes from organizational participation. Ideologically, also, communities can enforce traditional gender roles, which limit women's ability to enter the public arena. Politics remained largely, but not exclusively, a male preserve in Boston's working-class neighborhoods prior to the emergence of the 1974 antibusing movement.

This chapter analyzes the factors that allowed working-class women to become leaders in the antibusing movement, relegating men to more specialized roles. I argue that, paradoxically, it was the intense separation of women's and men's activities and daily lives in Boston that allowed women to early take command of the antibusing movement. Gender segregation reinforced women's control, since norms about gender roles assigned educational issues to women, an ownership they retained even when these issues generated a very large, militant, and intense political protest that convulsed Boston for several years. Moreover, because the movement remained confined to the city's working-class neighborhoods, the women who led it did not face competition from better-educated, better-connected middle-class women.

In addition, women retained leadership in Boston because the anti-busing movement did not use strategies that favored men. Even when struggles have a strong community component, women typically become secondary if key organizing strategies involve the use of organizational power or violence. Union struggles can involve whole communities, but even when they do, women traditionally are auxiliary supporters of male protesters, as occurred in the Flint sit-down strikes of the 1930s and in the British mining strikes of the 1970s. In these situations, fundamental power usually rests with male strikers (Ali 1987). The Boston protest, organized in neighborhoods rather than workplaces, did not favor men's leadership.

When political organizations take violence and intimidation as their central tactics, women also fall into auxiliary roles. Few aspects of political intervention are more sex-typed. Boston's antibusing women, however, were rowdy and disruptive; they specialized in organizing what I call "incitement marches," where disruption was key to their success. Incitement marches differ from violence directed at individual targets because they aim to draw the wrath of authorities by violating guidelines about march decorum or location, leaving authorities no choice except to move against women protesters, who can play on their gender to cause an outcry, or let an illegal or unsanctioned march proceed. Incitement marches, although disruptive, differ from hard-core acts of violence, which remain almost exclusively the province of men. This chapter analyzes the kind of violence found in the Boston antibusing movement as an aspect of gendered and age-segregated protest strategies. The question of how political tactics affect women's and men's political roles deserves far more attention than it has received from researchers, and here, too, the Boston case is informative.

In summary, I suggest that three factors deserve attention as central facilitators of working-class women's leadership in the Boston antibusing movement. First, because the movement sought to restore rather than challenge racial traditions (that is, because it was a right-wing move-ment), the women's activism did not pose any threat to the overall male domination of communities and families and thus received support rather than opposition from men. Second, because these were highly sex-segregated communities, certain issues were typecast as belonging to men or women, giving women early primacy on busing issues. Third, the antibusing movement had a violent component, but it was not centrally organized around violence. This essay locates working-class women's activism within a larger community context to assess how the growth and trajectory of the antibusing movement was affected by the women's leadership and how, in turn, participation in the movement affected the women themselves.

Method

The study is based on interviews with antibusing activists. The interviews were conducted in the course of four research trips to the city, including one of seven months in 1984 and one of three months in 1985; two later trips in 1986 allowed for further interviews and document collection. Other researchers have surveyed random samples of Boston residents to assess antibusing attitudes and to learn what differentiated activists from nonactivists (Useem 1980; Taylor 1986). Because my study focused on the rise and decline of the movement, I interviewed activists and leaders in the antibusing protest. To find such people, I gathered names of antibusing activists from Boston's citywide and neighborhood newspapers (including the *Boston Globe,* the *South Boston Tribune,* and the *Charlestown Patriot*). Further names came from study of document collections such as the papers of the Citywide Coordinating Committee. Nearly all antibusing activists I interviewed gave me names of additional people to interview.

Most of the interviews lasted around two hours, and, with only a few exceptions, they were tape recorded. Most interviews were conducted at people's homes, although some were done in bars, cafes, schools, offices, or parks. The study also draws on documents, leaflets, and meeting minutes given to me by movement activists. Antibusing publications such as the *South Boston Marshal* and the *Boston News Digest* provided insight into protesters' views. I also spent time at the South Boston Information Center, the original nerve center of the antibusing movement, talking informally with long-term antibusers and watching home movies they had taken of street protests and of South Boston High School during its time of turmoil.

It would have been hard to do this study during the antibusing conflict, as emotions ran high and the city was polarized. Ten years later, people's memories for dates and details had undoubtedly dimmed, but there was a corresponding gain in length of view. For most people, participating in the antibusing movement was the most dramatic thing they ever did, and they vividly recalled their emotions and actions during the movement's height.

Women's Early Lock on the Antibusing Movement

The women from Boston's white working-class neighborhoods did not so much thrust themselves into the political milieu as they were carried into it by the politicization of educational issues. In their gender-segregated communities, mothers oversaw their children's schooling as part of their maternal role. Before the arrival of busing, most did service work at their local schools, but they saw little reason to worry about the overall political direction of the school system. The white neighborhoods of South Boston, East Boston, Hyde Park, and West Roxbury were generally decisive in school committee elections. Although black residents made up about one-fifth of the city's population, they could not win a seat on the school board, which was elected at large and citywide. The school committee maintained patterns of student and teacher segregation (Dentler and Scott 1981). In 1973–74, nearly 90 percent of Boston's public school teachers were white; 8.61 percent were black, and fewer than 1 percent were Hispanic. Many of the teachers were upwardly mobile Irish-Americans who had attended parochial schools and local Catholic colleges. Imbued with conservative values, they made the public schools into a paler, secular copy of the parochial schools they had experienced. Promotion to principal or assistant principal occurred only from within, and the school district traditionally recruited teachers only from within the city (Schrag 1967, 55). Many Boston teachers opposed desegregation. They disapproved of ethnic studies and curricular innovation. Black parents found such teachers unresponsive and negative, but white parents in the city's ethnic neighborhoods respected and trusted them.[1]

Few parents in Boston's ethnic neighborhoods shared the harsh critique of the city's public schools offered by the city's more elite groups and by educational writers. Jonathan Kozol's *Death at an Early Age* (1967) described a repressive and racist school system. Peter Schrag's *Village School Downtown* (1967) attacked the Boston public schools as educational graveyards. Well-educated, cosmopolitan professionals deplored the rote learning and the dreary curriculum of the Boston schools. They pointed to the failure of Boston's high schools to send many children to college. In the city's ethnic neighborhoods, parents judged the schools by other criteria. They saw the schools as symbols of neighborhood pride and identity. High school sports teams won fierce loyalty from their communities. Most white working-class parents neither expected nor desired that their children would be taught to question the assumptions on which they had been raised. In the city's insular ethnic neighborhoods, the outside world was a threat. One antibusing South Boston mother summed up this attitude when she declared that when her daughter went to school, she wanted her "right in her neighborhood, no field trips, nothing."

Most mothers only did service work at their own children's schools, helping out on field trips or in the cafeteria, but some parents became active at regional and citywide levels. These parents had exposure to systemwide issues and debates. Active parents joined the Boston Home and School Association, the city's equivalent of the Parent-Teacher Association (PTA), an organization with a strong provincial cast. A charter clause outlawed any criticism of the school committee, which effectively ruled out any discussion of school desegregation. The school committee could impose this restriction on the Home and School Association because the district funded the organization. The rule generated little conflict, since the association operated almost exclusively in white neighborhoods. Over the years the association's members had rejected attempts to have the Boston group affiliate with the national Parent-Teacher Association because PTA affiliation might have raised questions about the Boston's group's racial practices or its relations with the school committee. Critics charged that the Home and School Association was a "vest pocket trinket" for the school committee (Dentler and Scott 1981), but such criticisms had no more effect than did educational complaints about the Boston schools. However limited the Boston Home and School Association, it helped create a network of activists who knew each other across neighborhoods.

In 1965, the Massachusetts legislature passed the Racial Imbalance Act, a law aimed primarily at Boston (Ross and Berg 1981, 56–57). It required the school committee to take steps toward desegregation, which committee members vowed never to do. Nearly ten years of skirmishing followed (Sheehan 1984, 86; Lupo 1988). City-wide Home and School Association activists heard rumors about desegregation and traded information back and forth from neighborhood to neighborhood. They understood before most parents that desegregation could become a reality and saw organizing as essential to keep it from happening. They became prophets to a fearful, but doubting, majority. Some spoke during meetings at local schools and urged the parents to take this threat seriously. For many parents, their first awareness of busing came through their Home and School Association's regional representatives. This spreading of the word through face-to-face contact accorded with the personalistic political style that was traditional in Boston's neighborhoods. Women returned from these meetings and alerted their husbands to what they had heard and then the men started coming themselves in greater numbers.

The nonpolitical nature of school activism changed with the threat of school desegregation. By then, the early antibusing activists had had a decade to learn organizing skills and to develop political identities (Ross and Berg 1981). The Boston activists, like most other social movement organizers, had strong roots in their local communities (Useem 1980), but most were not known outside of them. As the people most involved in educational issues, mothers had staked out the schools as their turf before the busing issue arose. By initially defining the educational arena as nonpolitical, these women did not view themselves as involved in a public conflict. Local activists had support from politicians, including, most notably, Louise Day Hicks from South Boston, who had won a national reputation as a candidate of white backlash; her evocative slogan, "You know where I stand," said all that was needed. Hicks faced eventual challenge in the antibusing movement (Lukas 1985), but she retained enormous symbolic importance as the best-known antibusing leader. Although other politicians jostled for position, their struggles took place on a plane one step removed from the day-to-day organizing and control of the antibusing movement. De facto control of the movement rested with a set of leaders—primarily women—who were generally known in their neighborhoods before busing but who were not known city-wide, apart from the antibusing struggle.

These women leaders emerged from the activist ranks mainly because they pursued their early neighborhood-based antibusing commitment with energy and boldness. Most had served as regional representatives in the Home and School Association, after an apprenticeship working at their own children's schools. The regional posts were not hotly contested when most first ran. Later, when the antibusing movement became a major force, factional struggles arose over some of these positions. Originally, however, the posts mainly went to those who showed eagerness to work, in line with the self-selection that operates in many civic groups (Oliver 1984). Early leaders organized mass demonstrations to bring pressure on the state legislature to repeal the Racial Imbalance Act. On April 3, 1973, five thousand demonstrators gathered at the state house. Although the demonstration was officially led by four school committee members, in fact lesser-known figures had done the organizing work. Activists received their first experiences in getting parade permits, setting up telephone trees, and running press conferences. They also organized many smaller-scale events to keep the protest in the news. Friends hatched plans at kitchen-table discussions. The Home and School Association's representative from Hyde Park joined a friend in buying lollipops for every legislator and attaching to each the message "Lick the Racial Imbalance Act."

The escalated activity brought the organizers new skills but did not require that they raise their sights far above the neighborhood. Boston is one of the few large cities that is also a state capital. State legislators from outside Boston have long believed they need to keep the city on a short leash (Taylor 1986), and the city lacks basic elements of home rule. The weakness of the Boston city council, combined with the interventionist stance of the legislature, has helped to make the city's legislative representatives the officials of first resort for citizens. Legislators from the white ethnic neighborhoods of Boston welcomed the antibusing protesters, who could gather at the state house merely by taking a city bus or the subway. One of the most vocal opponents of busing, Raymond Flynn, a state senator from South Boston (who was elected mayor of Boston in 1984), allowed antibusers to use his large office in the state house. The protesters did not have to travel far, either geographically or psychologically, to battle the racial imbalance act.

The antibusing struggle changed decisively when the venue shifted from the state legislature to the federal courts. On June 21, 1974, federal district judge W. Arthur Garrity Jr. ruled that the Boston school committee had intentionally segregated the schools. He ordered that a desegregation plan prepared by state officials be implemented in the fall. The plan did not cover the whole city, but it did require that busing between South Boston and Roxbury begin that September. Boston became the second big-city school system in the North ordered to desegregate, and it faced a more comprehensive desegregation program than had been implemented elsewhere.

Antibusers organized quickly, focusing their preparations on the school opening in September. Despite attempts by Boston's elite to downplay violence and conflict over busing, it soon became clear that the resistance was even wider and more intense than had been expected. Thousands of people turned out for meetings, motorcades, and marches. A school boycott drastically lowered attendance of white students. South Boston took the lead in organizing; its two regional Home and School Association representatives, Virginia Sheehy and Rita Graul, both housewives, became the heads of the South Boston Information Center, the core of the antibusing struggle. A new citywide antibusing organization, ROAR (Restore Our Alienated Rights) began meeting in city council chambers, courtesy of council member Louise Day Hicks.

Domestic Identities and Political Organizing

Boston's white working-class neighborhoods operated according to strict gender roles. In the Boston antibusing movement, mothers merely extended their maternal interests from the household to the neighborhood. Newly active women did not forsake their domestic identities but used them to ease the transition to activism. Many antibusing women relied on an ideology of motherhood to explain and justify their political involvement and to help them meet political demands. They saw their absences from home as serving the larger purpose of protecting their children from the danger and inferior schooling they associated with desegregation. The ideology of motherhood helped relatively uneducated women, with little experience in public speaking, to enter the public arena and believe they had something to say.

Catholic tradition had long emphasized parents' rights to decide about their children's schooling (Lee, Holland, and Bryk 1993). Parents first made the basic choice between the parochial and public systems. They then made choices within each system, since different parochial schools had different emphases and standards of academic performance. Within the public system, parents could decide whether to have their children aim for one of the exam schools, Boston Latin and Girls Latin. Mothers active in the antibusing movement went a step further in emphasizing choice by stressing their maternal awareness of each child's needs and their jobs as their children's protectors. A South Boston housewife with three children explained that mothers had been more active in the movement than fathers because mothers possess "that animal instinct in protection of your children." The fathers might have the same instincts, but they had their own responsibilities as wage earners. As a South Boston mother of four put it, "I always say it's like a lioness in her den. You know, these are my children. The father, I'm sure, feels that way, but the mother had a little more time. The fathers were out working. . . . My husband gets up at four in the morning to go to work." From the perspectives of these women, mothers played a special role in resisting busing, because they had a protective instinct and freedom from job constraints.

Active women pressed their husbands into greater domestic labor. While women went to meetings, men stayed home more often than before with children. The division of political labor thus led to a change in the division of domestic labor. A Dorchester antibusing activist said that her husband minded the children. "He agreed that the two of us couldn't be active at the same time because [the children] were fairly young. So he said, 'no problem, you go into the meetings, you find out what you can,' and we used to talk about it at home and so forth. And it became a learning process for both of us." Sometimes both husbands and wives were very active, but this seems to have occurred in only a minority of families. In several of these cases, the men were unemployed, giving them more time to devote to the movement; otherwise the tension and time demands became too great. As a male Hyde Park antibuser commented, "I think most of the people you find in any movement, one partner is active and the other one is passive. Someone has to take care of the family. Most people that get involved in these types of issues are family people. You wouldn't get involved if you didn't have some vested interest and mainly, I guess, it would be your children and what kind of future they're going to have." Families sometimes coped by adopting their own division of political labor, with mothers going to daytime meetings in their local communities, while men went to downtown ROAR meetings held in the evenings.

By emphasizing their maternal roles, antibusing women created an unchallengeable claim to authority, a strategy followed by women in earlier eras (West and Blumberg 1990a, 22; Thomis and Grimmett 1982, 58). The ideology of motherhood legitimated emotional pronouncements on busing; each mother had the right to state her feelings, and others could not question the way she did so. Women who had never spoken at public meetings got the courage to speak because they believed their feelings could not be gainsaid. They did not need to prepare talks in advance or gather facts or figures. The president of the major Charlestown antibusing organization, a mother of nine and a resident of a public housing project, explained that she hadn't known how to do public speaking but that "I just got up and said what was in my mind and in my heart." She did not have experience running organizations, but she had the emotional prerequisite, anger. "I was so angry and so mad that I kind of more or less watched others that had more experience than myself. I guess you'd say I learned the hard way." An antibusing leader from Dorchester concurred, saying that she learned how to speak by doing it: "You got up on your two feet and did it. And I think that having the personal experience, I think that the subject matter was so vital that in the beginning, even though your knees were knocking, you were so fired up, that you wanted to tell people, hey, this is the way that it is."

Other women also described themselves as fueled by emotion. One found the time to go to meetings every night because of anger. "Anger, anger. I know that's what it was. It made me strong. It scared me a couple of times, that anger could get such a grasp on your body that it controlled it." A nonpolitical mother of four children who became an antibusing leader in South Boston learned to speak up: "Your love for your child takes over and you just do it." An official of Massachusetts Citizens Against Forced Busing had been shy earlier in her life, but shyness was no barrier in dealing with busing: "Any time you spoke on this, it was coming from the heart."

The ideology of motherhood operated at the organizational as well as the personal level, reinforcing a gendered division of political labor. Within social movements, women often face a sex-typing of tasks. In the civil rights movement, male leaders tried to relegate women to office work and to keep them away from the more dangerous but more exciting and visible voter registration and organizing jobs (McAdam 1988, 107). This affront to politically engaged women helped to precipitate the feminist movement (Evans 1980). The sexual stereotyping of tasks has occurred in many social movements, but only in some does it dominate the movement's public face. In the civil rights movement, men and women did not routinely participate in separate demonstrations, and no special symbolic role attached to mothers or other women. In the anti-busing movement, in contrast, there was an ironic reversal. In practice, women probably faced less sexual stereotyping of tasks than they had in the civil rights movement, but they created a symbolically separate women's role.

The antibusing movement underscored mothers' symbolic roles by organizing special "mothers' marches." These served as vehicles for challenging authorities, becoming in practice what I term "incitement marches." A Charlestown antibusing leader explained the idea of moth-ers' marches as deriving from Charlestown's history. Boston's working-class neighborhoods have supplied many sons for the country's armies; South Boston is reported to have lost more men in Vietnam than any other community of its size. During World War II, when many Charles-town men were overseas, women decided to honor them and pray for their safety by organizing mothers' marches. When the conflict over busing arose, grandmothers who remembered the marches put the idea before antibusing women. The Charlestown women took up the idea eagerly. Pushing baby carriages and fingering rosaries, women marched to a churchyard, where they knelt in prayer. "We said the whole rosary for the busing. It was really beautiful. It was done at night, and we had the candles. It was really just lovely. We had a lot of prayer marches. Mothers and grandmothers and great-grandmothers." The women were disappointed that they could not persuade Catholic priests to bless them. In Charlestown they had to settle for a local Protestant minister who did not have to answer to his superiors. The heavy religious and maternal symbolism of these marches did not impress all observers, some of whom grimaced at their "crude contrivance" (Hillson 1977, 169–70), but with their domestic emphasis they fit the tone of the antibusing movement.

The women at the mothers' marches often engaged in raucous shouts directed at Judge Garrity and other enemies. In this and other respects, the marches harkened back to women's political history. Women de-fending their communities' traditional prerogatives in earlier eras have startled observers by their vulgarity and aggressiveness (Kaplan 1995). In nineteenth-century England, the "preservation of life and living stan-dards roused [women] to heights of unfeminine verbal and physical violence" (Thomis and Grimmett 1982, 57). The Boston women too violated norms of femininity; as their protest went outside normal politi-cal institutions, so the women went outside the boundaries of normal public behavior for their sex. They were, however, protected from police attack when they violated rules about where marchers could gather, as police hesitated to attack the mothers' marches.

The movement also adapted its tactics to women's availability. While few women could put in big blocks of time, many could participate when there were special calls for involvement. Women used their networks to create extraordinarily effective telephone trees. When news of some crisis flashed to different households, the antibusing movement could turn out hundreds, or sometimes even thousands, of people on very short notice. This happened on December 11, 1974, when a white student was stabbed at South Boston High School, and on many lesser occasions.

In spite of adjusting their activism to the rhythms of their households, politically engaged mothers faced an ironic situation. They were active in the names of their children, but their political involvement took them away from their families. The blurring of lines between personal and political responsibilities eased the conflict, as activism was viewed as an extension of the maternal role. In communities with traditional attitudes toward mothers' employment, being away from home was not so common as in middle-class communities. Some mothers worked out their own specific arguments on why their frequent absences would not harm their children. An intensely active woman from Hyde Park, the single mother of two boys and a girl, reversed the traditional argument about when children most needed their mothers. She believed that when her children were young, they did not need her guidance as much as they would when they were teenagers. Over time, as success appeared more unlikely for the antibusers, the "family claim" reasserted itself and many women, as I discuss later, found themselves concerned about the cost of their activism for their children.

The Division of Political Labor by Gender and Age

While women and, particularly, mothers claimed special roles in resisting busing, the division of political labor between men and women was not rigid. Women's preeminence did not rest on any absolute principle but sprang rather from their early identification with children's concerns. As fathers had always played some role in educational matters, in joining the antibusing movement they were not entering an arena that was entirely foreign to them. Further, the antibusing movement transcended the educational concerns that traditionally engaged mothers and became a clearly political enterprise. Men did not dominate the movement, however, as they did other political activities in Boston, but took a back seat to the women. A woman leader from Charlestown elaborated on the men's supporting roles: "Men backed us, men did everything for us, you know, anything we asked them to do, but they kind of let us run the show, us give the orders, and they just . . . any time we had a motorcade, the men would ride or be there. . . . It was mainly the women in Charlestown that did all the organizing and the hustle and bustle of running papers off, going to your meetings in Powderkeg [the Charlestown ROAR group] and everything, but the men were a big part of our organization, but kind of silent." Other women also saw the men as taking direction from them. The men were "in awe of the women" and "were quiet. They wanted to help. They just kept saying all the time, tell me what you want me to do and I'll do it."

In response to the mothers' marches, antibusing men organized a fathers' march. The first took place in South Boston and drew men from across the city. This march had a different character from those organized by the women. It also drew a different response from the police. The Charlestown mothers' marches had tried the patience of the police, as the women violated crowd control rules about how close they could come to schools (Lukas 1985). During one confrontation with police, a Charlestown mother of nine told old women and mothers with young children to fall back. She then told the marchers, "We're going through," and the women put their heads down and charged the police lines. The women had confidence that their status as mothers would protect them from attack, and, in fact, the police negotiated a compromise. In South Boston, however, the police faced no such constraints in dealing with the fathers' march. They waded into the crowd with batons swinging, and the march ended in a bloody melee. The fathers' and mothers' marches had a formal similarity but in practice conveyed a different symbolism and evoked different responses. The marches also occurred with different frequency. Just as women specialized in the daily work of relating to children's schools and running the antibusing movement, so they organized frequent mothers' marches. The fathers' march, in contrast, became a once-a-year event.

While women did not face relegation to secondary roles in the antibusing movement, active men gravitated to tasks that fell to them by the conventional division of labor. A South Boston antibusing leader said the movement relied on men to set up loudspeakers at rallies and to organize lines of traffic for motorcades. Men fixed up storefronts for antibusing offices. They also took on what they saw as the physical defense of the community, a role with overtones of violence. In February 1975 men formed the South Boston Marshals, a paramilitary organization whose members wore identifying jackets. The marshals had a simple organizational structure. The group elected a chief marshal and two assistant marshals ("South Boston Information Center News," 1975). Twelve deputy marshals were charged with forming, instructing, and controlling squads of at least ten friends or associates. The marshals patrolled the area at night and stationed members at the main roads leading into the South Boston peninsula. If they saw people they thought were suspicious, they relayed word to other marshals. Jimmy Kelly, the president of the South Boston Information Center and later a member of the Boston city council, explained that the marshals adopted a tougher, more hard-line style than would have been appropriate for women.[2] The marshals were an auxiliary to the main antibusing protest, albeit an intimidating one.

Some men became leaders in the antibusing movement. More so than the women, the male leaders tended to develop a specialized area of expertise. Jimmy Kelly's history provides a case in point. Kelly, a sheet metal worker when busing started, did not at first join the movement because his children attended parochial schools. When he became active about a year later, a leadership hierarchy had already been established. He was, in his words, a Johnny-come-lately. As another South Boston activist commented, "In South Boston, you know your place." Kelly needed a way to be active without stepping on toes. He succeeded by finding jobs he could do better than the women leaders who were already in place. Kelly had been active in the Sheet Metal Workers Union and had broad union connections. He concentrated on linking the unions (particularly the conservative building trades) and the antibusing movement. He managed to get many Boston unions to pass antibusing resolutions. Kelly had been astute enough to find an area where greater access to institutional power gave him leverage that the women leaders lacked. He also did other work where he had an advantage over the women. When Louise Day Hicks visited neighborhoods where she feared a hostile reaction, Kelly served as her driver and protector. His energy and dedication paid off in advancement through the movement's ranks. When the two women who originally led the South Boston Information Center gave up their posts, Kelly took over as the center's president. He also became the chief media spokesperson for the South Boston group. These two jobs gave him sufficient visibility that he later successfully campaigned for a seat on the Boston city council.

Other men also developed specialties. A Hyde Park father worked two jobs to support his family but spent all his available spare time on antibusing activities. Although without training in law, he took a particular interest in legal issues and served as a member of the Home and School Association's three-person legal committee. Sal Giarrantani specialized in writing political columns for local newspapers and for the *Boston News Digest*, a paper that billed itself as the official voice of ROAR. Charlie Ross, a retired longshoreman from Dorchester, also developed a role as a movement news analyst, although from a harder-core right-wing perspective. A man from Charlestown became known for a rather different specialty. A major figure in Powderkeg, he openly advocated violence. He stood out from many of the women leaders because of his emphasis on physical toughness. When some parents objected that their children might get hurt, he replied that it was a price that might have to be paid.

The men, in short, often found a movement niche if they aspired to leadership. They tended to claim roles where men traditionally had more political skills and leverage than women. These included the roles of ideologue, union liaison, physical tough, and legal expert. In a movement with a more middle-class membership, they might have had trouble adopting some of these informal identities. In a more middle-class movement, there would be actual lawyers, as well as self-taught aficionados, to specialize in legal issues. There would be better-educated men to serve as news analysts and ideologues, and the less educated might not find a voice. Particularly in the United States, with its lack of class-based politics, ideological confidence is strongly tied to education (McCarthy and Zald 1987). In the Los Angeles antibusing movement, which was based in the largely middle-class San Fernando Valley, women took the lead, but their husbands contributed by offering their professional skills. A public relations expert, for example, thought up the name for the new protest organization.[3] He called it Bustop, a name with more public relations savvy than ROAR or Powderkeg. Other men offered legal and accounting services. Even in broadly similar types of political protests, then, the division of political labor varied, with class and sex affecting the type of work people did and the allocation of tasks.

The division of labor on the busing issue went further, with working-class youth in Boston's white communities playing special, quasi-political roles. They made no attempt to assume any overall leadership in the movement, leaving that to their elders. Instead, they kept the pot boiling in the schools, forming "white caucuses" and engaging in melees with black students (Malloy 1986). The youth had friendly relations with political leaders such as Louise Day Hicks. Some male teenagers led assaults on blacks; they were responsible for most of the violence that marked the Boston antibusing movement. In a broader sense, they could be seen as taking on roles commonly adopted by juveniles in neighbor-hoods where residents repel a perceived racial invasion (Suttles 1970). Suttles describes the way adults in such communities often implicitly approve juvenile violence directed toward outsiders. The youth are not so much out of control as taking on a task reserved for those of their age and sex. This also took place during a bitter antibusing conflict in Canarsie, New York (Rieder 1985).

The participation of teenage boys in the protest, and their focus on brawling, led some mothers to question what they had wrought. They developed doubts about the division of political labor in their communi-ties once they saw its consequences for their children. This was particu-larly true in communities such as South Boston and Charlestown, where violence was part of the antibusing struggle. Even the most committed activists sometimes quailed when they saw their own children running wild. In Charlestown, night after night youths battled police; in South Boston and Hyde Park, white and black students brawled inside the high school. While the white youths received a measure of community sanc-tion for their activities, some parents began to feel their children were taking steps toward violent and possibly criminal behavior that could not be retraced. One Charlestown mother said, "It was just too much violence. You had to stop it. For the kids' sake, you had to stop it. You had to. Because that little lost generation out there, you got more kids in trouble since the busing than you ever would have in trouble before." She added, "The cops brought the violence into the town, and the kids kept it up. You had to call it quits after a while. It was sad for the children." She sent her youngest boy to live with her brother, afraid that he would be drawn into the violence. A South Boston mother had no regrets about participating in the antibusing movement, saying that she made many friends through her activism but that she worried about the effect on her kids. The protest made the youngsters politically aware: but it had a cost. "The only thing that I didn't like is that I find a lot of racism in them. Racist remarks. I don't know, I suppose in myself at times. I'll be honest. But I thought, well, it won't happen to them."

The contrast with black youth is instructive. During the busing conflict, adults in the black community campaigned against violence (Hillson 1977) and saw it as damaging to their interests. They formed task forces and worked to persuade young blacks to keep calm even in the face of provocation. Their efforts did not always work, as black students did engage in violence in the schools and on the streets, but the contrast between their control efforts and the lack of such efforts in the white community was striking. Youths cannot be entirely controlled by adults, but adults can shape the context within which violence is perceived as either serving a broader community purpose or as harming it.

Teenage girls played much smaller roles in the antibusing movement than did boys. They participated in fights inside schools but did not specialize in violence. Nor had they yet reached identities as mothers, so they lacked their own mothers' special identification with the busing issue.

Political Parochialism and the Antibusing Movement

The Boston antibusing movement was firmly rooted in the city's working-class neighborhoods. Not only did few middle-class Bostonians participate, but the movement's activists made almost no connections to intellectual circles. Working-class women and men faced little competition for leadership from the more privileged. This allowed them to develop their own leadership and political identities. It also reinforced reliance on a political style that had little attraction for those outside their own communities.

Middle-class Bostonians had little incentive to join the antibusing movement. While all blacks had suffered from racial discrimination and thus blacks of all class levels had motivation to join the civil rights movement, busing affected few middle-class children. Many prosperous families had given up on the public schools before busing started. The city of Boston encompasses only a small part of its metropolitan area;

the educationally concerned middle classes live in its huge suburban ring. The suburbs offered better-funded, more innovative school systems, and they also offered middle-class peers. Those educated, well-off parents who stayed in the city of Boston usually avoided the public schools.

There are other reasons for the relative absence of middle-class families from the antibusing movement. In Boston, municipal politics has long been the preserve of the city's ethnic groups, particularly the Irish (Erie 1988). Middle-class citizens tended to look askance at the brawling political world that surrounded them. They had little channel into the alien world of Boston's working-class neighborhoods. Those middle-class residents who had risen from the working-class districts had cultural ties with their old neighborhoods, but in their new homes they had less opportunity to build a political base and join a broader current of activists (Taylor 1986).

Because antibusers came so largely from one class and cultural tradition, they had a limited reach into other communities. The very meanings they attached to some concepts differed from those in other settings. In the antibusing movement, leaders gained from being perceived as having expert knowledge of the school system. Middle-class school reformers, such as the leaders of the Citywide Educational Coalition, also prided themselves on their expertise, but they meant something different by it. Antibusers relied on, and intensified, the gathering of informal information about the schools, the kind women had traditionally exchanged with each other. The middle-class reformers relied much more heavily on written information and on the presentation of their findings in cool, dispassionate language.

The lack of active middle-class support did not mean that antibusers were ideologically on their own. An advisory referendum and public opinion polls showed lopsided majorities (in the range of 90 percent) against busing (Taylor 1986). The antibusers maintained a high pitch of activity, with weekly demonstrations and motorcades. They also skirted the bounds of legality by conducting school boycotts, which were notably effective in such neighborhoods as South Boston and Charlestown. Some parents kept their children out of school for a full year, and a small minority kept them out even longer. The movement dominated people's lives. "We were absolutely consumed, totally, with busing. You couldn't have two people sit down at a dinner table or meet each other in the market or pass each other in the street without having the conversation going into busing."

In spite of this massive level of support and activism, the antibusers did not build a broadly based movement. As we have noted, because antibusers came so largely from one class and cultural tradition, their contacts with those in other communities were limited. Unlike the civil rights movement, which received money and volunteers from across the country, the antibusers had mounted a community-based protest, and it remained a community protest. The working-class women and men who formed it had far more strength in their city than outside of it; within the city, they had far more strength at the bottom of institutions than at the top. Their own suspicion of outsiders reinforced their isolation. Further, their political experience had not prepared them for formulating their protest in terms that would give it appeal outside their own circles. The division of political labor that led to sudden visibility for the protest's working-class women leaders did not mean that they could turn that visibility to political advantage outside their communities.

Movements with an ideological bent toward universalism try to maximize ties based on common convictions and to minimize other divisions. Left-wing unions and political parties urge unity across race, class, and regional lines. Boston's antibusing activists had no ideology that would encourage them to see others as potential supporters. Their community-based vision led to distrust and exclusion of outsiders. Neighborhood women ran the protest movement, and they tried to keep it a neighborhood event. Because ROAR meetings were held in the city council chambers (courtesy of council member Louise Day Hicks), outsiders could not officially be barred. Yet each meeting began with an injunction that attendees should look to the left of them and look to the right of them. Any person who wasn't known and could not be vouched for was asked to leave. This also occurred at neighborhood antibusing meetings. Even if a person claimed to live in the community, if not vouched for, he or she faced the risk of expulsion. Antibusers circulated stories about how they had unmasked police agents or reporters. Some of the movement's members became known for their penetrating questioning of outsiders to check their bona fides.

Suspicion was pervasive from the beginning of the movement. One activist recalled attending an early Home and School Association meeting where a regional representative and key antibusing leader gave a presentation. Afterward, she approached the speaker. "I said, 'Can I ask you a question?' She said, 'Only if you tell me who you are.' And I said,

'Oh, the guard's up already. I mean, this early on.' And I think they could have organized better if everyone wasn't as suspicious."

Not only strangers at meetings were met with suspicion. Antibusers quickly developed a dislike of the press. They believed the liberal media deliberately distorted the antibusing protest. A Dorchester antibuser said protesters distrusted the media "because the press was so hostile to our point of view and because they so maligned us. For example, whenever they showed a person at the meetings, it was never, say, a person such as myself or somebody like me; it was always the woman with the curlers in her hair, the gum-chewing, wise-cracking one who was not afraid to use vulgar words. You see, so we came across, the media painted us as rather coarse."

Antibusers pointed to an agreement among representatives of the establishment media, arrived at before school opened in September 1974, to downplay violence. While the *New York Times,* not a party to the pact, had headlined its early stories with reports of violence, the *Boston Globe* presented a determinedly optimistic view in the early stages of busing. When this pact was exposed, antibusers claimed vindication. The *Globe* became a particular target, with antibusers denouncing its editorials and news stories (Ross and Berg 1981, 506). Antibusers tried to stop *Globe* delivery trucks. After shots were fired into the windows of the newspaper's press room, the *Globe*'s managers installed a bulletproof shield. More generally, volunteer workers at the South Boston Information Center claimed the press so consistently distorted their statements that they saw no reason to talk with the media.

Some antibusers feared that the media and other outsiders would focus attention on any racist remarks that were made at antibusing meetings. Movement organizers encouraged the development of a highly emotional response to busing, legitimating it by the focus on parents' rights. Far from discouraging or prohibiting emotional outbursts, antibusing meetings became forums where parents could vent their emotions. These included racist emotions. Others found such comments damaging and embarrassing and over time moved to have the meetings more tightly structured. One antibusing woman summed up the problem:

> You took women who were housewives, they were the best organizers. You took people who had never done anything like this before, they'd never been involved politically. . . . The apathy, I would say, among them

was great, great. They took care of the kids, they went to their downtown in their own neighborhoods, and they met somebody for coffee, and that was it. I mean, they were lucky if they read the paper. And that was a very large part of this movement. They bought their local paper over a citywide one or the *New York Times*, they never heard of it. They were insulated. But Boston's neighborhoods are insulated. They always were.

The housewives showed they could organize, but they did not always know, or care, how their movement would appear elsewhere in the country. From the standpoint of the larger society, the racist comments at meetings, the antiblack slogans on the walls, the occasional assaults on blacks tainted the movement and made political association with it damaging, even though the overwhelming majority of whites opposed busing.[4]

Antibusers became increasingly aware that their movement's racist taint damaged it, but many responded with a sense of grievance about the injustice of the charge. After racial incidents occurred, they usually called for more media attention to black assaults on whites. Significantly, antibusers attacked the Boston Chamber of Commerce for taking out full-page newspaper ads deploring racial violence. The antibusers' already strong "us versus them" attitude intensified as powerful people and institutions increasingly distanced themselves from the violence they associated with the antibusing movement.

Public opinion surveys have shown that even through racial gulfs persist in American society, there has been declining tolerance for overt racism (Schuman and Steeh 1996). The antibusing movement's racist image made it harder to attract supporters from outside the affected neighborhoods. Organizers often sought in vain for well-known speakers to address their rallies. Whatever they might think of busing, few outsiders were interested in becoming so publicly identified with the Boston protest. Antibusers had some links with their counterparts in Louisville, Kentucky. The 1975 Louisville protest, however, with the Ku Klux Klan leading street marches, had image problems that at least rivaled Boston's (Hillson 1977). Its leaders could not add respectability to the Boston antibusers. Ultimately the Boston organizers found a black man from Texas, Clay Smothers, who came to Boston to address antibusing rallies. The mere fact that a black speaker had to be imported from Texas undercut the effort to present a multiracial image.

Busing protesters did have one reliable, articulate, middle-class speaker for their rallies; their ambivalent relations with him made plain the difficulties of going outside their own circle. Avi Nelson, who hosted a four-hour radio talk show, was the son of a rabbi and had been educated at Harvard. While antibusers did not find the *Boston Globe* or local TV stations open to them, they were welcome on radio talk shows. On Nelson's show, antibusers could speak informally and reach large audiences. Nelson became a hero to many in South Boston, Charlestown, East Boston, and other antibusing areas. He was a featured speaker at big rallies and obliged by giving rousing speeches (Ross and Berg 1981, 545–564). Crowds responded with chants of "Here we go, Avi, here we go" (Hillson 1977, 78). Yet all was not smooth. Neighborhood people were troubled by his speaking style. As one person remarked, Nelson spoke not in sentences but in paragraphs. People could not always understand him. Others suspected that Nelson was laughing at them. The *Boston News Digest,* a publication of the antibusing movement, ran a column accusing Nelson of jeering when ordinary people mispronounced words. The columnist detected an ugly disrespect in Nelson's attitude, even while acknowledging his aid to the movement. Antibusers had taken a risk in building ties with Nelson, as they exposed themselves to possible class-related scorn.

Historically, left-wing movements have often won the services of committed intellectuals. Movements of workers and the dispossessed have used such ties to create a sympathetic larger audience for their protests. Intellectuals have publicized their causes and helped interpret them for others. Right-wing movements have also won support from intellectuals, with fascist movements particularly notable in this regard. The Boston antibusing movement took place as part of a larger white backlash against the civil rights movement, but it remained a limited countermovement more than an ideologically based attempt to restructure the society. As such, it attracted few intellectuals. Its organizers were culturally very distant from the intellectual circles of Boston and did not find sympathizers willing to help them bridge the gap.

Without links to intellectual circles, antibusers had a very limited national network. Some joined the National Association of Neighborhood Schools (NANS), a loose organization that tried to build ties between antibusing groups. While those who joined found it broadening and informative, only a handful of Bostonians participated. NANS remained a weak organization that could not provide more than moral support to local groups. The national organization did contain a college professor from Iowa who acted as an intellectual leader. Boston antibusers appreciated his writings attacking busing. It is noteworthy, however, that this professor wrote under a pseudonym. He was unwilling to merge his professional and his antibusing identities, evidently fearing that his professional standing and career would be damaged. Antibusing groups carried a stigma that made it hard to win support from intellectuals, and even those few who actively supported the movement remained cautious.

Even on a local level, antibusers had a hard time winning institutional, rather than personal, support. Across a wide range of institutions, they had more support from rank-and-file members than from policymakers at the top. This applied to their relations with the police, the church, the press, the business community, the school system, the unions, and the political system. Even in the organization that helped nurture them, the Home and School Association, antibusers found they could not secure the type of unqualified institutional support they felt they were due. A neighborhood-based movement built on informal ties lacked the leverage to secure broader, institutionally based support.

The antibusers' relations with the church illustrate this problem. Many parish priests sympathized with them; this was particularly true in South Boston, where conservative priests predominated. At higher levels in the hierarchy, however, the antibusers got less support (Ross and Berg 1981, 185). Cardinal Humberto Madeiros angered antibusers by ordering Catholic schools not to accept students who were fleeing busing. In practice, most parents found ways around the ban, which was laxly enforced. Catholic schools were facing declining enrollments; the appeal of new students made the authorities reluctant to enforce the rule, and many parents, especially those who had previously supported their parish, succeeded in enrolling their children. The more militant antibusers, though, found it hard to forgive the cardinal for even having enunciated a policy that undermined their struggle. They denounced the cardinal, and some declared that the archdiocese would receive no further support from them. Some antibusers were blunt in their hostility. The antibusing leader Elvira "Pixie" Palladino was known for her outspoken style. An East Boston housewife, she used her post as a regional representative of the Home and School Association to build a network and name recognition that later led to her election to the school committee. Palladino dismissed the cardinal as "a jerk."[5] The historian John McGreevy concludes that the busing issue drove a major wedge between Catholic leaders and parishioners (1996, 261).

The antibusers did more than criticize the cardinal, also targeting him for a special form of protest that they reserved for prominent opponents. The antibusers organized horn-honking motorcades to the homes of those they wished to pressure, with the intention of embarrassing him when he lacked the protection of his official position and surroundings. This public display of hostility showed the extent of the alienation from the church hierarchy felt by antibusing activists.

The antibusing movement won considerable support from local police. Many came from South Boston and other white working-class neighborhoods. Deeply angered by court-imposed affirmative action plans, many white police officers already felt a sense of grievance against blacks. The president of the Boston Police Patrolmen's Association, Chester Broderick, militantly opposed both busing and affirmative action. In discussing busing, he declared, "You've got to understand one thing. We all had children in the Boston schools. And we knew one thing that was loud and clear. We were going to have, they were creating, a generation of idiots."[6] In spite of this grass-roots support, antibusers developed very hostile relations with the police chief, Robert di Grazia. They railed at him as a "neo-Nazi" for his use of the Tactical Patrol Force against demonstrators.[7] Equally important, many beat cops did not dare to make their antibusing feelings publicly known. Broderick, as president of the police union, had the freedom to express his views, but he counseled ordinary police officers not to make public statements that could get them in trouble with the hierarchy.

The same pattern of greater grass-roots than high-level support occurred in the labor unions. Many local Boston unions passed antibusing resolutions. And, in a major coup, antibusers also succeeded in getting the Massachusetts state labor federation to pass an antibusing statement. When the national AFL-CIO learned of the antibusing resolution, however, it ordered the state federation to rescind it. The national labor body did not want its state affiliates to enter such racially charged conflicts. The state federation complied with the AFL-CIO order (Hillson 1977, 103).

Antibusers had much closer ties with neighborhood newspapers than with citywide ones. Their hostile relations with the Boston Globe have already been described. They got more favorable coverage from such local papers as the South Boston Tribune and the Charlestown Patriot. These local papers helped publicize antibusing events and ran columns by neighborhood activists. Even the local papers, however, did not want to become semiofficial organs of the antibusing movement, since their main stock in trade was reporting on local people and neighborhood happenings. This led antibusers to establish their own publication, the *Boston News Digest,* which came out for several years. The South Boston Marshals also put out a newspaper. The neighborhood papers had geographically limited audiences, but the movement's own publications reached a still narrower circle.

The Boston school committee displayed unremitting hostility toward busing (Dentler and Scott 1981). Historically, the school committee's stance had been of great political importance in stalling desegregation efforts and here the antibusers had their greatest political influence. This influence, however, was of declining importance as busing became a reality. When federal district judge W. Arthur Garrity took increasing control over the school system, the school committee was forced to operate within ever more circumscribed areas. Recalcitrant school committee members were threatened with contempt of court citations, and several backed away from open defiance of the judge. Equally important, the changes brought to the Boston school system by desegregation helped break the tradition of promoting superintendents from within the system. The old method had rewarded those tried and true administrators who had played the political game with the school committee. The new, more open search process brought in superintendents who had less regard for the committee's prerogatives and patronage practices. One, Superintendent Robert Wood, the former president of the University of Massachusetts, came into office with the goal of cleaning up the school system and making it run on an efficient basis. He viewed the committee members as engaging in meaningless political posturing and strove to get around them.[8] The attempt to run the schools in a more professional, technocratic manner weakened the historical influence of the Irish neighborhoods on the schools' administration. The Home and School Association, the original organizational vehicle for white parents in the schools, declined in importance as the judge set up new racial-ethnic councils at each school. The old mechanisms of school system domination weakened as busing proceeded. In addition, over time militant antibusers came into conflict with some Home and School Association leaders who wanted to maintain some independence from the antibusing movement.

In solid antibusing communities, activists won support from local businesses. They approached owners of beauty parlors, bars, restaurants, corner stores, and other local concerns and asked for money. Local businesses took out ads in antibusing publications and displayed anti-

busing flyers and posters in their shop windows. Critics charged antibusing leaders with employing intimidating tactics against local businesses.
It was clear to all that those businesses dependent on neighborhood
patronage would not survive if they antagonized antibusers.

Antibusers had much less success winning support or money from
large concerns. The president of the South Boston Information Center,
Jimmy Kelly, approached the Gillette Corporation, which had a facility
in South Boston. He strongly intimated that Gillette would do well to
provide aid; the Gillette manager responded with outrage. Large companies had no reason to bow to the antibusers. Similarly, the Boston
Chamber of Commerce showed itself willing to disregard the antibusers,
even though it operated cautiously (Ross and Berg 1981, 186–88). The
chamber took a stance against violence, which all understood to be
directed at the antibusing movement.

Antibusers targeted some businessmen's homes for motorcade visits.
A business leader with a spot on the board of United Way became a
target because he had voted to give money to a black organization that
supported desegregation. The personalistic motorcade tactic could only
further alienate the business elite, from whom in any case antibusers
were separated by a long-standing class and cultural gulf (Lupo 1988).

The pattern of parochial influence continued in the political sphere.
The antibusers had great clout in certain neighborhoods, but the larger
the political district, the less solid their power. They never succeeded in
electing a mayor who took a firm antibusing stance. Mayor Kevin White
temporized on the issue, angering many antibusers, but remained in
office all through the busing conflict. Louise Day Hicks won wide name
recognition as the champion of the antibusers, but she ended her political
career by working out behind-the-scenes deals with Mayor White. These
deals brought her some control over patronage but did not involve
policy concessions on the mayor's part. Even at the height of the movement, the antibusers' anger and activism never translated into broad
electoral success. The movement created new leaders who ran for political office; very few built lasting careers. The striking exceptions to this
generalization were Raymond Flynn, a former state senator from South
Boston who later became mayor of Boston, and James Kelly, who began
a long career as a city council member.

Raymond Flynn appears an exception to the relative political failure
of the antibusers (Clay 1991, 21–22). Although Flynn vocally opposed
busing, he escaped the tarnishing that often came with identification

with the antibusing movement, in part because he took care to avoid intemperate language or actions even at the height of the struggle. Flynn developed a reputation for being a reasonable man and more open-minded than many of the antibusers. He had large political ambitions, which may have helped him decide to temper his comments. More militant antibusers viewed him as an unreliable, self-interested politician. Stanley Lieberson, in his analysis of racial politics, comments that "Politicians representing an overwhelmingly white constituency may well take stands that they are prepared to drop when running for an office with a broader electorate that includes more black voters" (1981, 570). Flynn was in fact less parochial than many other antibusing leaders, which helped his career but made him suspect in antibusing circles.

The antibusers' parochialism was perhaps nowhere more clearly seen than in their mode of political participation. They came out of a political tradition where ideology customarily took a back seat to practical gain. Even when they had a highly emotional issue, practical issues intruded. Antibusers rapidly slid into standard Boston wheeling and dealing around jobs and favors. Although the Irish machine had declined from its height early in the century (Judd and Swanstrom 1994), Boston politics traditionally ran on material incentives, with the Boston school committee an eager dispenser of patronage (Sheehan 1984). As the antibusing movement catapulted new leaders into politics, they found opportunities for such rewards opening up to them. Women who had never before been in much of a position to enter the patronage network now found themselves receiving offers. Some activist women got jobs for their husbands or brothers or sons; some got jobs for themselves. Many of the jobs did not pay well, but they were the heart of Boston politics. Their offer, and rumors of their offer, helped divide the antibusing movement. Purists accused those who took jobs of selling out. Those in Charlestown thought people in South Boston were getting more jobs. Some who took jobs in the school system said they were doing it to bring back inside information; their critics noted, however, that after a few months, the information usually stopped. The price of jobs was political support for office holders, in the words of Jimmy Kelly, the job takers became "part of the club." [9]

Some leaders found themselves discredited because they held city jobs. Others questioned the leaders' motives. The movement could not unite on a mayoral candidate because many people had much invested in Mayor Kevin White's continuation in office, and a bitter faction fight

erupted in ROAR between Louise Day Hicks, who had secret connections with Mayor White, and Pixie Palladino. The personalistic world of
Boston politics meant that there was little tradition of unity for a cause.
Equally important, others in the movement assumed that activists would
be looking out for their own interests. The strategy of cooptation works
most easily when people have little economically and are accustomed to
seeing politics as a way to get some personal benefit. To coopt a middle-
class movement, the jobs would have had to be more attractive and
higher paying; in a movement with a firmer ideological viewpoint, cooptation would also have been more difficult (see Fendrich 1977). In
Boston, some of those in the antibusing movement who did not get jobs
became bitter. The suspicion that was directed against outsiders was
now directed toward insiders.

As the movement began to splinter, less-committed parents started to
drop away, leaving the harder-core activists to carry on. Lofland notes
that "membership maintenance" is a constant problem for social movement organizations, especially ones that do not achieve their goals.
Members begin to ask themselves, "How long does one strive to reach
seemingly 'impossible dreams'?" (1996, 238). The doubts can be particularly acute for those with heavy family responsibilities, who have less
"biographical availability" than the students, autonomous professionals,
and well-off retired who are disproportionately active in many social
movement organizations (231). Antibusing mothers who had been going
to meetings in the evenings and to motorcades and rallies on the weekends began to wonder if their children might be suffering from their
activism. Boycotters became bitter when other protesters began sending
their children back to school. An antibusing leader in Hyde Park reported,

> I kept my kids out until I saw that everybody wasn't doing what they said
> they were going to do. My kids were being deprived of education, as far
> as I was concerned. I was willing to make that sacrifice for all of the other
> children who were suffering in the city because we were supposed to stick
> together. Then I saw people sending their children to school and my kids
> were staying home.

Some parents succeeded in getting their children into Catholic schools,
but these were often in suburbs, as the cardinal's enrollment ban was
not taken to apply to schools outside the archdiocese. Families had to
put time and energy into transport, which made activism costlier. Moth-

ers also wanted to do service work in their children's new schools, which further drained time from the movement. Over the long haul, the demands of individual families reasserted themselves. "Mothers had to go to work to put kids in private schools. Fathers had to take two jobs. Their life reverted back to their immediate family and how they could find an alternative education for their kids. . . . Time took its toll, people got burnt out. How many times can you motorcade, march, demonstrate, picket? And we were doing it seven nights a week, seven days a week." [10] The division of political labor had helped propel mothers into a community-based political struggle, but eventually the demands of the household division of labor pulled mothers back into the family as the movement began to seem futile.

The Effects of Activism on the Protestors

After the antibusing movement ended, the active women and their husbands did not always go back to the status quo ante. The activism had imposed great strains on some families, particularly where the husbands grew tired of their wives' absence and preoccupation. Antibusers, rightly or wrongly, attributed a good number of divorces to the movement. Even when husbands did accommodate their wives' activism, the women sometimes had developed a new sense of their own abilities. Because more children were in private school, families also had new tuition bills, so more mothers went to work to help pay them.

With few exceptions, active antibusing women did not undergo the life-altering experience reported by college women who joined the civil rights movement. Doug McAdam (1988) interviewed white students who went to Mississippi for the 1964 Freedom Summer project. Their experiences in the South had a lasting impact on them. When he compared them with an otherwise similar group of students who had applied to join the Freedom Summer project and who had been accepted but did not ultimately attend, he found differences in lifestyle and values twenty years later. Those who had participated remained more political and were more likely to have social service jobs and less likely to have business jobs. McAdam found the biggest differences among the women. Those who had participated in the project were less likely to be married or have children and had clearly opted for less conventional lifestyles, an impression borne out by the interviews.

The Boston women, in contrast, were intensely active, but within a traditional framework. Their activism moved some of them along a political curve, but it did not seem to have shifted them to a new curve. The Mississippi Freedom Summer women, however, did shift to new curves; their lives took new courses. Why the difference? First, the students who traveled south for Freedom Summer were undertaking high-risk activism. Three civil rights workers had been murdered in the area shortly before the students' arrival. Their work had an enormous emotional charge, heightened by the genuine risk they faced. Second, the students were in entirely new surroundings, far from their comfortable college campuses or middle-class families. The project volunteers lived with black families. Many had never had close contact with blacks before, and certainly not with very poor blacks living in harsh conditions. For companionship, the volunteers had each other and local project supporters, all people committed to social change. These circumstances created the conditions for a transformative experience. Third, the students were at a life-cycle stage where they were just beginning the process of shaping their lives. They had not yet taken on domestic responsibilities; fewer than 2 percent of the volunteers had children, and only 10 percent had spouses (McAdam 1988, 44). They were free, and a change of life course did not have to be negotiated with recalcitrant family members. Their lack of obligations made them available for change. Women students also tried to renegotiate the division of political labor, directly challenging the men about who would do what work, an experience that ultimately helped create a new wave of feminism (Evans 1980).

Antibusing women also had an intense experience of activism, but it occurred under very different conditions. They did not face physical danger. While some demonstrations ended in violence, the local police tried to maintain good relations with protesters. Most of the police came from antibusing neighborhoods; many had large families and themselves strongly opposed busing. The elite Tactical Patrol Force was far more forbidding, and the antibusers had documented charges of brutality against them. Still, they faced no threat of harm at the average demonstration. The women were proud of their lack of fear. Pixie Palladino was perhaps typical in being exhilarated rather than overcome by challenge. When police tried to stop her and some followers from sitting in the street, she dared them to arrest her. When they did, she remained defiant. On one occasion, when Judge Garrity threatened to hold her in

contempt for refusing, with other school committee members, to produce a desegregation plan, she declared that, since her husband supported her, it would not cost her if she went to jail. The male school
committee members might be frightened; the lawyers among them feared
disbarment. But Palladino saw no reason for fear. The judge decided not
to hold her in contempt, reserving that for the three men (who quickly
folded). Even those women who were investigated by the FBI reported
no dismay. They felt, rather, some pride in having drawn so much
attention, although several confessed they had never expected that they,
respectable housewives, would ever be FBI targets. As a group, the
antibusing activists seem to have felt little sense of threat and certainly
did not experience the fear of violence felt by the Freedom Summer
volunteers.

Moreover, the antibusing women undertook their activism in their
normal surroundings. They did not expand their horizons by any geo-
graphic moves or by any new acquaintance with people very different
from themselves. And, nearly all the women had already made domestic
commitments. They were mothers and were not at a stage in their life
cycle when they could shape their lives with little reference to others.
When the antibusing movement ended, they went back to being
housewives or went out to work. Few changed their basic mode of
living. Even women who had played dramatic public roles returned to
their domestic worlds, a phenomenon researchers have noted among
participants in other social movements (West and Blumberg 1990a, 22).

Perhaps still more important than any of these reasons, the antibusing
women had not been led to any ideological shift by their experiences.
They learned new skills and developed new political identities, but they
did not rethink their world. Many became more conservative, but this
was part of a larger shift of the white working class away from the
Democratic Party at the national level and toward the Republican. These
voters were part and parcel of the "white backlash." They believed
affirmative action benefited blacks at the expense of whites (Useem
1980; Taylor 1986). Aside from this reactive response, most antibusing
activists did not venture far into the realm of ideology. They had a
grievance that cut close to home and did not require any broad reshaping
of their worldview. Although some became visible political leaders and
often outshone their husbands, they perceived themselves not as challenging the men in their communities but rather as performing a task
that had fallen to them in the gendered division of labor.

Interestingly, the Boston activists who did undergo significant change were the very small number of white residents of working-class neighborhoods who stood out against the antibusing movement. Their stance rapidly produced isolation and physical danger for them. It also led them into a new circle of acquaintances and friends. They met black people through joint work on parent councils; the councils met at "neutral sites," as the risk was too great for them to meet in such areas as South Boston. These people paid a high price for their activism. One South Boston couple had police officers stationed outside their house for six months to protect them. They moved out of their bedroom because it was at the front of their house and at risk from firebombing. On several occasions, threatening crowds gathered in front of their house. Another South Boston woman who opposed the antibusing movement had her car destroyed. Her sister, who was nonpolitical and owned a hairdressing salon on South Boston's main street, was forced out of business. These people's initial, almost instinctive, stance against the antibusing movement led them into another world, socially and, to some extent, ideologically. Their conditions and experiences were more similar to those of the Freedom Summer participants than were those of the antibusing women. The daily lives of the antibusing women changed, but their activism took place within a community framework that limited larger-scale change.

Conclusions

This article positions right-wing women's political activism in a broader analytical context, with detailed examination of the Boston antibusing protest serving to illuminate fundamental issues of when and how women enter the political arena. Antibusing activists did not make a demand for a change in the political division of labor. However far their activism took them from their pre-protest daily lives, as a right-wing movement it did not involve a fundamental rethinking of the gendered division of political labor. As soon as women make such a demand, they leave behind the shelter of community legitimacy, a legitimacy that made possible an enormous variety of actual political activities on the part of Boston's antibusing protesters but that did not allow them to contest the fundamental framework of their political lives.

As researchers analyze the dynamics of right-wing women's activism, they need to remain aware of the place that activism holds in the larger community and the extent to which it is, or is not, perceived as a challenge to the customary gender arrangements of that community. Behind what appear to be a "protopolitics" of protests and outbursts may lie, in fact, a semiordered world of political tasks divided along lines of age and gender, where participants, in the words of one leading antibuser, "know their place." The arrangements may work reasonably smoothly, with general endorsement of each group's activities by others, until one group is perceived as going too far, as male antibusing youths who engaged in violence were often perceived by their mothers as going too far. The parents seldom contested the youths' goals; rather, they saw their children's activities as ultimately self-destructive and made efforts to rein them in. In a community-based protest, people have the freedom to act only when others endorse their mode of activism and help make it possible. The very process of activism—the attendance at meetings, the speaking out, the being in the limelight—can change people, but the change is likely to be profound only when it is linked to an ideological shift in what people want or expect for themselves. Otherwise, as community and individual attention wane, the great majority of people fall back into the ordinary division of political labor (and of household labor), with new skills, perhaps, but without the ideological convictions or institutional supports to carry them toward a new definition of the division of labor within their homes or communities.

NOTES

1. Personal interviews conducted by the author in Boston from 1984 to 1986. Subsequent quotations are from interviews unless otherwise attributed. Antibusing leaders who became elected public officials or who headed major organizations are cited by name.

2. Personal interview conducted by the author with Jimmy Kelly, Boston, 1985.

3. Personal interview conducted by the author with a Los Angeles antibusing leader, 1983.

4. Personal interview conducted by the author with Robert Schwartz, education adviser to Mayor Kevin White, Boston, 1984.

5. Personal interview conducted by the author with Elvira "Pixie" Palladino, Boston, 1984.

6. Personal interview conducted by the author with Chester Broderick, Boston, 1984.

7. Personal interview conducted by the author with Jimmy Kelly, Boston, 1985.

8. Personal interview conducted by the author with Robert A. Wood, Newport, Rhode Island, 1985.

9. Personal interview conducted by the author with Jimmy Kelly, Boston, 1985.

10. Personal interview conducted by the author with Jimmy Kelly, Boston, 1985.

REFERENCES

Ali, Moiram. 1987. "The Coal War: Women's Struggles During the Miners' Strike." In Rosemary Ridd and Helen Callaway, eds., *Women and Political Conflict: Portraits of Struggle in Times of Crisis*. New York: New York University Press.

Chafetz, Janet Saltzman, and Anthony Gary Dworkin. 1986. *Female Revolt: Women's Movements in World and Historical Perspective*. Totowa, N.J.: Rowman and Allanheld.

Clay, Phillip L. 1991. "Boston: The Incomplete Transformation." In H.S. Savitch and John Clayton Thomas, eds., *Big City Politics in Transition*. Urban Affairs Annual Reviews, 38: 14–28. Newbury Park, Calif.: Sage.

Dentler, Robert A., and Marvin Scott. 1981. *Schools on Trial: An Inside Account of the Boston School Desegregation Case*. Cambridge, Mass.: Abt Books.

Erie, Stephen P. 1988. *Rainbow's End: Irish-Americans and the Dilemmas of Urban Machine Politics, 1840–1985*. Berkeley: University of California Press.

Evans, Sarah. 1980. *Personal Politics*. New York: Vintage Books.

Fendrich, James M. 1977. "Keeping the Faith or Pursuing the Good Life: A Study of the Consequences of Participation in the Civil Rights Movement." *American Sociological Review* 42: 144–57.

Hillson, Jon. 1977. *The Battle of Boston: Busing and the Struggle for School Desegregation*. New York: Pathfinder Press.

Hochschild, Jennifer. 1984. *The New American Dilemma: Liberal Democracy and School Desegregation*. New Haven: Yale University Press.

Judd, Dennis R., and Todd Swanstrom. 1994. *City Politics: Private Power and Public Policy*. New York: HarperColllins.

Kaplan, Temma. 1995. "Female Consciousness and Collective Action: The Case of Barcelona, 1910–1918." In Barbara Laslett, Johanna Brenner, and Yesim Arat, eds., *Rethinking the Political: Gender, Resistance, and the State*. Chicago: University of Chicago Press.

Kozol, Jonathan. 1967. *Death at an Early Age*. New York: Bantam Books.

Laslett, Barbara, Johanna Brenner, and Yesim Arat, eds. 1995. *Rethinking the Political: Gender, Resistance, and the State.* Chicago: University of Chicago Press.

Lee, Valerie E., Peter B. Holland, and Anthony S. Bryk. 1993. *Catholic Schools and the Common Good.* Cambridge, Mass.: Harvard University Press.

Lieberson, Stanley. 1981. *Piece of the Pie: Blacks and White Immigrants Since 1880.* Berkeley: University of California Press.

Lofland, John. 1996. *Social Movement Organizations: Guide to Research on Insurgent Realities.* New York: Aldine de Gruyter.

Lukas, J. Anthony. 1985. *Common Ground: A Turbulent Decade in the Lives of Three American Families.* New York: Knopf.

Lupo, Alan. 1988. *Liberty's Chosen Home: The Politics of Violence in Boston.* Boston: Beacon Press.

Malloy, Ione. 1986. *Southie Won't Go: A Teacher's Diary of the Desegregation of South Boston High School.* Urbana: University of Illinois Press.

McAdam, Doug. 1988. *Freedom Summer.* New York: Oxford University Press.

McCarthy, John, and Mayer Zald. 1987. "Appendix: The Trend of Social Movements in America: Professionalization and Resource Mobilization." In Mayer N. Zald and John D. McCarthy, eds., *Social Movements in an Organizational Society: Collected Essays.* New Brunswick, N.J.: Transaction.

McGreevy, John T. 1996. *Parish Boundaries: The Catholic Encounter with Race in the Twentieth-Century Urban North.* Chicago: University of Chicago Press.

Oliver, Pamela. 1984. "If You Don't Do It, Nobody Else Will: Active and Token Contributions to Local Collective Action." *American Sociological Review* 49: 601–10.

Randall, Vicky. 1987. 2d ed. *Women and Politics: An International Perspective.* Chicago: University of Chicago Press.

Reynolds, Sian, ed. 1987. *Women, State and Revolution: Essays on Power and Gender in Europe Since 1789.* Amherst: University of Massachusetts Press.

Ridd, Rosemary, and Helen Callaway, eds. 1987. *Women and Political Conflict: Portraits of Struggle in Times of Crisis.* New York: New York University Press.

Rieder, Jonathan. 1985. *Canarsie: The Jews and Italians of Brooklyn Against Liberalism.* Cambridge, Mass.: Harvard University Press.

Ross, J. Michael, and William M. Berg. 1981. *"I Respectfully Disagree with the Judge's Order": The Boston School Desegregation Controversy.* Washington, D.C.: University Press of America.

Schrag, Peter. 1967. *Village School Downtown.* Boston: Beacon Press.

Schuman, Howard, and Charlotte Steeh. 1996. "The Complexity of Racial Attitudes in America." In Silvia Pedraza and Ruben G. Rumbaut, eds., *Origins and Destinies: Immigration, Race, and Ethnicity in America.* Belmont, Calif.: Wadsworth.

Sheehan, J. Brian. 1984. *The Boston School Integration Dispute: Social Change and Legal Maneuvers*. New York: Columbia University Press.

"South Boston Information Center News," 1975. *South Boston Tribune*. March 31, p. 1.

Suttles, Gerald D. 1970. *The Social Order of the Slum: Ethnicity and Territory in the Inner City*. Chicago: University of Chicago Press.

Taylor, D. Garth. 1986. *Public Opinion and Collective Action: The Boston School Desegregation Conflict*. Chicago: University of Chicago Press.

Thomis, Malcom I., and Jennifer Grimmett. 1982. *Women in Protest, 1800–1850*. London: Croom Helm.

Tilly, Louise A., and Patricia Gurin, eds. 1990. *Women, Politics, and Change*. New York: Russell Sage Foundation.

———. 1990a. "Women, Politics, and Change." In Louise A. Tilly and Patricia Gurin, eds., *Women, Politics, and Change*. New York: Russell Sage Foundation.

Useem, Bert. 1980. "Solidarity Model, Breakdown Model, and the Boston Anti-Busing Movement." *American Sociological Review* 45: 357–69.

West, Guida, and Rhoda Lois Blumberg, eds. 1990. *Women and Social Protest*. New York: Oxford University Press.

West, Guida, and Rhoda Lois Blumberg. 1990a. "Reconstructing Social Protest from a Feminist Perspective." In Guida West and Rhoda Lois Blumberg, eds., *Women and Social Protest*. New York: Oxford University Press.

Chapter Fourteen

"We're Fighting Millionaires!"
The Clash of Gender and Class in Appalachian Women's Union Organizing

Sally Ward Maggard

In the early 1970s a group of ordinary, working class women waged a long and sometimes violent strike against the Pikeville Methodist Hospital, one of the largest employers in eastern Kentucky.[1] Their strike shook the very foundations of class relations in Pike County, Kentucky, and developed into a thorny, unsolvable problem for their union, the Communications Workers of America (CWA). When the national media focused on the strike, the stories and photographs that spread across the country challenged common "Daisy Mae" and "Granny Clampett" stereotypes of Appalachian women. Here were mothers, wives, daughters, and sisters from hard-working families leading a strike in the heart of the eastern coalfields. As they stood in front of cameras and microphones, they described harsh working conditions and exploitation, a desire to do their jobs well, and a faith that collective action would improve their lives.

After nearly a decade of striking and legal battles, the women finally outdistanced their powerful political and economic adversaries. Although they did not gain union representation, they won a back-pay settlement that remains one of the largest in the history of strikes in this country. Amendments to the National Labor Relations Act (NLRA) prompted by the strike brought nonprofit health care institutions under the Act and extended opportunities for service workers to organize unions (Thompson 1973).

The women involved in the hospital strike had jobs as housekeepers, nurses' aides, cooks, cooks' helpers, dietary aides, and clerical workers.

They worked out of economic necessity, supporting households on their own or making a major contribution to household finances. Despite the restricted employment opportunities for women in the coalfields, most of the women had been in the workforce a long time. Their hospital jobs were considered some of the best jobs available to women in eastern Kentucky. Yet, these women made the risky and difficult decision to go on strike.

In this chapter I examine the lives of white-working class women who participated in the Pikeville hospital strike and the activism that forever changed the way they saw themselves and their region. Since the CWA was able to incorporate women only in traditionally gendered ways that ultimately weakened the organizing drive, I also examine difficulties that emerge between militant women workers and their union. Data are drawn from structured in-depth interviews conducted with twenty-four female participants in the hospital strike.[2] Ten auxiliary interviews were conducted with male strikers, relatives of the women interviewed, members of the hospital administration and board, and selected observers of the strikes who were knowledgeable about eastern Kentucky politics and history. All interviews were conducted in eastern Kentucky in 1987, a period that included the fifteenth anniversary of the strike. I also consulted the archives of the Commission on Religion in Appalachia, housed at the University of Kentucky, records from the Methodist Council of Bishops, files of the Council of the Southern Mountains (CSM), arrest records, court hearings and trials, legislative hearings, the congressional records of Amendments to the National Labor Relations Act, newspaper archives, documents from strikers' personal collections, and photographic collections.

Access to the field was not a problem. During the 1970s, as a member of the CSM staff, I wrote about the hospital strike for the news magazine, *Mountain Life & Work,* and was involved in strike support. When I returned to Pike County a decade and a half after the strike, many of the strikers were ready to assist in the research, eager to have this dramatic time in their lives recorded. This research supports the position that familiarity and involvement with events can sharpen rather than taint a researcher's scholarship (Reinharz 1992; Thorne 1983). Far from compromising the research, my connection to eastern Kentucky, where I was born and reared, and to this strike in particular, was essential.

Regional Background

In the Appalachian coalfields, lives have been framed for much of this century by an economy dominated by mineral extraction and politically powerful economic actors (Gaventa 1980). Economic opportunity is restricted, class relations are polarized, and fluctuations in the demand for coal and labor periodically throw miners out of work and dependent households into crisis (Corbin 1981; Dix 1988; Seltzer 1985; Tickamyer and Tickamyer 1986). The economic system put in place with the industrial development of coal was supported by a system of gender relations and ideology that positioned women and men with different economic opportunities and vulnerabilities (Maggard 1994; Pudup 1990). Considered "family wage earners," men were assigned the higher paid but dangerous jobs in mining. In contrast, women's market labor was considered superfluous, leaving most of them dependent on the income that their husbands could earn in an unstable and dangerous industry.

The labor histories of the women in this study illustrate the limited nature of opportunity for women in the eastern coalfields. Before their employment at the Pikeville hospital, most had moved from job to job, steaming clothes in laundries, selling merchandise in discount stores, cooking hamburgers and hot dogs, washing dishes, and cleaning motels and middle-class homes. Many of these jobs were temporary or part-time and without benefits. In contrast, the hospital offered a wage and benefits package with a chance for long-term employment. Although hospital wages were quite low, these women reported that they believed they had some of the best jobs available to women in the early 1970s in Pike County.

Beneath the surface, however, there were tensions between the hospital and its women workers. Earlier, hospital management had instituted a "speed-up." Patient load nearly doubled for the nursing staff and other employees. Employees complained of lengthy and erratic work schedules, heavy overtime duty, difficulty collecting overtime pay, harsh and discriminatory supervision, lack of job security, and discharges imposed without proper cause. Nurses' aides reported having to do work for which they were not qualified (such as dispensing narcotics) or face the loss of their jobs. Employees had no promotion or seniority rights, few holidays or vacations, inadequate medical insurance, and no unemployment insurance. One striker said, "You get tired of people walking on you after a while, making a door mat out of you . . . after so long

you back something up in a corner, eventually it's going to fight back."
In every department, they complained of excessive work loads and
understaffing, a situation that prevented them from providing quality
care. One nurse reported that "I did everything but firing the furnace."
Another reported that

> You work like a dog. Work for 89 cents an hour for years trying to raise
> six kids. Then $1.05. Then $1.10. We just all got tired. After we moved in
> that big hospital, so many patients and you couldn't get them all fed and
> bathed. You couldn't take care of the patients because the work load was
> too heavy. It just got 'til you couldn't handle it, and I guess it was [strike]
> or quit.[3]

Such management practices pushed workers to organize, and the
CWA agreed to take on the organizing campaign. Most nonprofessional
and many professional employees signed union representation cards
with the CWA. The hospital responded with a position from which it
never wavered, insisting that "union representation is not consistent
with the purposes of the institution" (in Layne 1972). For eight months
the hospital refused all requests to meet with the union. On June 9,
1972, two employees were fired for union activities. The next day the
strike began.

Deciding to strike is one of the most difficult decisions workers may
reach once they have reasons and the resources to act collectively (Costello 1991; Sacks 1988). It is particularly difficult for women in a tightly
restricted labor market. However, the jobs these women held were
recognized as vital to household economies, and many family members
supported the strike for that reason. In addition, fathers, husbands, and
other male kin who had union experiences encouraged the women to
act. One woman recalled that her father threatened to disinherit her if
she did not participate: "That's what he said. He wanted me to stand
right there. Be right out there everyday.... He used to work in the
mines, and he worked for the C&O Railroad. He was a union man."
Another striker equated her union fervor with her husband's union
history: "I was all for it, because my husband was a union man for
twenty-three years. I'm 100 percent union." One of the most active
strikers had no family union history, but she had previously worked
under a union contract: "I knew the working conditions under a union.
I was just dying for a union because I had been under this union, and
my heart was broke whenever I seen that we'd lost it." Many expressed

strong commitment to the principle of unionism. As one striker said: "I believe in people having a choice. I believe whenever people has good workers, they shouldn't make it harder on them just because they think they can. They sure made it hard on us."

"We're Fighting Millionaires!," the women's strike slogan (Kirby 1972), captured the class distinctions that exist in bold relief in the Central Appalachian coalfields. In 1972, a small, very wealthy elite group of business and political figures dominated the thirty-member board of directors of the hospital. Opposing them were more than two hundred hospital employees earning near-poverty wages. The gulf of understanding that separated these two camps in the strike is illustrated by the issue of wages.

The pay scales at Pikeville shocked much of the country when the national media covered the strike. The average wage in 1972 among nonprofessionals at the hospital was $1.68 per hour. One nurse's aide reported that after thirty-one years at the hospital she was earning $1.87 an hour when she came out on strike. One nurse's aide confronted the chairman of the hospital board shortly before the strike:

> I told him that I'd like to see him buy his groceries and eat on what I made. I showed him my check. He said, "Well, that's not really very much, is it?" I said, "No, that's not enough to pay my grocery bill, and I have bills to pay out of this, too." He walked on off. He didn't have nothing else to say about it.

To compensate for their meager wages, many of the women held multiple jobs. An aide who worked three, and sometimes four, jobs at once to rear her four children described the economic necessity and determination that motivated her:

> I've did odds and ends work all my life. When I worked on the [hospital] day shift I used to work at a steak house in the evening three nights a week to make enough money for me and the kids. I have cleaned houses of an evening . . . worked at motels, cleaned rooms, worked in kitchens, washed dishes. Just anything to make an honest dollar.

Interviews with members of the hospital administration and board of directors, however, suggest that most saw the wages paid to workers at the hospital as fair, although many were closely affiliated with the coal industry and aware of the disparity between the wages paid by the mining industry and those paid by the hospital. Thus, it was not only the social distance between a small, privileged elite and the working-class residents in a coalfield county that served to justify the low compensation for hospital labor. More important was the ideology of gender in Appalachia in which women's wages were seen as supplements to male earnings. As a result, work done primarily by women, like the work done by nonprofessional women at the Pikeville Hospital, was systematically undervalued (see also Reskin 1984; Steinberg and Haignere 1984).

Moreover, the gendered nature of hospital work itself depressed the wages and the economic status of women. The women were hired to take care of people—to feed them, clean up after them, nurse them, and nurture them. People (almost always women) who work as caretakers work very hard. But the popular understanding that it is a woman's "duty" to take care of the needy, ill, and dependent members of society serves to justify lower wages (Melosh 1982; Reverby 1990; Sacks 1990, 1988). For those who do "caring" work, this results in a dilemma that the historian Susan Reverby describes as "the order to care in a society that refuses to value caring" (1990, 133).

The Strike

Twenty-four hours a day for twenty-eight months, strikers maintained a picket line at the hospital. The union's strike strategy hinged on strict behavior codes for strike participation. CWA wanted the public to see a nonviolent strike by well-mannered hospital employees who were requesting collective bargaining and improved working conditions. A gender alignment in picket-line organization helped produce this image.

Women were assigned to early-morning and day-shift picket duty, and they were instructed to behave in pleasant, "ladylike" ways. People driving by the picket line saw women quilting, sewing, waving, reading Harlequin novels, cooking over barrels, and just passing the time. One woman amused herself by making a quilt with all the strikers' names appliqued on it while she peacefully fulfilled her picket line assignments. Another woman said, "Well, hollering at Mr. Keene [a hospital administrator] was what made my day mostly." Men built a shack near the picket line so that strikers could take breaks and talk with visitors without breaking injunctions against mass picketing. They also came to the picket line during the day to unload and chop wood to keep fires burning for cooking and for warmth.

These patterns produced a public presentation of the strike as "nice" much of the time. Ladylike and "womanly" behavior, complemented by "manly" strike roles for men, helped to normalize the strike in Pike County. Over time, the presence of strikers sitting out by the guard rails on the road below the hospital became part of the Pikeville landscape. Evening and night shifts were supposed to be reserved for men, especially the "hoot owl" shift, when picketing was most likely to turn antagonistic and violent. According to one maintenance worker, "Mostly men did the eleven-to-seven. Save the women from being out on the picket line from eleven to seven." Since most of the strikers were female, "saving the women" kept these men busy. It also meant that most women would not be present during the most dangerous picketing hours.

"Proper" picket line behavior was an issue that divided the women. One woman who agreed with CWA traveled around the country to publicize the strike. "My idea was to try to get us a decent union," she said. "That's why I was willing to make all those trips. I felt that was helping in the right way. . . . I didn't do any of the dirty work. That wasn't my idea of the strike." In contrast, another woman who was impatient with CWA complained, "I think CWA has a rule that you're supposed to be extremely nice on the picket line. Let's face it. I wasn't out there for my health. I was out there for my job. I didn't want to be nice all the time."

Despite the union's policy, many women came to the picket line throughout the evening shifts and joined in much of the late-night action. One of the men said he was surprised by this: "A lot of [women] come around at night. That blonde-headed one, why she'd do anything with you!" On all the picket shifts women reported having to jump guardrails to get away from people driving at high speeds in and out of the hospital grounds, but the danger was greatest after dark. One woman's shoulder was dislocated when a strikebreaker rammed her with a pickup truck. Several women were beaten by strikebreakers or people who came to the picket line intentionally to harass them. Others were shot at from passing cars.

Interviews indicate that many male family members were nervous about the involvement of their female kin and took active roles in the strike. They became escorts, substitute pickets, and picket line "bodyguards." Some women said they never went to the picket line without a male relative, usually a husband or father. While a concern about women's safety prompted some "escorts" to join in the strike, others came because they had a hard time adjusting to the new idea of women as strikers.

As the strike wore on, some women found other jobs. They made certain their picket duty was covered, most often with the help of male family members. Fathers were the most typical standins, while some sons and a few daughters also pulled substitute duty. A number of these "substitutes" were so familiar on the picket line that they might as well as have been strikers. Such family participation helped women maintain their involvement in the strike.

For most women, household arrangements posed few problems. In fact, many said that being in the strike was a lot like going to work. One nurse's aide who picketed in the afternoons described the strike as "business as usual except I was striking during the daytime instead of having to work all night long." The women earlier had learned to arrange their work schedules around the needs of children and other dependents and housekeeping. As strikers they did not have to devise a new system to balance their household roles and strike participation. Strike work just replaced work at the hospital, and household labor continued as usual. Going on strike, then, did not require major renegotiation of gender roles and expectations as it has at other times (Maggard 1990). Strike involvement was understood as an extension of women's work at the hospital. In this sense, behavior by women that was out of the ordinary and even "disorderly" was accepted inside families.

Community Response

The strikers expected solid support from working-class people in the region served by the hospital. All major unions in the area and many other national and international unions officially endorsed the strike. Donations poured into Pike County from prolabor organizations all over the country. Locally, however, many working people who normally supported the idea of unionism were outspoken in their opposition to the strike. Members of union families crossed the picket line for routine examinations and nonemergency treatment. Others crossed the picket line and took jobs as replacement workers.

Even some unionized miners failed to honor the hospital strike, leaving the women strikers bitterly disappointed. One woman described an encounter with a United Mine Workers of America (UMWA) member:

> Old man Holbrook took [his daughter] to work. I got him on the street over here. I said, "You ready to haul them scabs back in? You're hauling one every day. You're supposed to be a UMW[A] member." He was! He was from Wheelwright mines. His daughter, he took her in. She's working over there yet.

Another striker expressed her anger this way:

> Any time you've got a strike going on if you're a union person I don't think you should cross any picket lines whatsoever. I think you should take your patients somewhere else. Some of the UMW[A] people would take their wives in there. . . . I told them they ought to be ashamed. If they was on strike at the mines, would they like it if we went in and worked in their place? Or went across and helped? No, they wouldn't have liked it.

Why didn't a local, unified, working-class base of support develop in this strike? The answer lies in the gendered nature of the opposition to the strike. The widespread sentiment that it was women's responsibility to care for others—at home and at work—made people reluctant to see them as workers who could organize collectively and strike. The strikers reacted with frustration to criticism of their efforts. One recalled that "[t]hey'd say that we was keeping them from taking care of the people in the hospital. They didn't understand that we was out there trying to get more money and better conditions and things." A hospital cook said, "We had some smarties come along the picket line. Told us we shouldn't be out there. We should be at work." To which she replied, "Well, I'll go home in about four hours, but it's our duty here. If we don't stand up for our rights there's nobody going to stand up for us." Discussing a nursing supervisor who turned over to hospital management the names of suspected union sympathizers, a nurse's aide recalled:

> She'd say, "I wonder when them old strikers, when are they going to have their strike? I just don't see why they want to strike the hospital. The hospital ain't no place to have a union." All the time her husband worked for a big union mines. He was UMWA, honey!

Solidarity might have developed in the strike along gender lines. Most of the hospital staff was female. Many of these women were friends, relatives, and neighbors. They all worked under difficult conditions at the hospital and they were well aware of the struggles women in the county faced in trying to earn a living. But divisions among women in the hospital tended to follow class lines. Many professional staff, like the nursing supervisor discussed earlier, did not support the strikers. Most supervisors aligned themselves with management and worked to break prestrike union momentum and intimidate pro-union employees.

Some women who did not go on strike nonetheless were supportive of the strikers. Licensed practical nurses (LPNs) were just a few steps above the nurse's aides and other nonprofessional employees. Most signed union cards and expected to strike. However, just before the walkout they were threatened with losing their state licenses and decided to remain inside. During the strike, many LPNs and RNs acted as a pro-union intelligence network of informal "spies." They leaked information to the strikers about the hospital's operating capacity and quality of care. Strikers used this information to describe inadequate treatment and to discourage hospital patronage. They also used it in unsuccessful attempts to challenge the hospital's state certification and to pressure the UMWA Health and Retirement Funds to drop the hospital from its list of participating health care facilities.

Over time, the general public settled into a position of tolerating the strike, even if sentiment ran against the right of these women to organize. Yet people were surprised that women could hold out so steadily for so long. A nurse's aide said: "They thought that we would all quit. Give up. They thought a week or two would kill us. 'They're just women. They'll just give up and throw their signs down and quit.' We didn't. We stuck it out."

In the Pikeville strike, gender functioned to blur traditional class lines, and a broad working-class support base did not develop as it traditionally did in coal strikes. Class divided women whose work situations and experiences in the region's economy might have generated solidarity based on gender. As a result, the legitimacy of the strike was challenged and class solidarity weakened. The union failed to deal with these problems.

The Union

Gender shaped a relationship between CWA and the strikers that can best be described as paternalistic. Women strikers depended on the union to negotiate for them with hospital officials, to represent them with the NLRB, and to solicit support from other unions and organizations. They also depended on CWA for strike benefits. In exchange, the union demanded that strikers follow certain behavior codes, pull picket duty, be available for strike support activities, and staff a strike office. But the CWA did not encourage or seek out input or leadership from the women on the direction of the strike. Thus, even as the strikers grew increasingly dissatisfied with their union, they were not able to directly influence or challenge the strike direction. Some of the strikers orchestrated a behind-the-scenes militant campaign against strikebreakers and hospital supporters. Others accepted CWA's control of their strike.

One of the main points of contention between the union and the women strikers was CWA's commitment of time and resources to lobbying the United Methodist Church (UMC). The Pikeville Methodist Hospital was neither owned, nor run, nor financed by the Methodist Church. It was merely "affiliated" with the denomination. This meant that one third of the hospital board were required to be clergy or members of the church, a requirement that was easily met, since many of Pike County's elite belonged to the Pikeville Methodist Church.

In the early 1970s, the UMC endorsed the principle of collective bargaining as part of its "Social Gospel." Lonnie Daniel, area director for CWA in Kentucky and Tennessee, believed that leaders of the church should be taken at their word, that they could and would pressure hospital officials into signing a union contract. He allocated a major portion of union resources to what the strikers saw as an expensive and misguided campaign of conscience. Daniel took groups of strikers all over the country to set up informational picket lines at various church meetings and to meet with church leaders and ran a national ad campaign questioning the morality of locking strikers out of a church-affiliated charity hospital. He reasoned that the church's national Council of Bishops could force the church's state organization to persuade Methodists in Pike County to convince the hospital board to recognize the union.

This proved to be a naive and costly strategy. Nationally, the bishops made public statements in support of the strike, and some traveled to Kentucky to see the situation in person. Many prayers were offered and sermons delivered. But the Kentucky "brothers" failed to see the light.

During the CWA's "Social Gospel" campaign, the strikers insisted that ministers outside Pike County could not or would not interfere locally to challenge a powerful elite and reorganize the hospital leadership. Even fifteen years later they remained bitter over the time and money invested in the strategy. One woman explained why she felt it would not work:

> I know this local Methodist Church over here at Pikeville. . . . A lot of the members there was against us. I couldn't see as it helped any. The [national and state] church leaders could never had done nothing with them board members, even if they'd wanted to.

A woman who had been a cook at the hospital described her feelings about a trip that strikers made to Louisville, Kentucky, to picket the offices of the Kentucky Bishop:

> I knew he wasn't going to help us. No! We all knew that! We knew before we went down there. Lonnie Daniel wanted us to go down there and picket the Methodist Church. We knew we wasn't going to get nothing from him before we went.

And another striker complained that the hospital "was really Methodist in name only, if you want to know quite truthful." She also traveled to lobby church leaders but said, "I just went because I was told to. . . . I really think that it was a lot of wasted money and effort."

Strikers wanted CWA to focus on Pike County and to target members of the hospital board and their allies, not Methodist ministers or bishops. As one striker said of their adversaries, "They was fifty millionaires in Pikeville. They don't believe in unions. . . . They all stick together. Too many millionaires in Pikeville."

In the strikers' estimation, CWA failed to put appropriate pressure directly on the people who controlled the outcome of the conflict. Frustrated by CWA's strike direction, a number of militant strikers began to devise alternatives. At their urging, a coalition of supporters formed the "People's Committee on Organized Labor" (PCOL) as a vehicle for activities CWA was reluctant to pursue. For a brief period the PCOL organized "informational picketing," which functioned as a secondary boycott. Picket lines were set up at area businesses connected to board members and maintained for several weeks until each owner was able to obtain court injunctions banning the pickets. In the meantime, one car dealership was threatened with the loss of its franchise and several retail stores reported substantial loss of sales. Although the strategy was reluctantly and temporarily endorsed by the strike director, he decided it was too controversial and instructed the strikers to abandon it.

Strikers were also frustrated by their inability to shut down the hospital and by the union's willingness to tolerate violations of the picket line. The strikers expected area residents to use the hospital only for emergencies, but people routinely crossed their picket line. Strikers wanted more resources directed toward building a broad base of community support but were not able to persuade the union to move in this direction. One said:

> I really think that money could have been spent on our own people. Invite people that weren't union. Let everybody come and hear our cause. Just let the people come and let us explain why. I really think that people would have [boycotted more].

Despite major disagreements with the union, the striking women were never in a position to demand changes. Dependent on CWA strike support, they often felt guilty about their frustrations with the union leadership. Many women reported being in better financial shape with CWA benefits than they were with hospital wages. As one striker said:

> Actually we lived better and had more after we came out on strike, after CWA took us over. We worked for nothing there. It was a struggle to keep something to eat and pay your rent. With CWA paying our bills we knew we was going to have something to eat off of and everything.

The women were officially linked to and dependent on the union. Few had experience with strikes, and none had experience in union leadership. They had no autonomous base from which to pressure the union, and they had no allies in the union leadership to help advance their positions.

For twenty-eight months, the striking women maintained a twenty-four-hour-a-day picket line, organized rallies and protest marches, attended strike meetings, worked in the union office, struggled through legal and court actions, raised money, worked on community and media relations, and traveled to generate support. After the picket line was disbanded, the strike was fought out in the courts for six more years while the women went to work in the menial, low-wage service jobs available in Pike County and tried to keep the hope of a victory alive. A series of unfair labor practice rulings favored the strikers, but the hospital board invested hundreds of thousands of dollars to contest every ruling. In 1980, the U.S. Supreme Court refused to hear the hospital's final appeal, and the hospital was forced to offer to reinstate workers and compensate them for their economic losses. Checks for court-awarded back pay, totaling $697,000, were not in the hands of strikers until early in 1981, nearly a decade after the night of the walkout. Most of the women never got their jobs back, although a few continue to work at the hospital today. In interviews, the women repeatedly question their choice of union and wonder if a different union would have led them to a contract.

Aftermath

Women in the Pikeville strike took part in activities they had never been involved in previously, and they did things they had never dreamed they would do. A comment from one of the hospital cooks suggests just how unusual the situation was: "If anybody had told me fifteen years before that I'd be on a picket line, I'd said, 'You're crazy!' Whoever hear'd tell of the women getting out there and being on a picket line?"

Participating in the hospital strike affected the people involved in tangible and intangible ways. Many women lost their jobs at the hospital. Some were not called to return. Some returned but were subsequently laid off. A few retired, although they had difficulty collecting retirement benefits from the hospital. Most of them were thrown back into the same labor market that had made working at the hospital attractive. They found work, once again, as dishwashers, short-order cooks, grocery checkers, retail clerks, motel housekeepers, and the like. Two women got skilled jobs weighing coal shipments for a coal tipple. Another woman works for a radio station, where she occasionally dedicates late-night music to the strikers. The women continue to work wherever they can find paid work.

However, the women did emerge from the strike with a new identity. When they traveled around the country to publicize the strike, they were introduced as "the hospital strikers from Pikeville, Kentucky." In Pike County people still refer to them as "one of those strikers." As one former kitchen worker said, "We made history. I mean, you know, what would Pikeville be without us strikers?" Most of the women enjoyed the strike. They described it as "an exciting time," "fun," "a challenge," and said that they missed the activity and excitement. One woman said, "It was just like a camping ground. Go over there and camp out and have a good time. . . . Nobody could have ever had any more fun than we did. No way."

All of the women referred to the strike as "an education." One woman who attended court hearings on violence during the strike said, "I got real educated listening. You do learn a lot going to court." The testimony of hospital officials and board members was instructive: "You could sit and listen to them. They tell a different story . . . looking right out at you. You know how it happened, but it would be different when they told it." And another striker said, "Although we didn't get it organized, I wouldn't give up what I learned about Pike County and the people in it for no amount of money."

These women express regret that they did not win union representation. Still, they are aware that their strike led to improvements in working conditions at the hospital, improvements enjoyed now by the workers who hold the strikers' former jobs. All of the women said they would go through the strike again, and half of them said they would be much more active the next time. Above all, the women believe that participation in the strike was a good thing to have done. "I think it's the best thing that we ever done when we came out on strike," one nurse's aide said. "I still say it's the best thing that ever happened to me." A hospital cook spoke for many of the women when, with some satisfaction, she said:

> They thought we was just a bunch of dumb women out there. Well, we was a bunch of women out there, but I don't think we was quite as dumb as they thought we were. We may not have got the union, but we got them straightened out a little bit. . . . [T]he experience of this now is worth more than gold!

The collective action of these strikers unsettled traditional images of Appalachian mountain women. These weren't coal miners who shut down mines against wealthy coal operators. These were women who took care of sick people and cleaned public spaces. They did "women's work," yet they seemed to expect the same support and union privileges that miners had won through union organizing. Their strike was an inconvenience, an annoyance that made people uneasy or hostile. And they wouldn't go away. They stood on their picket line, held rallies, confronted opponents, and filed legal appeals year after year. Their strike grew out of problems with conditions in a work place, just like mine strikes, but, beyond this, members of the hospital board, ordinary clients of the hospital, and even the strikers' union had trouble seeing any similarity.

In this strike, ideas about gender influenced the level of wages and the working conditions that led women to organize. Gender ideologies influenced the patterns of the strike and the way family members were involved. Notions of gender created community opposition when support was expected and led the CWA to disregard the strategic opinions of the strikers. The women at Pikeville had an enormous and remarkable capacity to organize and to fight a determined adversary. Their need for collective organization was unquestionable. But they were seen as people to be taken care of, and their voices were not considered powerful. The women needed to be heard, to be able to advise their union as it gave shape and direction to their protest. A participatory, inclusive model of the union-striker relationship, free of gender stereotypes, would have strengthened the protest and brought the women closer to changing their wages and working conditions in the hospital (Melcher et al. 1992; Shur and Kruse 1992).

NOTES

1. This chapter is based on a larger project that compared this strike with a coal strike in which women were also active (Maggard 1988). Funding for the larger project research was provided by an American Fellowship from the American Association of University Women, a Lena Lake Forrest Fellowship from the Business and Professional Women's Research Foundation, a James Still Fellowship from the University of Kentucky, an Appalachian Studies Fellowship from Berea College, and the Graduate School of the University of Kentucky. The author thanks Kathleen Blee, Deborah Tootle, Rachel Tompkins, and Nancy Naples for careful reading and insightful critique of this chapter.

2. A purposive sampling frame was used to identify respondents from all units in the hospital that employed nonprofessional women (clerical, nursing, special diets, kitchen and food service, and housekeeping). I selected respondents who varied in their hospital work experience and poststrike employment.

3. All quotations from strike participants are from the author's interviews. To protect their privacy, participants are not identified by name.

BIBLIOGRAPHY

Corbin, David Alan. 1981. *Life, Work, and Rebellion in the Coal Fields: The Southern West Virginia Miners, 1880–1922.* Urbana: University of Illinois Press.

Costello, Cynthia B. 1991. *We're Worth It! Women and Collective Action in the Insurance Workplace.* Urbana: University of Illinois Press.

Dix, Keith. 1988. *What's a Coal Miner to Do? The Mechanization of Coal Mining.* Pittsburgh: University of Pittsburgh Press.

Gaventa, John. 1980. *Power and Powerlessness: Quiescence and Rebellion in an Appalachian Valley.* Urbana: University of Illinois Press.

Kirby, Rich. 1972. "We're Fighting Millionaires." *Mountain Life & Work* 48: 10–13.

Layne, Gene E. 1972. Letter to Communications Workers of America Local 10317. In possession of the author.

Maggard, Sally Ward. 1994. "From Farm to Coal Camp to Back Office and McDonald's: Living in the Midst of Appalachia's Latest Transformation." *Journal of the Appalachian Studies Association* 6: 14–28.

———. 1990. "Gender Contested: Women's Participation in the Brookside Coal Strike." Pp. 75–90 in *Women and Social Protest,* edited by Guida West and Rhoda Lois Blumberg. New York: Oxford University Press.

———. 1988. "Eastern Kentucky Women on Strike: A Study of Gender, Class and Political Action in the 1970s." Ph.D. diss., University of Kentucky.

Melcher, Dale, Jennifer L. Eichstedt, Shelley Eriksen, Dan Clawson. 1992. "Women's Participation in Local Union Leadership: The Massachusetts Experience." *Industrial and Labor Relations Review* 42 (2): 267–80.

Melosh, Barbara. 1982. *The 'Physician's Hand': Work Culture and Conflict in American Nursing.* Philadelphia: Temple University Press.

Pudup, Mary Beth. 1990. "Women's Work in the West Virginia Economy." *West Virginia History* 49: 7–20.

Reinharz, Shulamit. 1992. *Feminist Methods in Social Research.* New York: Oxford University Press.

Reskin, Barbara F. 1984. "Sex Segregation in the Workplace." Pp. 1–11 in *Gender at Work: Perspectives on Occupational Segregation and Comparable Worth,* edited by Women's Research Education Institute. Washington, D.C.: Women's Research Education Institute of the Congressional Caucus for Women's Issues.

Reverby, Susan. 1990. "The Duty or Right to Care? Nursing and Womanhood in Historical Perspective." Pp. 132–94 in *Circles of Care: Work and Identity in Women's Lives,* edited by Emily K. Abel and Margaret K. Nelson. Albany: State University of New York Press.

Sacks, Karen Brodkin. 1990. "Does It Pay to Care?" Pp. 187–206 in *Circles of*

Care: Work and Identity in Women's Lives, edited by Emily K. Abel and Margaret K. Nelson. Albany: State University of New York Press.

———. 1988. *Caring by the Hour: Women, Work, and Organizing at Duke Medical Center.* Urbana: University of Illinois Press.

Seltzer, Curtis. 1985. *Fire in the Hole: Miners and Managers in the American Coal Industry.* Lexington: University Press of Kentucky.

Shur, Lisa A., and Douglas L. Kruse. 1992. "Gender Differences in Attitudes toward Unions." *Industrial and Labor Relations Review* 46 (1): 89–102.

Steinberg, Ronnie, and Lois Haignere. 1984. "Separate but Equivalent: Equal Pay for Work of Comparable Worth." Pp. 13–26 in *Gender at Work: Perspectives on Occupational Segregation and Comparable Worth,* edited by Women's Research Education Institute. Washington, D.C.: Women's Research Education Institute of the Congressional Caucus for Women's Issues.

Thompson, Honorable Frank, Jr. 1973. "Nonprofit Hospitals," Congressional Record—Extensions of Remarks. January 16, 1973. E 232.

Thorne, Barrie. 1983. "Political Activist as Participant Observer: Conflicts of Commitment in a Study of the Draft Resistance Movement of the 1960s." Pp. 216–34 in *Contemporary Field Research: A Collection of Readings,* edited by Robert M. Emerson. Boston: Little, Brown and Company.

Tickamyer, Ann R., and Cecil Tickamyer. 1986. "Gender, Family Structure, and Poverty in Central Appalachia." Pp. 80–90 in *The Land and Economy of Appalachia: Proceedings from the 1986 Conference on Appalachia.* Lexington: Appalachian Center, University of Kentucky.

Chapter Fifteen

Fighting for Environmental Justice
An Interview with Lois Gibbs

Multinational Monitor

Lois Gibbs first came to national attention in the late 1970s, when as a housewife in Niagara Falls, New York, she discovered that her children were attending an elementary school built on top of a chemical waste dump. Gibbs organized her neighbors into the Love Canal Homeowners Association, eventually forcing the federal government to pay for their relocation. Gibbs's efforts brought the problem of hazardous waste disposal to public attention and helped spur passage of Superfund hazardous waste disposal legislation. Determined that others should not face the difficulties she confronted in organizing against toxic waste dumpers, Gibbs formed the Citizens Clearinghouse for Hazardous Waste (CCHW). For a dozen years, CCHW has worked with grassroots environmental justice groups across the United States, providing organizing and technical support. CCHW has also been involved in numerous national grassroots environmental campaigns and has now initiated a Stop Dioxin Exposure Campaign. In conjunction with the campaign, CCHW released the book *Dying from Dioxin*.

Multinational Monitor: Why did you form the Citizens Clearinghouse for Hazardous Waste?

Lois Gibbs: I formed CCHW because I discovered during the struggle at Love Canal that there was no organization that was established for the purpose of helping local, average, grass-roots people, moms and dads, with the issues of environmental threats. When I worked at Love Canal, I kept trying to find somebody who could answer questions like, "What do you do when there is a dump site across the street from you?" or "How do you find out what these chemicals mean and what they will do to your body?" CCHW has been established primarily to focus on those needs of grass-roots people.

MM: What do you mean when you call CCHW an environmental justice center?

Gibbs: Plenty of people in this country who are faced with environmental threats are low-income people, people of color or blue collar workers—they are people who have been targeted by corporations, and to a lesser extent by our own government, for being poisoned.

These people's health and well-being is really more than an environmental issue. It is a justice issue. Very wealthy people for the most part do not have waste facilities located in their communities and are not faced with these threats. Our campaigns really come down to justice, not specific environmental issues—the right to clean air, a clean environment, a safe place to work, play and live.

MM: How do you distinguish the environmental justice approach from "environmentalism"?

Gibbs: Environmental justice is really about people and communities. It is about children and grandchildren.

Most of the environmental groups work only on natural resources—air, water and soil—without looking at the bigger picture of the people. In most environmentally threatened communities, it is not just a matter of an environmental threat; they are also faced with issues of education, of how to build an economically sound community.

Our approach, then, is very different in that we look at the whole community and focus on people; that is in contrast to the environmental groups' focus on natural wildlife and habitat, not that those are not important.

MM: Are your strategies different as well?

Gibbs: I think one of the biggest differences is the goal. For the most part, environmental groups look at regulation as the answer to the problem. They look at how much can be discharged from a smokestack, how much can be discharged into our water supply, how much can be discharged into our air, before harm is done.

The environmental justice movement's goal is not on a control system like the traditional, mainstream groups. We are more focused on prevention. We ask, "Why do we have to have the smokestack in the first place? Why are we discharging into the air?" There are no safe levels for our children. We have to come up with other ways to manufacture products; we have to come up with other ways to deal with our environment that prevents hazardous exposures and releases altogether.

Based on those goals, the strategies are very different. Our strategies are not to go and change or introduce a piece of legislation. Our primary efforts are directed to closing down this incinerator, or putting together a recycling program in our city that takes care of the waste stream without jeopardizing the environment and public health.

MM: The main criticism of the environmental justice approach is the notion that it is a just a NIMBY (not in my backyard) movement, that people are only concerned about eliminating the hazards that affect them and are unconcerned about who eventually will end up accepting the hazard. How do you respond to this criticism?

Gibbs: At one time, I think that was true. If you go back to the early 1980s, people really were concerned about their backyard and their backyard alone. But the movement has matured and grown; people have met the people from the other backyards in the United States, Canada, and Mexico, and the criticism is no longer true.

People are not saying, "Take it out of my backyard, and I don't care where you put it." In fact, people worked very hard under the Superfund legislation, which is meant to clean up the worst sites in this country, to include a regulation that says you cannot move Superfund waste from one site to another. And that was accomplished and included because of the grass-roots effort.

People are not saying, "Don't put it in my backyard; put it somewhere else." People are saying, "Don't manufacture it, don't dispose of it this way, and use reduction in the manufacturing process so that we don't generate the waste in the first place." They really do see the bigger picture.

MM: The environmental justice movement has adopted a more aggressive posture than the mainstream environmental groups. Is it correct to say that you are less willing to talk to the other side, to the polluting corporations?

Gibbs: It is not that we are less interested in talking to the other side. It is really that the other side doesn't come to the table to play fairly. The other side instead works behind the scenes to sabotage what community groups are doing.

The mainstream environmental groups can meet with the other side, but that is generally to compromise away issues and goals that grass-roots groups are looking at.

Let me give you an example. One of the things we are doing now is looking at dioxin. We are asking the paper and pulp facilities—the paper companies—to not use chlorine in their bleaching process, to use a closed-loop system, and to use hydrogen peroxide. It is a process that can be changed over without job loss, without closing down mills and so forth. The Environmental Defense Fund (EDF) met with Time Warner and several of the major corporations that have financial ties to the paper industry and cut a deal that said it was okay for them to use chlorine dioxide—which is less toxic than straight chlorine but is a form of chlorine nonetheless. EDF cut that deal knowing there are affordable alternatives, that Time Warner and the paper companies could still make their product and still have major corporate growth and major corporate profits, without poisoning people.

MM: But hasn't EDF achieved some successes through negotiation with corporations, such as McDonald's?

Gibbs: EDF does not deserve any credit for McDonald's getting rid of styrofoam sandwich packaging. That entire effort was done by the grass-roots groups, which launched a campaign in 1987 and pushed McDonald's to the point where McDonald's had to do something. McDonald's as a corporation does not want consumers to know that a grass-roots campaign impacted company policy. So they cut a deal with EDF which gave credit to EDF for persuading them on the basis of their argument alone.

But the truth is, it was not EDF that won that fight; it was the local people in communities across the United States.

The grass-roots groups and CCHW in particular were especially angry with EDF because we wrote letters to all of the mainstream groups, saying that McDonald's is likely to come and try to negotiate with you. We had been trying to get McDonald's to sit down with the grass-roots leaders. We were willing to sit talk about it, but they were not. EDF was the only environmental group which violated that strategy, and went ahead and met with McDonald's, violating people's trust and their working relationship with people on the grass-roots level.

MM: As a general matter, how does race fit into the environmental justice equation?

Gibbs: The issue of race and income fit very tightly into environmental justice. As conscious policy, the dirtiest industries, the things that are going to pollute and poison the environment and the public are, more often than not, put in communities of color, indigenous people communities or poor communities—places some government documents call "communities that are least likely to resist."

There are two documents that talk about this, one by Cerrell and Associates, contracted with the Solid Waste Division of the state of California, and another one by a consulting firm called Epley, which was contracted in North Carolina to site a low-level radioactive waste facility. In both of these cases, they said they were going to site the facilities where people were least likely to resist, not where there is the best environment for the facilities, where there is no nearby water table, or where the soil structure is a certain pattern that would reduce the risk of such a facility. Instead, it was in a community where people don't have the resources to fight back, where people are already struggling with so many survival issues each and every day.

The siting is deliberate and intentional. I would say the majority of waste facilities in this country are located in low-income communities, communities of color, or blue-collar communities.

MM: Why is CCHW now turning its attention to dioxin?

Gibbs: There are two things motivating us. One, it is a campaign that can broaden our network of people, because everybody is affected by dioxin poisoning across the country, every man, woman, and child in this country. Second, most of the facilities that we currently work on have a dioxin component to it.

MM: What is the campaign's agenda?

Gibbs: We are asking to stop dioxin exposure. We are looking at where dioxin sources are across the country and what it is that we can do locally to stop dioxin exposure.

Dioxin exposure is easy to resolve. We can stop using chlorine in products like paper; we can close solid-waste incinerators and limit waste and switch to other methods of waste disposal; we can stop the manufacturing of plastics from chlorine; and we can stop burning nonhuman tissue waste in medical incinerators and switch to alternative disinfection methods such as microwaving. So it is something that is very winnable; because there are alternatives, we don't have to go live in a cave somewhere with candlelight and eat over an open fire.

MM: So it is not the case that dioxin exposure is just one of the prices we pay for receiving the benefits of industrial society?

Gibbs: Absolutely not. In fact, we can have all the same products,

including white paper and plastics, without dioxin exposures and releases. The problem is that there is not the political will, and there are
not economic incentives for the corporations to change. And without
either one of those, corporations are not going to change their processes;
they are not going to stop making particular products.

MM: Is the campaign calling for the complete elimination of dioxin
or just a reduction?

Gibbs: A complete elimination of dioxin exposure.

At this point, we are not asking for a ban on chlorine, which is really
where dioxin comes from—it is combustion and chlorine. We need
chlorine for some other areas, like pharmaceuticals and drinking water
supplies. So until we have more alternatives, we are starting with the
biggest sources of dioxin exposure and will look to a phase out of
chlorine over time.

MM: On whom is the campaign focused?

Gibbs: It is focused on the producers of dioxin at the local level. It is
not focused nationally as it relates to some type of regulation or legislation. We are asking people to go out and be dioxin detectives, to identify
dioxin sources in their communities—hospital medical waste incinerators, community solid waste incinerators and so on. Once we find those
sources, then we can work with the corporations, if they are willing, or
outside of the corporate circle if they are not, to try and shut down those
dioxin sources.

MM: Why focus on production rather than consumption?

Gibbs: That is the other piece. We are focusing on consumption as
well. We are asking college campuses, state houses, and other institutions
to adopt procurement policies which say they will only buy paper that
has not been rebleached with chlorine or is totally chlorine free. (The
rebleach part applies to recycled paper that already has chlorine in it but
does not need to be rebleached with chlorine.)

We are also looking at other alternatives for products. We are asking
people to go to the store and look at items like their shampoo bottle. If
it has a "V" in it or a number "3" (both of which symbolize that the
bottle is made of polyvinyl chloride), we are asking them to not buy
that product. Instead, they should call the corporation that makes the
product—there is usually an 800 number on the bottle—and tell them
why they did not buy that bottle of shampoo, why they bought a
different product.

So we are working on the marketplace incentives and the local dioxin sources at the same time.

MM: Are there any companies that stand out as the main targets of the campaign?

Gibbs: Dow and Occidental Petroleum are the biggest manufacturers of chlorine-based products that later get incinerated. Those companies stand out as a chlorine producer and a manufacturer of plastics with chlorine in them.

We haven't targeted the companies yet. We are still choosing targets, based in part on which company we think we can most successfully pressure.

MM: Have you had any kind of response to the campaign from dioxin-producing companies?

Gibbs: We have had a fairly strong response from the Chlorine Chemical Council and the Chemical Manufacturers Association and other trade associations. Pretty much that response has been at the local level, because our activities have been local.

We had a young woman in Midway, Texas, who attempted to pass a local high school Parent-Teachers Association (PTA) resolution calling for the elimination of dioxin exposures. DuPont showed up and said that the PTA had no business talking about dioxin, that the PTA's business is educating students and not talking about environmental pollutants. Needless to say, the people—the moms and dads at that PTA meeting—became pretty outraged that someone would think they have such a narrow view of their responsibilities, and they passed the resolution.

The woman and the other Midway parents went to the state PTA level, to pass a dioxin resolution within the Texas state PTA. When that happened, all heck broke loose with the Texas Chemical Council and the Texas Manufacturing Association, and Dow Chemical and Occidental, who sent reams and reams of data to PTA leaders all across the state. These PTA leaders had no clue why all this stuff was coming.

The big companies pressured the local leader to sit down and have a meeting with them. She refused. Then they called her state senator, who pressured her to meet with the corporate guys. She finally agreed to do it, so there was this meeting with six of these big corporate giants and her, trying to compromise on this PTA resolution.

The other thing industry did was buy two exhibit spaces at the PTA convention. It was the first time the convention had ever had a Chemical Manufacturers exhibit space; usually the exhibits are devoted to school educational materials and stuff like that.

All in all, 1,400 delegates came to the convention, and the dioxin resolution was passed by seventy-two votes. But it was a real tough fight.

The woman who organized the resolution was frightened to death that all these people were faxing things and banging on her door and demanding to meet with her. It reached the point where the Texas PTA appointed a bodyguard for her prior to the convention.

The response has been pretty heavy-handed at the local level, where we are working. If that is the response to a PTA resolution, I can't imagine what would happen if we ever tried to pass a state law, or a federal law.

MM: Isn't Dow now considered to be one of the more environmentally sensitive companies?

Gibbs: You would think they would be more open and responsive.

Dow has a terrific public relations department, but from what I understand from Greenpeace activists, Dow already has alternatives available for the products they manufacture which have chlorine that later turns into dioxin. But they are not using them, because there is not the political will to make them use it.

If Dow were such a great corporate citizen, they would be the first one out the door with the alternative chemicals and the alternative products, and they could put commercials on—honest commercials— saying, "We were the first ones to say dioxin is a problem and we are dealing with it, because we had this bad experience with Agent Orange and the Vietnam vets." But I don't see that happening.

MM: Who are the participants in the campaign?

Gibbs: The participants are grass-roots leaders and environmental groups across the country at one level. Six hundred of those folks came together in Louisiana in March [1996], to figure out what the strategies are and how to go about doing the struggle.

The other people who are beginning to join the campaign—because it is going to be a broad-based campaign—include: the Vietnam Vets of America; the Endometriosis Society, because endometriosis, which is a uterine disease, is directly connected to dioxin; the breast cancer groups across the country; the paper workers, because they are front-line dioxin exposed; the lobster fisherpeople; the Council of Churches; and the

American Association of Retired People. So the coalition is very broad-based. In different regions, it is broader than in other regions.

Essentially it is being nurtured and pushed by grass-roots environmental groups across the country, who are introducing, educating, and holding meetings to bring together this coalition and to figure out what do we do in states across the country.

Contributors

Karren Baird-Olson is assistant professor in the Department of Anthropology, Sociology, and Social Work at Kansas State University, where she teaches criminology and race and ethnic relations courses. She is currently completing, with coinvestigator Dr. Carol Ward of Brigham Young University, a research project funded by the Louisville Institute on reservation women and spirituality and resistance. She is also working on a project funded by the National Institute of Justice on rural community policing.

Kathleen M. Blee is professor of sociology and director of women's studies at the University of Pittsburgh. She is the author of *Women of the Klan: Racism and Gender in the 1920s* and a forthcoming book with Dwight Billings on the historical origins of chronic poverty and violence. She is currently completing a book on women in contemporary organized racist groups in the U.S.

Cynthia Costello, Ph.D., has her own research and policy consulting business. She has held positions as research director of the Women's Research and Education Institute, director of employment policy for Families USA Foundation, and director of the Committee on Women's Employment at the National Academy of Sciences. Her publications include *The American Woman 1996–97: Women and Work*; *The American Woman 1994–95: Women and Health*; and *We're Worth It: Women and Collective Action in the Insurance Workplace*. She lives in Bethesda, Maryland, with her husband and her eight-year-old son.

Pam E. Goldman is a lawyer and political activist. She is working on a book about the 1975 grand jury investigation in Lexington, Kentucky, and its impact on the community. She lives in Pittsburgh.

Shirley A. Jackson teaches in the Department of Ethnic Studies at Bowling Green State University. Her research interests are African American women's organizations, African American women in the Black Power movement, and media depictions of race and gender issues. She teaches courses on minority social movements, the literature of Black nationalism, and African American images in literature and film.

Sally Ward Maggard is an associate professor of sociology and anthropology, adjunct associate professor of history, Regional Research Institute faculty research associate, and women's studies faculty associate at West Virginia University. Her research centers on gender, class, and collective protest and on the economic and social development of the Central Appalachian and Hungarian coalfields. She has held research fellowships from the American Foundation, the Mellon Foundation, the Rockefeller Foundation, the Kentucky Foundation for Women, and the Pro Kultura Foundation of Hungary. She is the editor of the *Journal of Appalachian Studies*.

Jane Margolis received her doctorate from the Harvard Graduate School of Education in 1990. Her research and teaching focus on equity issues in education. Currently she is visiting research scientist at the Carnegie Mellon University School of Computer Science, where she is studying gender inequities in computer science. She is writing a book on her political experiences and groupthink.

Susan E. Marshall is University Distinguished Teaching Professor of Sociology at the University of Texas at Austin. She has written extensively on women's participation in U.S. antifeminist movements. She is the author of *Splintered Sisterhood: Gender and Class in the Campaign against Woman Suffrage*.

Multinational Monitor is a periodical published in Washington, D.C.

Sonya Paul and *Robert Perkinson* traveled with Winona LaDuke and the Indigo Girls on the "Honor the Earth" tour.

Belinda Robnett is assistant professor of sociology and women's studies at the University of California, Davis. She is the author of the forthcoming book *How Long? How Long? African-American Women in the Struggle for Civil Rights*. Her research interests include race and ethnicity, identity, culture, gender, social movements, and social change.

Margaret Rose is an historian and directs a professional development program for educators at the Interdisciplinary Humanities Center at the University of California, Santa Barbara. She received her Ph.D. from UCLA in 1988. Her dissertation dealt with Chicanas and Mexicanas in the United Farm Workers, 1950–1980. Other work has appeared in *Frontiers, The Journal of Women's History, Notable Hispanic American Women, Latinas! Women of Achievement,* and *Not June Cleaver: Women and Gender in Postwar America, 1945–1960.* She is currently researching an article on Dolores Huerta.

Beth Roy lives in San Francisco, where she studies case histories of racial and religious conflict using oral histories of participants. She is the author of *Some Trouble with Cows: Making Sense of Social Conflict* and is presently studying the lives of people touched by the desegregation of Central High School in Little Rock, Arkansas. She is also a mediator of family organizational disputes and a counselor in private practice.

Amy Dru Stanley is assistant professor of history at the University of Chicago. Her forthcoming book, *Contract Bonds in the Age of Slave Emancipation,* focuses on freedom, marriage, and wage labor. She teaches courses on nineteenth-century history, gender, law, and labor.

Julia Wrigley teaches in the sociology program at the Graduate Center of the City University of New York. She is currently studying the cross-class socialization of children and is the author of *Other People's Children.*

Index